Criti
Th

T   nts

GORSUCH SCARISBRICK, PUBLISHERS
Scottsdale, Arizona

Editor	John W. Gorsuch
Consulting Editor	Gerald R. Miller
Developmental Editor	Gay L. Orr
Production Manager	Carol H. Blumentritt
Sales & Marketing	Sandra Byrd
Copyeditor	Carolyn Acheson
Design	R Design Associates
Typesetting	Publication Services
Printing & Binding	BookCrafters

Gorsuch Scarisbrick, Publishers
8233 Via Paseo del Norte, Suite F400
Scottsdale, AZ 85258

10 9 8 7 6 5 4 3 2 1

ISBN 0-89787-342-4

CONTENTS

PREFACE

We are all consumers and producers of arguments. Arguing may be more characteristic of human life than is any other activity. No aspect of our existence, it seems, is lived out in the absence of arguments. Commerce, religion, politics, romance, education, medicine, science, family life, sports, the arts, and even humor, involve advancing and evaluating arguments. Conversation, books, periodicals, the media—all are sources of arguments. To think critically is, above all, to think well about the arguments we read, hear, and make.

The goal of this book is to assist you in becoming a more capable critic and advocate, a person skilled in argument, a responsible and critical thinker. The approach taken in pursuing this goal is to introduce you to the structure, vocabulary, types, and tests of arguments. Thinking skills are developed by analyzing example arguments in the narrative and the exercises. The skills acquired should be useful in evaluating arguments in any context and presented in any form.

Chapter 1 introduces some of the basic vocabulary of argument, as well as a method for finding the structure of arguments. Chapter 2 explores the responsibilities of arguing reasonably and ethically. Chapter 3 takes up the important topic of evidence and its sources, and chapter 4 discusses the types of conclusions at which arguments can arrive and the structure of arguments arriving at each.

Chapters 5 through 11 offer a detailed analysis of seven broad categories of arguments: analogies, generalizations, causal arguments, category arguments, division arguments, arguments from essential nature, and nonpropositional arguments such as emotional appeals. These chapters provide descriptions and tests of thirty of the most commonly encountered forms of argument, grouped according to similarity of structure. This in-depth discussion of the types and tests of arguments is the text's most distinctive feature.

1 THE STRUCTURE OF ARGUMENTS

Chapter Preview

THE ELEMENTS OF ARGUMENTS

An introduction to some of the basic vocabulary of argument and critical thinking.

IDENTIFYING ARGUMENTS

The signs indicating that an argument is being presented and the contexts in which arguments are often found.

TOOLS FOR ANALYZING ARGUMENTS

Presentation of a system for discovering the content and structure of an argument.

Key Terms

argument	reservation	rhetoric
reason	intermediate	evidence
conclusion	conclusions	connective
logical sense	qualifier	value
inference	independent reasons	provisions
indicator	dependent reasons	motivating the
statement	supplying missing	argument
linguistic cue	indicators	rule of charity
scanning	supplying missing	straw man fallacy
standardizing	reasons	
diagramming	enthymemes	

This book is about arguments. **Argument**, however, has several meanings in English, so clarification is important at the outset. We often speak of people "having an argument," by which we mean they are disagreeing, perhaps angrily, about some matter. We also speak of someone "making an argument," by which we mean presenting reasons in support of a point. In fact, in the midst of the first kind of argument, the second kind of argument is often advanced. This leads to some confusion surrounding the meaning of the term "argument."[1]

❖ THE ELEMENTS OF ARGUMENTS

This text is concerned only about the second kind of argument. For the purposes here an argument is *a reason or reasons advanced in support of some conclusion*. This definition contains two additional terms that also require definition—reason and conclusion. A **reason** is *a statement advanced as justification for believing some other statement*. A **conclusion** is *a contention advanced with attending reasons*. As I have defined the term, an argument always will involve at least one **inference**, or *movement from a reason or reasons to a conclusion*.

With these definitions in mind, consider the following argument:

Competency tests should be required for all public school teachers, because studies show that such tests improve the quality of education, and whatever improves the quality of education should be aggressively pursued.

The first task involved in understanding and assessing arguments is to determine which statements are advanced as reasons, and which as conclusions. As you read the example, you probably decided that one of its statements was its conclusion and the others were reasons. This process of differentiating reasons and conclusions is part of understanding the argument. But how did you know which was which?

Three means are employed to identify reasons and conclusions in arguments. First, *our sense of how arguments develop*, what we might call **logical sense**, is often a reliable guide to the inferential structure of arguments. From having heard and read a lot of arguments, we know that it just "makes sense" that some statements are reasons and others are conclusions. Logical sense suggests that the first statement in this example is the conclusion of the argument:

3

Conclusion: Competency tests should be required for all
               public school teachers.

But, in separating reasons from conclusions, we have more to go on than logical sense alone, as important as this may be as an aid to understanding arguments. How do we know which statements are the reasons in this argument? The word "because" provides an important clue to its inferences. This word functions in the argument as an **indicator**, *a word or phrase signaling that a reason or a conclusion will follow.* As an indicator, "because" signals that a reason will follow. Among the many other indicators for reasons are "since," "for," "my reason being," and "as shown by." Indicators for conclusions include "therefore," "thus," "so," "which shows that," and many others. Later in this chapter the usefulness of indicators in making and analyzing arguments will be discussed.

Not all arguments have indicators, and sometimes indicators show up in discourse that is not intended to contain arguments. Indicators only tell us where a speaker or writer has drawn an inference, not whether the inference is a good one. Finally, not all of the inferences in arguments are signaled by indicators; indicators may be used for some inferences and not for others. With these cautions in mind, indicators can signal that an argument is being advanced, and they can tell us something about the structure of arguments.

Returning to the example, the indicator "because" shows that one reason in the argument is the second statement. We can show more clearly the relationship of the indicator, its reason, and the conclusion by putting the argument in the following form, and by labeling its parts:

Indicator: *because*
Reason: Studies show that competency tests improve
               the quality of education.
Conclusion: Competency tests should be required for all
               public school teachers.

The third clue for identifying the reasons and the conclusion in the example argument is the word "and." In this argument, "and" functions as a **linguistic cue**, *a word or phrase that reveals relationships among statements within an argument other than reason-conclusion relationships.* In most cases the word "and" suggests a parallel relationship between the statements it joins. Thus, according to the linguistic cue, the third statement in this argument is also a reason. Other linguistic cues include the words "although," "in addition to," "nevertheless," and "moreover." The meanings of these cues will be discussed as we encounter them in arguments.

We now can set out the entire argument so as to reveal its inferential structure:

Indicator:	*because*
Reason:	Studies show that competency tests improve the quality of education.
Linguistic cue:	*and*
Reason:	Whatever improves the quality of education should be aggressively pursued.
Conclusion:	Competency tests should be required for all public school teachers.

The reasons in this argument did not originally appear as the first two statements but, instead, as the last two. Here the reasons are placed before the conclusion to clarify the inferences in the argument. *A statement's location in an argument is usually* not *a reliable clue as to whether the statement serves as a reason or a conclusion.*

WRAP UP

A general picture of arguments can be sketched as units of discourse involving at least one reason, at least one conclusion, and at least one inference. Indicators or linguistic cues may be present. This picture will be helpful in identifying other arguments, though sometimes differentiating an argument from other kinds of discourse that share certain similarities is difficult.

❖ IDENTIFYING ARGUMENTS

As has already been suggested, some kinds of discourse sound like arguments, when some other label might be more accurate. Reports and informational discourse are at times confused with arguments, but to treat them as arguments would, in most cases, be inappropriate. In addition, some claims achieve general agreement, whereas others can be clearly demonstrated to be true or accurate to the satisfaction of most people. Such claims may not require reasons and inferences in their support.[2]

Therefore, being able to distinguish arguments from other types of discourse is important. This can be difficult at times. Consider the following example:

During the first thirteen years of its existence, Social Security enacted a maximum employer/employee contribution of $60 per year per worker. As recently as 1958 the maximum combined Social Security tax was only $189; by 1965 it was still only $348. Today it is $6,006, and by the end of the decade it will approach $8,000.[3]

Is this an argument? Probably not, because we cannot see an inference being made. There is no apparent movement from reason to conclusion. This paragraph may be part of an argument but, as it stands, it is more accurately labeled a report or an explanation.

Distinguishing between arguments and other types of discourse is a skill acquired with practice. As you develop a sense of when arguments are being advanced, you will become more confident of the distinction. But some signs and situations are characteristic of arguments, and these can help us in making this distinction. Signs that arguments are likely to be advanced, or contexts in which arguments are frequently found, include:

1. *The need for reasoned support.* Sometimes we have a sense that a statement requires reasons to support it, that by itself it would not be accepted by a reasonable person. Thus, the statement "Elvis is still alive" has to have some support before most reasonable people would accept it as true. By itself it raises the question, "Why do you think that?" It is a conclusion, or contention, in need of a reason.

2. *The context of controversy.* When we know that an issue is controversial, we expect arguments. If someone says, for example, "The AIDS epidemic is destroying our entire medical establishment," we would expect that an argument is being made and that reasons will be advanced in support of this conclusion.

The context of controversy is not always a sign of argument, however. For example, the statement, "AIDS cannot be contracted by shaking hands with an infected individual," might not be followed by reasons if the claim is thought to be generally accepted. Though it occurs in the context of the AIDS controversy, this statement is not itself controversial in most settings. Another way of making this point may be to say that when we are aware that reasonable people disagree on a point, we expect arguments. When we are aware of general agreement, we may not hear arguments.

3. *Statement of personal opinion.* Expressions of an opinion, especially a controversial opinion, may involve advancing supporting reasons. Thus, a statement such as, "I think George Bush is a good President," is often followed by a reason such as, "because he has not tampered with Reagan's agenda," making an argument, a statement of an opinion along with a reason in its support. When we state an opinion, we are not surprised to hear someone else ask us, "Why do you think that?" The other person is asking for our reasons, and in providing reasons we are advancing an argument.

4. *Proposal of policy.* When a course of action is being suggested, reasons are often advanced. If someone were to say, "The U.S. space program should be abandoned," he or she would be proposing a policy or a course of action. We would expect the person to advance reasons supporting this proposed action, such as, "because the money is needed to solve social problems."

5. *Rendering of a value judgment.* Most value judgments require some substantiation, especially if they are controversial judgments. Thus, if someone were to say, "Abortion is morally wrong," we would expect this statement to be supported with reasons. The person making the claim might follow it with the reasons, "because I think abortion involves killing a person, and killing people is morally wrong."

6. *Inference based on evidence.* If I were to say, "Someone is home because the lights are on in the house," I would be making an argument. I have presented an observation as evidence and have drawn a conclusion on the basis of that evidence. Inferences from evidence usually are treated as arguments.

WRAP UP

The six signs of argument overlap a great deal, and none is a certain signal that an argument is being advanced. Even skilled critics can mistake a writer's or a speaker's intent in this regard, and we sometimes have to say that, although the author meant some statement as a simple report, an argument was really called for. Still, distinguishing between arguments and other types of discourse is important. It makes little sense to analyze a report as if it were an argument, because the rules governing the one are quite different from the rules governing the other.[4]

❖ TOOLS FOR ANALYZING ARGUMENTS

We are all accustomed to reading or hearing arguments, and we usually think that we have grasped what we have read or heard. But at times it is simply not clear what an arguer intended. At other times we want to be absolutely certain that we have thoroughly understood an argument, because an important decision will be based on it, or because we have to respond to it. Five analytic tools that can be of great help in ascertaining the inferential structure of an argument, so as to better understand and respond to it, are scanning, standardizing, diagramming, supplying missing indicators, and supplying missing reasons.

SCANNING

The analytic tool of **scanning** involves *identifying and marking the statements in an argument.* **Statements** in an argument are *sentences or portions of sentences that have their own inferential function or play some other important role in the argument.* In the process of scanning arguments, underlining indicators and linguistic cues can be helpful. Individual statements can be marked using numbers, letters, or some other symbol system. Marking statements with letters, the earlier example argument would be scanned as follows:

A: Competency tests should be required for all public school teachers, <u>because</u> B: studies indicate that such tests improve the quality of education in our schools, <u>and</u> C: whatever improves the quality of education should be aggressively pursued.

Even though we may not always be confident that we have accurately identified all of the statements in an argument, scanning can often help in our getting a grasp of the argument's structure.

STANDARDIZING

The second tool for ascertaining an argument's inferences is called **standardizing** the argument, *making each statement a complete sentence, placing reasons above the conclusions they support, and setting out indicators and linguistic cues.*[5] When standardizing an argument, the letters assigned to statements when the argument was scanned might be retained, as in the example:

---

　　because
B:　Studies indicate that competency tests improve the quality of education.
　　and
C:　Whatever improves the quality of education should be aggressively pursued.
　　[thus]
A:　Competency tests should be required for all public school teachers.

In this example we have supplied the indicator "thus" to clarify the inference from the reasons to the conclusion. Adding indicators is a tool for analyzing arguments, and this will be discussed momentarily.

Standardizing an argument to understand its inferential structure is not always necessary. When the relationships among reasons and conclusions are not clear, however, standardizing can help clarify them.

DIAGRAMMING

The third analytic tool for arguments is **diagramming**, which involves *using only the letters assigned during scanning, and drawing lines from reasons to the conclusion they support.* This process helps us to *see* the inferences that make up the argument. To illustrate this process, a simplified version of the example argument is:

A: Competency tests should be required for all public school teachers, <u>because</u> B: studies indicate that such tests improve the quality of education.

In standardized form, the argument looks like this:

     <u>because</u>
B: Studies indicate that [competency tests] improve the quality of education.
     [<u>thus</u>]
A: Competency tests should be required for all public school teachers.

Brackets have been placed around the term "competency tests" in statement B to show that this did not appear in the original statement and has been inserted. Any indefinite reference in an argument should be made definite in a standardization, as we have done here.

Now it is easier to see that the diagram for this argument would require a line from B to A, from the reason to the conclusion. An argument's diagram should follow closely its standardization. Thus, the diagram looks like this:

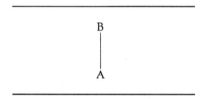

Even if we did not know the content of this argument, we could "read" this diagram as saying: In this argument, statement B is offered as a reason for conclusion A.

Were we to rewrite the argument by reversing the order of reason and conclusion, we would have a different diagram. In that case, the argument could be presented as:

A: Competency tests would improve the quality of education in our schools; <u>therefore</u>, B: they should be required for all public school teachers.

In this example the reason precedes the conclusion, and "therefore" indicates that a conclusion will follow. Standardized, the argument looks like this:

A: Competency tests would improve the quality of educa-
    tion in our schools.
    <u>therefore</u>
B: [Competency tests] should be required for all public
    school teachers.

The diagram for this version of the argument looks like this:

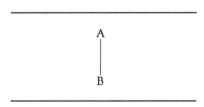

An argument can have any number of reasons, and it may arrive at several conclusions. Though the diagram may become complex, diagramming can be used to illustrate the inferential structure of nearly any argument. More reasons can be added to the example argument to show what might be done with somewhat more complex arguments:

<u>Though</u> A: some educators object to the idea, B: compe-
tency tests would improve the quality of education in our
schools <u>because</u> C: they would eliminate from the teaching
profession some people who shouldn't be teaching. <u>Thus</u>,
D: competency tests should certainly be required for all public school teachers. <u>In addition</u>, E: teachers who did pass
the tests could claim that their services are worth more, <u>so</u>
F: teaching salaries might rise.

We have scanned this argument and underlined the indicators "because," "thus," and "so," and the linguistic cues "though," and "in addition." This argument contains a **reservation**, or *a statement presenting a reason* *opposing the argument's conclusion.* In this case the linguistic cue "though," signals the reservation. Among the other cues signaling that a reservation has or will be stated are "nevertheless," "however," and "regardless of the fact that." Reservations occur frequently in arguments, especially when reasons opposing some conclusion are well known or widely accepted. A broken line will be used to diagram reservations.

Taking the evidence available to us from the indicators and linguistic cues, this argument can be standardized as follows:

<u>though</u>
A: Some educators object to the idea of [competency tests].
<u>because</u>
C: [Competency tests] would eliminate from the teaching profession some people who shouldn't be there.
B: Competency tests would improve the quality of education in our schools.
<u>in addition</u>
E: Teachers who did pass the tests could claim that their services are worth more.
<u>so</u>
F: Teaching salaries might rise.
[thus]
D: Competency tests should certainly be required for all public school teachers.

Scanning this argument reveals that one sentence may contain more than one statement. A diagram of this argument is:

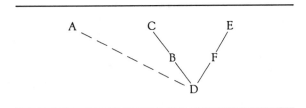

Notice that the conclusion of this argument appears in the middle of the argument (as the fourth of six statements), not at the beginning or the end. Again, the order of statements in an argument does not tell us anything in particular about which statement is the argument's conclusion.

Notice also that statements B and F are *statements that serve as both conclusions and reasons* and therefore function as **intermediate conclusions** in this argument. The word "certainly" in this argument is a **qualifier**, or *a term or phrase indicating the degree of certainty the arguer attaches to a conclusion.* Other qualifiers include "probably," "possibly," and "it must be the case that."

The arguments considered so far have involved only **independent reasons**, *reasons that by themselves tend to add support to a conclusion.* Some arguments, however, involve **dependent reasons**, *reasons that must be accompanied by other reasons to support their conclusion.*[6] The original example argument contains dependent reasons:

A: Competency tests should be required for all public school teachers, <u>because</u> B: studies show that such tests improve the quality of education, <u>and</u> C: whatever improves the quality of education should be aggressively pursued.

Notice that, to allow an inference to the conclusion A, the reasons B and C must be accepted together. When reasons in an argument have a dependent relationship, they are diagrammed in such a way that this will be clear. The w/ symbol (meaning "when combined with") is a convenient means of showing the dependence of reasons. A diagram of the argument above, then, would look like this:

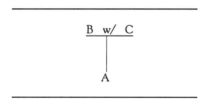

An argument may have both independent reasons and dependent reasons. By combining the examples we have been working with, such an argument might be:

A: Competency tests should be required for all public school teachers, <u>because</u> B: studies show that such tests improve the quality of education, <u>and</u> C: whatever improves the quality of education should be aggressively pursued. <u>In addition</u>

D: teachers who did pass the tests could claim that their services are worth more, <u>so</u> E: teaching salaries might rise.

This argument can be standardized as follows:

<u>because</u>
B: Studies show that [competency] tests improve the quality of education.
<u>and</u>
C: Whatever improves the quality of education should be aggressively pursued.
<u>in addition</u>
D: Teachers who did pass the tests could claim that their services are worth more.
<u>so</u>
E: Teaching salaries might rise.
[<u>thus</u>]
A: Competency tests should be required for all public school teachers.

The argument is diagrammed as follows:

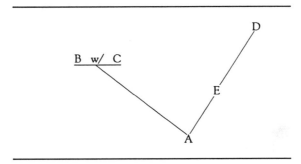

To this point we have examined arguments containing indicators, linguistic cues, or both. Now, how do we go about figuring out the inferential structure of an argument when no indicators or linguistic cues exist to tell us what the person making the argument intended? Sometimes all we have to go on is logical sense. Logical sense can be tested by using our last two analytic tools.

SUPPLYING MISSING INDICATORS

The structure of some arguments is not apparent even after we have scanned, standardized, and diagrammed them, employing all of the evidence we can derive from indicators, linguistic cues, and logical sense. Moreover, the indicator words present in an argument may not tell us about all of the inferential connections an author intends. As they make their arguments, most writers and speakers are not quite that conscious of indicators. Thus, sometimes we have to make educated guesses as we plot the inferential structure of an argument. One way of testing the correctness of these guesses is to **supply missing indicators**, *to insert indicators at various points in the argument where we suspect a reason-conclusion relationship between two statements.* Supplying missing indicators is a useful tool for getting at the inferential structure of some arguments. Consider the following example:

A: Stock car racing is a dangerous sport which needs to be more carefully regulated. B: Drivers should be screened for drug use, and safety regulations more carefully monitored. C: Fatal, drug-related accidents occurred last year in Mobile and Atlanta, and safety violations were behind the deaths of at least seven drivers in 1985.

What is the conclusion of this argument? Placement of the first sentence, along with its urging a policy and its nature as a sweeping generalization might lead us, on the basis of logical sense, to think this is the argument's conclusion. It also seems to bear some reason-conclusion connection to the second sentence. One way of testing our guess is to standardize this part of the argument and to insert an indicator word between the two sentences to see if the first sentence sounds right as a conclusion drawn from the second:

B: Drivers should be screened for drug use, and safety regulations more carefully monitored.
    [therefore]
A: Stock car racing is a dangerous sport which needs to be more carefully regulated.

Somehow this doesn't sound right. Let's see if the second sentence makes more sense as a conclusion, by again inserting an indicator word:

A: Stock car racing is a dangerous sport which needs to be more carefully monitored.
[therefore]

B: Drivers should be screened for drug use, and safety regulations more carefully monitored.

This sounds more likely as an arrangement of reason and conclusion. What about the other two statements? They are more clearly reasons, and they probably support the first contention, which in turn supports the final conclusion in the second sentence. We can test this idea by inserting indicator words:

C: Fatal drug-related accidents occurred last year in Mobile and Atlanta, and safety violations were behind the deaths of at least seven drivers in 1985.
[these facts prove that]

A: Stock car racing is a dangerous sport which needs to be more carefully regulated.
[therefore]

B: Drivers should be screened for drug use, and safety regulations more carefully monitored.

Now we can see the likely logical structure of this argument.

Returning to the argument about stock car racing, we can now provide the following diagram:

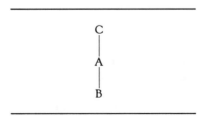

The logical structure of the argument was clarified by supplying missing indicator words.

SUPPLYING MISSING REASONS:
ENTHYMEMES AND RHETORIC

Another analytic tool that is useful in understanding arguments is to **supply missing reasons**, *to fill apparent gaps in arguments by providing reasons a speaker or writer left out.* Because arguments in public discourse—speeches, editorials, essays, sermons, advertisements—are written with a specific audience in mind, they may not yield easily to formal or logical analysis. Supplying unstated reasons can play an important role in analyzing and understanding this kind of argument.

As Aristotle pointed out in his work *Rhetoric*, speakers often advance *arguments in which the evidence, connectives, or even the conclusions may not be stated and are supplied by the reader or listener* when arguing before an audience of the general public.[7] He called arguments such as this **enthymemes**, and he referred to *persuasive discourse involving enthymemes and other arguments constructed with an audience of the general public in mind* as **rhetoric**.[8] Rhetoric, then, is argumentative discourse composed with a view to a particular audience, usually one made up not of experts but, instead, of members of the general public.

Moreover, rhetoric usually deals with issues that are not of a technical nature and thus do not belong properly to a science such as medicine. Rhetoric is the discourse we hear, read, and advance when trying to decide what is a good or a bad use of funds or resources, distinguish the just from the unjust, and differentiate good from evil.[9] The arguments considered throughout this text would fit Aristotle's definition of rhetoric.[10]

The missing pieces of a public argument are often crucial to understanding and evaluating the argument. These elements are frequently supplied subconsciously as we read or listen to the arguments. Even so, when we supply a missing reason while analyzing someone else's argument, we are making the best guess we can about something we cannot know for sure: how another person is reasoning. In fact, in some cases the person arguing is not even sure about the specific nature of reasons missing from his or her arguments.

You may wonder why speakers and writers would fail to state all of their reasons in making an argument. They may do this for at least four reasons. First, speakers may simply be unaware of some of the reasons that make up their arguments and, thus, not think to state them. Second, the person speaking may assume that the reason is widely believed and, thus, that stating it is not necessary. Third, not stating a reason is a way of affirming that the speaker and the audience are in agreement on the point, which serves to unite the speaker with his or her audience.

Fourth, by making the audience member supply the missing reason, a speaker or writer may be involving the audience in the argumentation process, which is itself an aid to persuasion.

In some cases we have to supply a missing reason if we are to understand or respond to a given argument. The tool of supplying missing reasons, to the extent that our guess has been accurate, helps us to see the full inferential structure of some arguments. Consider the following example:

A: The canyon should be maintained as a wilderness area, <u>since</u> B: wilderness areas are rare.

From the indicator "since" we can see that the second statement is reason for the first, but why does moving from statement B to statement A make sense? What connection does the canyon being rare have with the conclusion that it ought to be preserved? If you find the argument to be reasonable, you might think that the connection is obvious. But, still, something is missing. What is it?

Let's look at the argument again, standardizing it and leaving room for the missing reason connecting the reason we have to the conclusion:

     <u>since</u>
B: Wilderness areas are rare.
(*): Missing reason
    [therefore]
A: The canyon should be preserved as a wilderness area.

At this point we need to differentiate two types of reasons: **evidence** and **connectives**. Evidence is a name for *reasons intended as rational support, confirmation, or proof of some conclusion*. Common types of evidence are *direct observation, testimony*, and *statistics*. Statements serving as evidence are often capable of being shown to be true or false in some definite or demonstrable way. In some arguments, however, the evidence can be identified only because it is the most specific statement or statements in the argument. Types and tests of evidence will be discussed in chapter 3 and at other points later in the text.

But not all reasons constitute evidence. A connective is *a belief, a value, an assumption, or a generalization linking evidence to a conclusion*.[11] Connectives often are not capable of being shown demonstrably or definitely to be true or false; in many arguments they are treated as assumed, presupposed, or "taken for granted." If challenged, however, evidence in their support might be advanced. Connectives frequently are the most general statements in an argument.

An argument usually involves some evidence, a connective, and a conclusion. Very often, however, one or more of these elements is left unstated, and more often than not, the unstated element is a connective—a belief, a value, or an assumption. We have already discussed why speakers or writers might leave out connectives from their arguments, and we do not always bring them to mind when reading or hearing an argument. When an unstated connective is not obvious, or is likely to be contested, it is a good idea to attempt to formulate it into a statement. In the example, then, the missing connective reason (and here we are only guessing, because the author does not tell us what it is) is something like:

(*) Whatever is rare ought to be preserved.

The **value** expressed in this statement—the value for preserving rare things—seems to be necessary for connecting evidence to conclusion in this argument. Let's plug this reason into our example, marking it with an asterisk to show that we have supplied it, and see if the argument makes sense:

B: Wilderness areas are rare.
(*): Whatever is rare ought to be preserved.
   [therefore]
A: The canyon ought to be preserved as a wilderness area.

Without the value expressed in this or some similar missing reason, the connection between reason B and conclusion A cannot be made. You originally supplied the connective reason, probably without even realizing it. This is often the case when reading or hearing arguments. We supply missing elements, consciously or subconsciously, as we seek to understand or make sense of the arguments.

The process of subconsciously supplying missing reasons may become conscious when an argument does not make sense to us. Consider an argument that a young child might make:

A: Don't sit on that log, <u>because</u> B: an elephant sat on
   that log.

The argument is silly, though perhaps not to the child. What is the missing reason? It seems to be the connective reason:

(*) We ought not to sit where elephants have sat.

We can construct an inferentially reasonable argument by supplying this
missing reason:

B: An elephant sat on that log.
C*: We ought not to sit where elephants have sat.
     [<u>therefore</u>]
A: Don't sit on that log.

Clearly, supplying missing reasons can help us grasp the inferential structure of an argument, as well as inform us about important connecting
reasons which might be unstated. Sometimes supplying missing reasons
is the only way to really know what someone is arguing, and only then
can we know if we agree with the argument or reject the reasoning.
Returning to an earlier example, suppose you were to encounter the
following argument:

A: Competency tests should be required for all public
school teachers, <u>because</u> B: studies show that such tests improve the quality of education.

Here we have a conclusion, and one reason that seems to be intended
as evidence. If we were to guess what connective reason is being employed to link evidence to conclusion in this argument, we might suggest
the following:

C*: Whatever can be shown to improve the quality of education should be required.

If we accepted the original argument, we would be accepting this or some similar, unstated connective reason as well, perhaps without even realizing it, and perhaps without even agreeing with the value expressed in it.

To illustrate this possibility, we can develop another argument that might employ the same connective reason:

A: Studies show that reducing class sizes by half improves the quality of education.
C*: Whatever can be shown to improve the quality of education in our schools should be required.
    therefore,
B: All class sizes should be reduced by half.

Many people would reject this argument, even though they might accept the first reason. Thus, of the two reasons, the second—the missing reason from the example—is the one they are rejecting. Again, not until we have some idea what reasons are missing from an argument can we be sure we accept or reject the argument.

Of course, the person making the argument concerning competency tests probably has in mind certain **provisions**, or *conditions governing acceptance of the connective reason*. Provisions often are introduced by linguistic cues such as "provided that" or "as long as." Thus, this connective might be accepted only "provided that: (a) the improvements are practicable, or can be accomplished given the means available, and (b) the improvements do not violate existing laws or personal rights." Just as people often do not state their connective reasons, so they often do not state the provisions governing these connectives.

In *attributing to another person a reasonable argument*, which is sometimes called **motivating the argument** or **the rule of charity**, it is important not only to make the best guess possible about connectives but also to try to imagine the provisions that might be intended to govern the connective and the argument as a whole. *To attribute to an opponent a weak argument, or one that no reasonable person is likely to make, is sometimes called the **straw man fallacy**. The straw man is a weak opponent that you have constructed and attacked, not the actual opponent. In face-to-face controversy, questions regarding missing reasons possibly can be cleared up by asking one's opponent about unstated connectives and provisions. When dealing with written or broadcast arguments, however, such direct inquiry is not possible and we have to rely on the best guess we can make. Still, making the effort to motivate any argument we intend to answer is vital.

To supply missing reasons in arguments is not always possible. Sometimes we simply don't know what a writer or speaker was thinking, or the argument is constructed in such a way that missing reasons are difficult to reconstruct. In rare instances a reasoner provides us with all of his or her reasons. But many times we have the sense that some reason has been left unstated in an argument, and that we have to get it out in the open. In these cases we must look for a reason that would connect the reason we do have with the conclusion of the argument.

WRAP UP

Getting a clear picture of the full inferential structure of an argument is sometimes important, either because we must respond to it or because we are not sure we understand it. Five tools for analyzing arguments in an effort to clarify their structure and content are: scanning, standardizing, diagramming, supplying missing indicators, and supplying missing reasons.

Chapter Review

Arguments—reasons advanced in support of conclusions—occur in various contexts. We all make, hear, and evaluate arguments, and if we are to do these things well, we must know about the nature and structure of arguments. Here we have examined the basic structure of arguments, discussed contexts in which arguments are likely to occur, presented some terms that help us to talk about arguments, and advanced a set of analytic tools for understanding arguments.

EXERCISES

A. Scan the following arguments:

1. We should give Jones the new car because it would serve to motivate the other employees to work harder.

2. We should give Jones the new car because the company bylaws state that new vehicles should go to the "most deserving" employee. This term, "most deserving," should be taken to mean the employee who has done the most to advance the company's image, and that's Jones.

3. AIDS testing should be required of everyone applying for life insurance policies because it would save insurance companies a great deal of money in the long run, and thus bring down rates for everyone.

4. AIDS testing should not be required of those applying for life insurance, since it is a violation of a person's right to privacy.

5. Public schools should conduct their classes only in English because education laws read, "Education should be provided in the common language of the people." "The common language" must be taken to mean the language common to the most people in the school system—English.

6. "Death" is the utter and final cessation of consciousness. Thus, anencephalic babies—babies born with a brain stem but little or no cerebral cortex—are dead, since they are not and never will be conscious.

7. Every year 2,000 to 3,000 children need organ transplants. Each year 2,000 to 3,000 anencephalic babies are born. With so many potential lives saved, shouldn't we allow organs from anencephalic babies to be used in transplants?

8. The canyon area ought to be developed since more people then would have access to it.

9. Nuclear chemistry and biology have produced significant improvements in the human condition, especially in the areas of agriculture and medicine. Thus, even though a threat of nuclear annihilation still exists, you more likely will be helped by nuclear medicine than killed by a nuclear explosion.

10. Bilingual education must not be opposed on patriotic grounds. Language is not a matter of national loyalty. It is a skill, and the more skilled a person is, the more likely that person will be to succeed.

B. Standardize the following arguments, and supply the missing reason for each:

1. Of course I love you, darling. I love all women.

2. Bob must have gone bowling because he came home drunk.

3. All men are mortal, so Socrates is mortal.

4. The recent U.S. invasion of Panama was immoral, since it was a case of intervention in the internal affairs of a sovereign nation.

5. The Warren Commission determined that Lee Harvey Oswald acted alone in killing President Kennedy. Therefore, Oswald did act alone in killing the President.

6. Four out of five dentists recommend sugarless gum to their patients who chew gum, so you should chew sugarless gum.

7. Marx theorized that all societies would eventually become socialist, so we can expect America to become socialist.

8. Since the plant could have been knocked off the shelf only by you, by a ghost, or by an earthquake, we both know how the plant got knocked off the shelf.

9. Cats eat fish, so Frisky eats fish.

10. You should not accept his ideas, because they are ridiculous.

11. All religions teach about the same thing, and so they should be regarded as equally legitimate.

12. Gambling is something that cannot be stopped. Therefore, gambling should be legalized.

13. It's only a story, so I don't have to prove it.

14. Because interest rates are going up, home sales can be expected to decline.

15. Military aid will not stop the flow of drugs from South American countries, since military aid does nothing to solve the problems of poverty in those countries.

C. Scan, standardize, and diagram the following arguments. Supply missing indicators in your standardizations, and missing reasons where these are important.

1. Nuclear chemistry and biology have produced significant improvements in the human condition, especially in the areas of agriculture and medicine. Thus, even though a threat of nuclear annihilation still exists, you will more likely be helped by nuclear medicine than killed by a nuclear explosion.

2. "Today . . . desperate patients and their families are still willing to risk unproved therapies when nothing else helps. Ambitious doctors can persuade some of the media to report untested cures with anecdotal research. Economic factors still influence the choice of treatments. [The lobotomy scandal] could happen again.

There is need to remember lobotomy."
(Joan Beck, *Detroit Free Press*, Feb. 23, 1987)

3. Some people oppose the idea of a joint Mars mission with the Russians, but clearly such a mission would benefit both countries. This program would require extensive cooperation between the two powers, so the tensions created by our traditional competition with the Soviets would be greatly reduced. The technological advances from a joint Mars mission are also important to both nations, for both have fallen behind the West Germans and Japanese in critical technologies during the past two decades. Moreover, Americans are losing their pioneering spirit and exploring Mars would help us to recapture that spirit. Finally, a successful mission to Mars would improve the credibility of the U.S. and USSR in the international community.

4. The focus of any sound economic policy must be jobs. People with jobs have money to invest in the economy. Thus, more jobs are created, and so the standard of living rises continually. Moreover, people with jobs are not people who commit crimes.

D. Find a brief argument in a newspaper or magazine. Scan, standardize, and diagram the argument. Bring your example to class and be prepared to discuss it.

ENDNOTES

1. For a detailed discussion of this issue, see D. J. O'Keefe, "Two Concepts of Argument," *Journal of the American Forensic Association* 13 (1977), pp. 121–128.

2. See Chaim Perelman and L. Olbrechts-Tyteca's discussion of facts and truths as the starting points of argument in *The New Rhetoric* translated by John Wilkinson and Purcell Weaver (Notre Dame, IN: University of Notre Dame Press, 1969), pp. 61–70. These authors hold that a fact maintains this status only as long as it garners "uncontroverted, universal agreement" (p. 67). Once it is seriously challenged, it loses its status as a fact. I intend to extend this criterion to some explanations and reports; as long as they do not elicit a serious challenge to their status as explanations or reports of facts, they do not require substantiation.

3. William Hoffer, "Taking Social Security Private," *Nation's Business*, July 1986, p. 30.

4. One of the best discussions of the characteristics of argumentative discourse is found in Edwin Black's book *Rhetorical Criticism* (Madison: University of Wisconsin Press, 1979), chapter 6, "The Genre of Argumentation" (original work published 1965).

5. Standardizing arguments in this way is suggested by Trudy Govier, *A Practical Study of Argument* (Belmont, CA: Wadsworth, 1985), pp. 21–26.

6. See also Stephen N. Thomas, *Practical Reasoning in Natural Language*, 2d ed. (Englewood Cliffs, NJ: Prentice Hall, 1981), p. 52.

7. Aristotle, *Rhetoric*, translated by W. Rhys Roberts (New York: Modern Library, 1954), p. 28. Aristotle wrote, "The enthymeme must consist of few propositions, fewer often than make up the normal syllogism. For if any of these propositions is a familiar fact, there is no need even to mention it; the hearer adds it himself."

8. For a detailed and helpful discussion of enthymemes, see Lloyd F. Bitzer, "Aristotle's Enthymeme Revisited," in *Quarterly Journal of Speech* 45, (1959), pp. 399–408.

9. In his book *Rhetoric*, Aristotle divided discourse into three categories: deliberative (the rhetoric of legislation), forensic (the rhetoric of justice), and epideictic (the rhetoric of ceremonies).

10. If you wouuld like to read more about rhetoric and its history, see James L. Golden, Goodwin F. Berquist, and William E. Coleman, *The Rhetoric of Western Thought*, 3d ed. (Dubuque, IA: Kendall Hunt Publishing Company, 1984). For a good introduction to some contemporary thinking about rhetoric, see Sonja K. Foss, Karen A. Foss, and Robert Trapp, *Contemporary Perspective on Rhetoric* (Prospect Heights, IL: Waveland Press, 1985).

11. The terms "evidence" and "connective" correspond approximately, though not in every case exactly, to Toulmin's terms "data" and "warrant." As I employ the term, "connective" ignores the distinction between warrant and backing. As a result, some of the connectives advanced later in the text do not match well with either of Toulmin's categories. See *The Uses of Argument* (Cambridge: Cambridge University Press, 1958), pp. 94–106. I would like to thank Professor Michael Leff for originally suggesting the term "connective."

2 ETHICAL AND REASONABLE ARGUMENTS

Chapter Preview

BASIC AGREEMENTS

A brief description of some of the types of basic agreements that are present in the process of argumentation.

ETHICAL ARGUMENTS

Presentation of some guidelines for arguing in an ethically responsible way.

REASONABLE ARGUMENTS

Definition of general criteria for reasonable arguments and discussion of what it means to be a critical thinker.

Key Terms

argumentation	reasonable argument	refutation
procedures	support	repudiation
goals	validity	relevant community
evidence	linguistic consistency	critical thinking
fallacies	acceptance	
context of	consideration	
argumentation	rebuttal	

Argumentation, *the whole process of advancing and responding to arguments*, occurs because some statement or proposition is in dispute. Because disagreements about statements or claims mark nearly every aspect of human life, argumentation is one of the most common human endeavors.[1] And we should not limit our view of argumentation to public discourse; we advance and respond to arguments in private conversation, and even argue with ourselves.[2]

❖ BASIC AGREEMENTS

Theorists of argument note that the process of argumentation cannot take place without some basic *agreements* between the people advancing arguments, or between the individual advancing an argument and his or her audience.[3] Perhaps the most basic agreement is that of entering into argumentation rather than resolving disagreement by some other means such as coercion or violence.

Agreements about other matters attend argumentation as well. Argumentation often involves some agreement about **procedures**, as it does in courts of law. Both sides agree to present their cases according to the procedures prescribed in the law. The judge should ensure that this agreement is realized in the actual presentation of arguments in court. In competitive debate, both sides agree that the contestants recommending a change in the way things are currently done get to speak first. This is an agreement about the procedures of debate.

Argumentation also may involve agreements about the **goals** of the dispute. For instance, legislators may agree in some disputes that the goal of their argumentation is to formulate legislation that benefits the largest number of people, or makes the best use of available funds, or provides the most expedient solution to some pressing problem. In court, advocates may agree that their goal is to justly resolve the case at hand. Even a disagreement between friends about what to do for an evening's entertainment may involve an unstated agreement that the goal is to have the most fun within the limits set by the available money and time.

Even though disagreements about the quality of evidence, interpretations of evidence, and what should count as evidence in a controversy are common, argumentation also may involve some agreements about **evidence**. For instance, both parties to a court case might agree that the defendant wrote a certain letter, though they may disagree about the intent, interpretation, or significance of the letter. Legislators might agree about evidence that shows their state is facing a serious waste disposal problem but disagree about how the problem should be solved.

Arguments often move from the agreements that make argumentation possible to the disagreements that make it necessary. Even parties engaged in disputes as heated as that concerning nuclear power agree on some points that make argumentation possible—for instance, the agreement that adequate sources of clean and inexpensive energy must be developed. But this controversy also involves serious disagreement about what those sources ought to be.

Almost any public controversy involves a mix of agreements and disagreements, as do controversies on a more personal level. Our point here is that, though we think of argumentation as taking place when persons disagree, the process of productive argumentation occurs within a framework of agreements. Thus, we can summarize by saying that *argumentation occurs because people disagree, but it cannot take place without some basic agreements*.

We have noted that argumentation often involves agreement about things such as the value of argumentation, procedures, goals, and even evidence. But this text takes the position that two other agreements should function as ground rules of all responsible argumentation: the agreement to be *ethical* in arguing, and the agreement to seek to be *reasonable*. That is to say, when we enter into argumentation, we have a responsibility to operate within ethical standards appropriate to argumentation and to seek to advance reasonable arguments.

Much of the rest of this text deals with the standards of reasonableness applicable to several specific kinds of argument. The last section of this chapter additionally will take up some general concerns for reasonableness that are relevant to nearly any argument. The following discussion sets out some of the ethical principles that seem appropriate to argumentation.

❖ ETHICAL ARGUMENTS

Any time we try to change someone's thinking, we are engaged in an endeavor with a clear moral dimension. The business of persuasion ought not to be entered into lightly or unreflectively, and this is certainly true of efforts to persuade using reason and argument. Of course, you probably know, without special instruction, some of the ethical principles that should govern responsible argumentation. For example, you likely are aware that lying and attacking an opponent on a personal level do not reflect a high level of ethicality in debate. Nonetheless, a brief review of some principles of ethical argumentation can be helpful in thinking through the ethical considerations involved in trying to persuade others by advancing arguments.[4]

Perhaps that statement is a good place to begin our discussion of argumentation ethics. When we advance arguments, we are attempting to persuade other people by one available means—the use of reasons. Our very willingness to enter into argumentation rather than to persuade by some other means suggests that we value reasons and the reasoning process. It also suggests a principle that is less obvious: We value the reasoning processes of others. We could say, then, that when we argue, we recognize the value of other people as reasoners. At the same time, we are expressing that we wish the same consideration to be extended to us. From this observation we can derive a principle that may provide a foundation for our thinking about ethical argumentation:

Ethical argumentation shows respect for people as givers and hearers of reasons.

Ethical argumentation, then, involves a commitment to demonstrating our respect for people as reasoning beings. Adhering to this principle in our own argumentation means developing arguments that reveal our own respect for others as intelligent, reasoning, and reasonable people. Thus, ethical argumentation avoids persuasive approaches that seek to "get around" reason, or reveal a failure on our part to view others as forming reasonable opinions and making reasoned choices.

What kinds of argumentative activities would reveal our own failure to respect other people as givers and hearers of reasons? Perhaps the most obvious violation of this principle is intentional dishonesty in argument. Thus, an important guideline for ethical argumentation is:

1. Ethical argumentation carefully avoids dishonesty.

When we lie to others, we show them disrespect. When we lie to those with whom we are engaged in argumentation, we show disrespect for them as reasoning people. Moreover, lying undermines the whole argumentative process by rendering it impossible to make reasonable choices, which is a major goal of much argumentation. Thus, when we engage in argumentation, we must scrupulously avoid dishonesty.

Argumentative dishonesty can take various forms, including advancing conclusions or reasons we know to be false, or suggesting a false conclusion without directly stating it.[5] By the same token, twisting or distorting evidence in argument is dishonest, as is using evidence that we know to be inferior to other available evidence—for instance, old evidence that has since been replaced by better evidence.

The choice and identification of sources of evidence also raise questions of honesty in argumentation. Employing sources of information we know to be unreliable violates our guideline, as does plagiarism—presenting ideas or evidence as our own when they actually originated with someone else.

This is not intended as an exhaustive list of dishonest argumentative behavior, but it suggests some of the most common forms of such dishonesty. Ultimately the decision about what constitutes dishonesty in argument is up to us as individuals. In some instances the decision about honesty in difficult or questionable situations can be answered by asking yourself whether you would be comfortable if your audience knew exactly what you had done in inventing, presenting, and documenting your argument.

Approaches other than dishonesty also show disrespect for others as givers and hearers of reasons. The arguer may advance arguments that he or she knows are weak, misleading, or fallacious. Can these arguments be demonstrations of respect for others as givers and hearers of reasons?

2. Ethical argumentation avoids knowing presentation of bad arguments.

In our efforts to persuade others, employing an argument we know to be flawed is unethical. Here, we can define a bad argument as *one that fails in some significant way to satisfy the appropriate standards of reasonableness for that type of argument*. Some of these standards are considered later in this chapter, under the heading "Reasonable Arguments." Other standards are discussed throughout the text. In making ethical arguments, we also might consider whether we find that presenting a particular argument is unethical even if it *does* appear to pass the appropriate tests. For instance, an argument may be reasonable and persuasive but might suggest actions that are unacceptable on moral grounds.

Bad arguments can take several forms. Some of the more common are called **fallacies**, *arguments that are, by their very nature or form, nearly always flawed.*[6] Bad arguments further include those based on inadequate evidence, as well as those that are not fallacious (formally flawed) but still fail to pass some test of reasonableness. Chapters 4 through 11 of this text are intended to help you distinguish between good and bad arguments.

We also may fail to respect others as givers and hearers of reasons not by dishonesty or bad arguments but, instead, by violating the context or environment in which argumentation occurs. Perhaps you have witnessed a speaker being shouted down by an angry crowd, as happened to Eldridge Cleaver (a noted writer and black leader) during a speech at the University of Wisconsin several years ago. Many people in Madison considered Cleaver to be an opponent of socialism, and members of local organizations sympathetic to a socialist political perspective determined that the best way to "answer" Cleaver was to not let him speak at all. After several unsuccessful attempts to present his message, Cleaver gave up and left the stage. Under this criterion the protesters had acted unethically by effectively destroying the context of argumentation. Ethical argumentation allows argumentation to continue as long as necessary to ensure that arguments are fully presented and reasonable choices are thoughtfully made.

3. Ethical argumentation seeks to preserve the argumentative context.

A **context of argumentation** is *any situation in which arguments are being advanced and heard*. Such a context can be intentionally violated in a variety of ways. Failing to let others make their arguments by shouting them down or in some other way preventing their argumentative efforts is one clear violation of the argumentative context. Launching a personal attack on an argumentative opponent, an attack that belittles the opponent and distracts attention from his or her arguments, is also a violation of the argumentative context. Attacks such as these do not encourage arguments to be advanced and heard and do not encourage audience members to act as reasonable judges.

Recently the nation witnessed violent confrontations on television talk shows. The violence was a response to the expression of controversial viewpoints. By physically preventing the expression of these unpopular points of view, the principle of preserving the argumentative context was violated.

WRAP UP

One responsibility of all parties to argumentation is to seek to argue ethically. The fundamental principle of ethical argument is that all argumentation should respect, and seek to enhance, the status of people as reasoning beings. Three guidelines of ethical argumentation derived from this principle are as follows:

1. Ethical argumentation carefully avoids dishonesty.

2. Ethical argumentation avoids knowingly presenting bad arguments.

3. Ethical argumentation seeks to preserve the argumentative context.

❖ REASONABLE ARGUMENTS

People engaged in argumentation are also under an obligation to advance reasonable arguments. A **reasonable argument** is *an argument that moves from good reasons by means of proper inference to a thus substantiated conclusion*. Three criteria of reasonable arguments are implied here:

1. Reasonable arguments advance good reasons, or exhibit **support** for their conclusions.

2. Reasonable arguments involve good inferences, or have **validity**.

3. Reasonable arguments involve clear and consistent definitions of key terms, or show **linguistic consistency**.

Arguments advanced on opposite sides of an issue may satisfy these criteria, and seldom are all of the reasonable arguments on a single side in a controversy.

The criteria for determining whether reasons and inferences are good will be developed later in this chapter and throughout the rest of the text. The clear and consistent use of definitions is discussed in chapter 8. Each of these three criteria—support, validity, and linguistic consistency—must be satisfied by a reasonable argument. At this point a closer look at the term "reasonable" may be helpful, because it is integral to this text and is widely used to describe arguments.

I have suggested that persons engaged in argumentation should seek to advance reasonable arguments, and I have defined a reasonable argument. This is not to say, however, that every reasonable argument is one we ought to accept. Reasonable people disagree about a wide range of topics on the basis of reasonable arguments. This is why we have controversies such as those over abortion or nuclear energy.

We should not make the mistake of thinking that these controversies occur because all of the people on one side are uninformed or stupid. Each of us inevitably finds some arguments to be more reasonable than others. Some arguments emerge for us as strong, convincing, or even compelling. But we should not reject too hastily arguments advanced by apparently reasonable people, nor should we in most cases think that all of the arguments advanced by those defending our own position are utterly compelling to all thinking people.

A number of responses to any argument we hear or read is possible.[7] We may reach **acceptance** of the argument at one level or another. We may be convinced by the argument and accept the arguer's point of view, or perhaps just agree that a reasonable person could arrive at the conclusions advanced using the evidence advanced. When we accept an argument, we usually are not inclined to formulate an answer to it.

A second response to an argument is **consideration**. *To consider an argument is to think about it further, to withhold judgment for the time being, to explore the possibility that it might have merit.* Consideration is not acceptance, and neither is it rejection—though either of these may follow consideration.

A third way of responding to an argument is to offer a **rebuttal**, *an argument offered in response to another argument.* This is not to say that rebuttals must be good or successful responses to arguments, only that they are argumentative responses to arguments. Thus, a rebuttal includes evidence and conclusions, as well as stated or implied connectives, and must be tested like any other argument.

Refutation is a fourth possibility for responding to an argument. A **refutation** is *a successful counter-argument, one that wrecks the original argument.* If we can show, to the satisfaction of a reasonable and relatively objective listener, that we have thoroughly discredited the original argument, we have advanced a refutation. Of course, the individual advancing the original argument may not acknowledge that he or she has been refuted.

A fifth way of responding to an argument is **repudiation**, *dismissing the argument without advancing arguments or evidence as part of the dismissal.* Repudiations take several forms, including the use of phrases such as, "That's just ridiculous" or "That's crazy." Ridicule in argumentation is discussed in chapter 11. Repudiation also may take the form of a personal attack, such as, "Well, I'd expect someone like Bill to say something like that." Repudiation may involve labeling the person or group making an argument. As examples, "That's just a fundamentalist talking" and "What do you expect from a liberal?" constitute labeling. Finally, repudiation may take the form of a refusal to respond to the argument in any way at all. Some argument theorists contend that repudiation by silence is reasonable in certain special cases, because to answer some arguments is to attribute to them a status they don't deserve. Michael Billig wrote that:

> The refusal to enter a debate can itself be a rhetorical strategy, based upon the recognition that the mere act of answering a question imparts legitimacy to the question. Thus, the serious historian would be well advised to refrain from discussing the reality of the Holocaust with the self-styled, anti-semitic "experts," because to do so implies a legitimate controversy between two schools of thought.[8]

What should be noted again about repudiation is that it does not involve a stated (though it may involve an implied) argument.

Acceptance, consideration, rebuttal, and refutation offer several potentially reasonable responses to arguments we encounter. In most cases, repudiation does not offer a reasonable alternative for responding to arguments. As Billig has argued, however, repudiation by silence may be reasonable in some contexts. Of course, uncritical acceptance or consideration, or a weak rebuttal, may not be reasonable either. Moreover, in response to a rebuttal or a refutation, we may decide to modify or even to reject our own previous position on a topic. Argumentation, then, is a process that involves complex and ongoing mental and verbal activity. This process can be engaged in responsibly or irresponsibly, ethically or unethically.

Again, reasonable people do disagree about what constitutes a reasonable argument on a specific topic, and reasonable people advance and accept both reasonable and unreasonable arguments. Our attitudes and actions likely are based on unreasonable arguments at times. To the extent possible, however, we should aim to base belief, action, and debate on the most reasonable arguments we can marshal. This is the obligation of all parties to argumentation and constitutes one agreement that should accompany all responsible argumentation.

These thoughts raise the question: Who ultimately decides which arguments are reasonable and which are unreasonable? Each of us makes many such determinations, and in decisions that are ours alone to make, such as where we will live and what kind of work we will do, we are the final judges of reasonableness. We may listen to arguments others advance and consider evidence they present, and may modify our views in response, but the final judgment about which arguments will be accepted rests with us.

When arguments affect groups or communities of people, however, the final judgment about the reasonableness of arguments usually does not rest with a single individual. Most argument contexts involve a **relevant community,** *a group of people charged with making final judgments about which arguments are most reasonable.* In a court of law, a jury often functions as the relevant community. Lawyers on both sides set forth the most reasonable cases they can, witnesses present their testimony, evidences are advanced, but the jury is left with the judgment as to whose arguments were most reasonable. In an election the voting public is the relevant community. Campaign speeches are presented, commercials are broadcast, letters are sent, but the final judgment about the reasonableness of the candidate's arguments is rendered by the voters.

This is not to say that relevant communities are always accurate in their judgments about arguments. Any given community is capable of reasonable or unreasonable judgments about arguments. It is to say, however, that democratic societies leave many such judgments to relevant communities. One conclusion to be drawn from these two observations, taken together, is that education in argumentation and critical thinking is important to ensure that good decisions are made in a free society.

⋆ The search for reasonable arguments involves some effort, along with a commitment to careful **critical thinking**—*thinking informed by an awareness of the criteria for judging the ethicality and reasonableness of arguments, and a willingness to apply these criteria consistently.* Being critical thinkers means that we try to separate reasonable from unreasonable arguments in our own rational commitments, a difficult thing to do when we have all accepted propositions on some basis other than careful thought. Critical thinking also means that we must carefully scrutinize the arguments others ask us to accept. Thus, to be critical thinkers we must understand something about arguments and what makes them reasonable.⋆ Enhancing understanding of arguments is a goal of this text.

WRAP UP

Reasonable arguments move from good reasons by means of good inferences to thus substantiated conclusions. They also exhibit consistent definitions of key terms. We are not obliged to accept all reasonable arguments. Reasonable people disagree on many issues on the basis of careful and critical thought. Responding to an argument may involve acceptance, consideration, rebuttal, refutation, or repudiation. It is important to try to be reasonable in our own arguments, and to be careful in assessing arguments advanced for our acceptance. Only in so doing can we claim to be critical thinkers.

Chapter Review

Argumentation usually develops out of disagreement among individuals, but it does require some agreement to proceed productively. Both sides may agree on procedures, goals, evidence, or other matters. This chapter suggests two additional agreements crucial to responsible argumentation: the agreements to argue ethically and to argue reasonably. Some of the contours of ethical and reasonable argumentation have been sketched, as have the basic components and commitments of critical thinking.

EXERCISES

A. Provide an instance of argumentation that you have read or heard, which you consider to have been unethical. Explain why you think the argument you have in mind was unethical. Does it violate some principle mentioned in this chapter, or should some other principle of argument ethics be added to the ones already discussed?

B. Think of an argument you have read or heard recently that has struck you as particularly unreasonable. Try to identify what it was about the argument that seemed unreasonable. What group would constitute the relevant community for determining the reasonableness of this argument? In which of the five ways discussed in this chapter (acceptance, consideration, rebuttal, refutation, repudiation) have you sought to respond to this argument? Explain.

C. Provide an example of an argument you find to be both ethical and reasonable. Given the guidelines discussed in this chapter, explain why you think that a person who thinks critically could accept or consider the argument.

ENDNOTES

1. For a helpful discussion of the argumentative nature of human social and personal life, see Michael Billig, *Arguing and Thinking* (Cambridge: Cambridge University Press, 1987), especially chapter 2.

2. See Chaim Perelman and L. Olbrechts-Tyteca, "Self-Deliberating," in *The New Rhetoric*, translated by John Wilkinson and Purcell Weaver, 1969 (Notre Dame, IN: University of Notre Dame Press), pp. 40–45.

3. See "Agreement," in Perelman and Olbrechts-Tyteca, pp. 65–114.

4. I would like to thank Allen Verhey for several helpful suggestions regarding ethics and argument. For a detailed discussion of ethics in communication, as well as an extensive bibliography on the subject, see Richard L. Johannesen, *Ethics in Human Communication*, 2d ed. (Prospect Heights, IL: Waveland Press, 1983).

5. For a discussion of suggestion, see chapter 11.

6. For a good discussion of fallacies, see T. Edward Damer, *Attacking Faulty Reasoning*, 2d ed. (Belmont, CA: Wadsworth, 1987).

7. I would like to thank Professor Yehudi Webster for suggesting these categories of response to arguments.

8. Billig, p. 222.

3 THINKING CRITICALLY ABOUT EVIDENCE AND SOURCES

Chapter Preview

THINKING CRITICALLY ABOUT EVIDENCE

Presentation and discussion of several general tests of evidence.

TESTIMONY AS EVIDENCE

Discussion of how to evaluate testimony—evidence drawn from the experience of other people.

THINKING CRITICALLY ABOUT SOURCES

Guidelines on how to evaluate periodicals, books, and television as sources of evidence.

SPOTTING A SOURCE'S POLITICAL PERSPECTIVE

Discussion of some clues to look for in figuring out a source's orientation.

Key Terms

consistency of evidence
accessibility of evidence
adequacy of evidence
recency of evidence
relevance of evidence
testimony
ordinary testimony

expert testimony
biased source
reluctant source
unbiased source
individual testimony
concurrent testimony
source's political perspective

C hapter 1 pointed out that evidence is usually derived from observation, testimony, experiment, or some other type of experience. Connective reasons, on the other hand, are usually beliefs, values, assumptions, or generalizations. Connectives are specific to the kind of argument in which they occur. In fact, the type of connective employed often identifies the kind of argument we are reading, hearing, or advancing. For these reasons, connectives and their tests will be discussed in more detail in subsequent chapters dealing with various types of argument.

Evidence, on the other hand, is subject to a number of general tests, which apply regardless of the kind of argument in which the evidence is advanced. What, then, are the marks of good evidence? When does evidence provide reasonable support for a conclusion? Answering these questions requires asking and answering other questions regarding the evidence, as well as its sources. We can begin with questions about the evidence itself.

❖ THINKING CRITICALLY ABOUT EVIDENCE

One requirement of evidence is that it be generally consistent in what it relates or suggests. Evidence that contradicts itself is usually not good evidence. Good evidence should be consistent with the best of other available evidence as well. The requirement of consistency, the first test of evidence, can be formulated into the following question:

Test 1: Is the evidence internally and externally consistent?

Two tests are actually present here, the tests of internal consistency and of external consistency. Evidence in an argument has internal consistency when it is not at odds with other statements in the argument, whether reasons or conclusions. Internally inconsistent evidence can render an argument unreasonable, and perhaps even self-refuting; the argument casts doubt on its own integrity. In a brief argument such inconsistency might be immediately apparent. For example:

The Reagan administration made drastic cuts in research and development of alternative energy sources, cutting some programs by up to 80 percent and setting back development of these sources by years. Federal funding of research and development of solar, wind, and water power has led to steady advances in these technologies in the 1980s. Clearly the Reagan administration was no friend to alternative energy development.

In this argument, the evidence presented in the first sentence seems inconsistent with that presented in the second sentence, thus creating some doubt about the argument's reasonableness. Another speaker was heard to affirm the following in a presentation on genetic engineering:

Because of the tremendous potential benefits of genetic engineering I have outlined, we need to proceed immediately with experimentation on recombinant DNA research using human genetic materials. Because of the dangers associated with human genetic research, current legislation allows for experimentation on animal and plant genetic structures only. It is my view that the current laws should remain in place until adequate safeguards are established for human genetic research, and such safeguards may take years to develop.

In this example, the claim that "we need to proceed immediately" with human genetic engineering research seems inconsistent with the claim that current laws which prohibit such research should remain in place, perhaps for years.

These examples are brief, so the inconsistencies are relatively easy to spot. In a longer argument, however, internal inconsistency is often difficult to recognize. Since internal consistency is one criterion of reasonable evidence, we have to listen and read carefully for any contradictions or inconsistencies in arguments.

The external **consistency of evidence** also should be considered in making judgments about its quality. Evidence ought not to be sharply at odds with the majority or the preponderance of other available evidence. It also ought to be generally consistent with the best available sources on the topic. An example of inconsistency with both the majority of evidence, and the best available evidence was alluded to in chapter 2. Recently, arguments have been advanced by groups in both Europe and the U.S. that the Nazi holocaust either did not occur or was not nearly as serious as has been reported. These arguments rest on evidence that flies in the face of massive physical and testimonial evidence to the contrary.

Other, less dramatic, examples of externally inconsistent evidence are also apparent. Books that explain unusual ancient artifacts as the result of visits to earth by extraterrestrials often are opposed by the findings of qualified anthropologists. Remarkable medical claims resting on questionable evidence may be inconsistent with vast research by established medical experts. This is not to say that externally inconsistent evidence may not be accurate and reliable, but some question about the credibility of evidence is raised when it is clearly at odds with the best or the majority of other available evidence.

Some arguments present evidence directly. Other arguments allude to evidence, and still others may be essentially without evidence. If we are at all inclined to question an argument's evidence, the evidence must be accessible to us. We all are inclined to accept some arguments in which the evidence is not immediately available, especially if we already agree with the claim being advanced, or if we think the point has been well established in other arguments, or if we don't see that the claim being advanced is particularly important. Sometimes we are willing to simply believe the person arguing because he or she is a highly credible source. Even in such cases, though, we should ask whether the evidence would be available were we to seek to obtain it. Thus, the second general test of evidence asks:

Test 2:   Is the evidence accessible?

Accessible evidence is either presented directly, or can be retrieved and examined. If an argument presents its evidence, or presents sources that can be consulted, then the test of accessibility has been met. Sometimes the actual evidence would be too complex or unwieldy to present. In such cases, citing an accessible source may be satisfactory.

Inaccessible evidence presents a problem when we doubt the truthfulness of a claim. When an argument advances a questionable claim, and when the evidence for the claim is unavailable in the argument, or the evidence's sources are unknown or inaccessible, we are under no obligation to accept the argument.

One important exception to this guideline should be noted. In some cases evidence in a reasonable argument may simply not be accessible— for instance, when the appropriate evidence would be too complex to decipher without special expertise. When visiting an orthopedic surgeon for help with a painful knee, I may be shown x-rays that represent clear evidence for the doctor to conclude that I have a torn ligament and bone fragments in my joint. Still, in looking at the evidence, I may not see what the doctor sees. Don't I have good reason for accepting the doctor's word that the evidence can be interpreted in a certain way? In such cases, assuming a decision has to be made, the test of accessibility may have to be set aside temporarily in favor of trusting the expert's interpretation. But even in such cases we can consult a second or third expert if we are unsatisfied with the quality of the first interpretation.

Suppose we are satisfied that the evidence for a conclusion is accessible and consistent. We still may want to ask whether that evidence is sufficient to reasonably support its conclusion. Putting this test in the form of a question, we can ask:

Test 3: Is this evidence adequate to support this conclusion?

Asking whether sufficient evidence has been advanced in support of a conclusion is vital. But how much evidence is enough? This question can be answered in two ways. Asking whether *you* are satisfied that the evidence advanced is adequate is always important. At times, however, we are aware that our own desires, ignorance, or biases may prevent us from making good decisions about evidence. In such cases we can ask whether *some other reasonable person* would find the evidence adequate. The argument theorist Chaim Perelman has suggested that imagining whether some highly reasonable individual or group would be willing to accept the evidence as adequate might be helpful. Perelman called this imagined audience the "universal audience."[1]

When assessing the **adequacy of the evidence** in an argument, just to ask yourself about the *seriousness* of the question being decided can help. If I am being asked to risk my own or someone else's life on the basis of the argument before me, I may require that the evidence be both good and plentiful. We would face such a situation when sitting on a jury hearing arguments in a case in which the accused might receive a death sentence. If I am being asked to sign a petition to allow a local restaurant to serve wine, I may not require as much or as good evidence that the claims I am being asked to accept are reasonable. The seriousness of claims ranges from trivial to gravely serious, and assessing the adequacy of evidence often requires placing a claim somewhere on that continuum.

Another important consideration in evaluating some evidence is its recency. We are all aware that what is considered good evidence today may be worthless as evidence in a few years, or even a few weeks. In controversies that involve changing technologies, as do many of the controversies in the fields of medicine and energy, new evidence is constantly coming to light. In political controversies, changes in a nation's or a region's political situation can render the best evidence antiquated almost overnight. Thus, it is important to ask:

Test 4: Is the evidence recent enough?

In some cases, having the most up-to-date evidence is not crucial. Geological controversies exist in which evidence gathered more than a hundred years ago is still considered important. Arguments about human nature may draw on reliable evidence as old as the ancient Greek philosophers.

In many controversies, however, ensuring that the evidence we are being asked to accept is the most recent available is important. Evidence that has been overturned by more recent findings does not provide a good foundation for a reasonable argument. For instance, evidence from five years ago tending to show that room temperature superconductivity was either impossible or out of reach for at least twenty years would not be good evidence in light of more recent advances in superconducting materials. Thus, in testing evidence we need to be concerned with whether the issue at hand requires the most **recent evidence** available.

Another important consideration is whether evidence is relevant to the conclusion it is advanced to support. This concern can be expressed as the question:

Test 5:   Is the evidence relevant to this conclusion?

In many arguments, it is relatively easy to see that the evidence advanced *does* have some bearing on the conclusions it supports. For example:

Because 60 percent of U.S. electricity is produced from coal, electric utilities produce more carbon dioxide than any other single industry—35 percent of the nation's total. Thus, any serious efforts to curb carbon dioxide emissions must take electric utilities into consideration, and possibly would involve reevaluating how electricity is produced in our country.

Some evidence, however, doesn't seem to have any bearing on its conclusion. For example, someone argues:

The city should not hire a city manager. After all, the county board recently voted not to fund a new building for the high school.

In this example it is difficult to see what the county board's failure to fund a new building for the high school has to do with the decision to hire a city manager. Possibly the missing connective in this argument would suggest the relevance of this evidence to this conclusion but, as it stands, the former seems irrelevant to the latter.

If we doubt that some evidence bears directly on the conclusion it is advanced to support, we might be able to ask for clarification of the relationship between evidence and conclusion. In other instances, as with written arguments, such direct questioning of the person arguing may not be possible, and we are left to make the best judgment we can about **relevance**. The test of relevance also should serve to remind us to make every effort to clarify the relationship between our own evidence and our conclusions. We can readily assume, falsely, that a connection between evidence and conclusion that makes sense to us will make sense to others.

WRAP UP

The strength of an argument is directly dependent on the strength of its evidence. The five general tests of evidence are:

1. Is the evidence internally and externally consistent?
2. Is the evidence accessible?
3. Is the evidence adequate to support the conclusion?
4. Is the evidence recent enough?
5. Is the evidence relevant to the conclusion?

Later chapters will take up specific types of evidence and their tests. The next section, however, focuses on one particularly important type of evidence not covered in subsequent chapters.

❖ TESTIMONY AS EVIDENCE

Testimony, *the reports of others about their experiences or knowledge*, is an important source of information about the world because the experience of any one person is necessarily limited. We seek and value testimony in situations in which our own experience does not allow us direct knowledge, or when our own knowledge is limited.

The two major kinds of testimony are **ordinary** and **expert**. Ordinary testimony is *the experience or opinions of others presented in their own words, and on topics not requiring special expertise*. Ordinary testimony may be used as evidence when the issue at hand does not require evidence from expert sources. Expert testimony is *the opinion of an expert concerning a matter within his or her realm of expertise*.

All testimony can be categorized according to the source's relationship to what he or she is testifying about.[2] First, some people will benefit in some way if what they say is accepted as true. For example, a defendant in a trial certainly would stand to gain if his or her testimony that he or she did not commit a certain crime is accepted as true. A **biased source** is *a source who stands to gain if his or her testimony is accepted as true*. This designation does not by itself mean that the testimony is unreliable, though it does mean that the testimony should be viewed with some suspicion and accepted only after careful efforts at verification.

Second, some people stand to lose if their testimony is accepted as true. If my testimony means that I likely will be socially ostracized, I stand to lose if it is accepted as true. *A source who stands to lose if his or her testimony is accepted as true* is termed a **reluctant source**. This designation does not ensure that the testimony is reliable, but it does create a strong presumption that it is true. Testimony from reluctant sources is generally considered to be the strongest type of testimony.

Third, some testimony comes from sources who stand neither to lose nor to gain if their testimony is accepted as true. When a psychologist who has no relationship to an individual on trial testifies that the individual is sane, we would tend to assume that the psychologist has nothing to gain or lose if the testimony is accepted as true. *A source who stands neither to lose nor to gain if his or her testimony is accepted as true* is called an **unbiased source**.

Introducing one other basis of dividing testimony will be helpful. We may hear *testimony from one person*, which can be called **individual testimony**. *Consistent testimony from two or more individuals* can be termed **concurrent testimony**. Though concurrent testimony is not always more reliable than individual testimony, there is usually a presumption that it is more reliable when it conflicts with individual testimony.

The following diagram illustrates the categories of testimony we have introduced to this point:

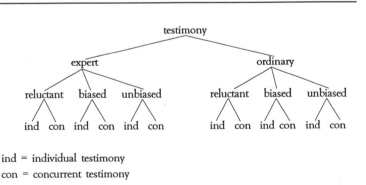

ind = individual testimony
con = concurrent testimony

In general, the strongest type of testimony is concurrent-reluctant testimony of either the expert or the ordinary type. The least reliable is individual-biased. Reluctant testimony usually is held to be more reliable than unbiased testimony.

EVALUATING TESTIMONY

Evaluating the strength of testimony you are being asked to accept as evidence is important. The following tests can be helpful in this regard. We will begin with some tests of ordinary testimony, looking both at the sources of the testimony and at the events testified about.[3]

Tests of Ordinary Testimony

First we will want to ask an obvious question concerning the veracity or truthfulness of the source of testimony:

Test 1:   Is the source known to be honest or reliable?

There is generally a presumption in favor of a person with a record of honesty and against a person with a record of dishonesty. This does not mean, however, that a person with a record of dishonesty cannot present truthful testimony, or that a person with a history of honesty might not be dishonest on occasion. The test simply expresses the belief that we will more likely hear accurate testimony from people who have in the past shown themselves to be honest.

Beyond inquiring about the honesty of the individual whose testimony we are examining, determining the relationship of the source to what he or she is testifying about is also important. Thus, we should ask:

*Test 2:   Does the person testifying have anything to gain
            by the testimony being accepted?*

This, of course, is a question designed to ascertain if the source is *biased*. Again, a biased source is not necessarily unreliable, although the presumption is that the testimony might not be reliable. The test simply expresses that we want to be cautious about accepting the testimony of persons who will benefit by their testimony being accepted. Some would go so far as to say that this sort of testimony ought never to be accepted.

Because ordinary testimony is often about someone's experience of an event, we have to ascertain if reliable experience of the event was possible. Thus, we might have to ask:

*Test 3:   Did the person testifying have the opportunity to
            clearly observe the event in question?*

One obvious question is suggested here: Was the witness in the area when the event occurred? More specific questions might include: Was it dark when the event in question took place? Might any objects have obstructed the witness's view? As for the witness's frame of mind, we would certainly want to know if he or she had been drunk, frantic, mentally unstable, or in some other condition that would have prevented accurate observation and reporting.

Finally, determining whether the testimony we are being asked to accept is consistent with other available testimony is important. This test can be formulated as follows:

Test 4:   Is the source consistent with other witnesses?

This question asks whether any other testimony is available and, if so, whether it is concurrent with the testimony we have. In cases where testimony conflicts, we might have to determine what the preponderance of testimony tends to indicate. Again, a single, uncorroborated source may be more accurate than several witnesses making contrary reports. The test is simply expressing the presumption favoring consistent testimony.

Tests of Events

Testimony is usually a report about some event or set of circumstances. In assessing testimony, we must ask certain questions about the events being reported. Among the questions we should ask of an event are:

Test 1:   How close in time is the event to the testimony regarding it?

The accuracy of testimony depends on the accuracy of memory. Moreover, recountings of events may change with each telling. Thus, events occurring close in time to when testimony regarding them is advanced usually are more easily supported than are events occurring a long time before the testimony regarding them. This is why the dating of ancient historical documents is often hotly debated. Documents that can be shown to have been written close in time to the events they record are taken to be more accurate than documents written long after the events they describe.

The probability or likelihood that an event occurred is also a consideration in making judgments about testimony. Thus, a good question to ask is:

Test 2:   How unlikely is the event being reported?

The more unlikely an event is, the more testimony we will require to be satisfied that it occurred. Although this is generally true, cases certainly exist in which we are willing to accept the testimony of one highly reliable witness to support some unlikely event. In general, the more unlikely the event is, the stronger is the testimony required to support the event.

The occurrence of events may be established by evidence other than testimony, and testimony may be confirmed or dismissed on the basis of other evidence. Thus, the third test of events asks:

Test 3:   *Does any other evidence support the reported event?*

The search for corroborating evidence often accompanies the examination of testimony. For example, testimony regarding the cause of an airliner crash may be supported by physical evidence from the scene of the accident. If we can find other evidence either confirming or disconfirming some event, we will want to weigh this evidence against the testimony we have in making any final determinations.

Tests of Expert Testimony

Two special tests should be applied to expert testimony. First, we should ask about the source's field of expertise:

Test 1:   *Does the individual have credentials as an expert in the appropriate field?*

This obvious question must be asked of sources of expert testimony. In some cases an individual's expertise is generally recognized. In other cases the person's expertise might have to be established. This usually can be accomplished by stating the individual's qualifications. The expert's testimony should be employed solely concerning questions germane to his or her field of expertise. Only then are we dealing with expert testimony. Expertise is not transferable from one arena to another.

The consistency of expert witnesses with other experts in the same field also must be tested, by asking:

Test 2:   *Is the expert's testimony consistent with that of other experts in the field?*

Finding an expert to support a point of view is almost always possible. But if many other experts in the field contradict the testimony of a given authority, that person's testimony is called into question.

GUIDELINES FOR USING TESTIMONY

When employing testimony as evidence in your own arguments, be sure, first, to *accurately quote sources*. If you paraphrase, always indicate clearly that you are doing this, and have the original quote ready in case you are called to produce it. Second, *identify your sources*. Be sure to let your audience know whom you are quoting and where you found the testimony. Third, *avoid biased sources*. A biased source is often an unreliable source. Audiences will be suspicious of sources they know to be biased. Fourth, *use qualified sources*. Be sure that whether you are employing expert or ordinary testimony, your sources meet the tests set out herein. Fifth, when using quotations in a paper or a speech, *be brief*. A brief quotation that makes your point is better than a long quotation that requires interpretation or generally makes more demands on an audience.

WRAP UP

Ordinary testimony is the reported experiences of others about matters that do not require expertise. Most of us find it reasonable to accept ordinary testimony at least some of the time. But we also must be cautious of ordinary testimony, especially when the reliability of the source of testimony, or the likelihood of the reported event, is questionable. Sources of ordinary testimony can be classified as biased, unbiased, or reluctant, depending on their relationship to what they are reporting about. Ordinary testimony also can be classified as being from an individual, or consistent testimony from more than one person—concurrent testimony.

Expert testimony is an expert's report on matters within his or her field of expertise. Experts must be qualified and expert in the appropriate field. An expert who is consistent with other experts in the same area is most desirable.

❖ THINKING CRITICALLY ABOUT SOURCES OF EVIDENCE

Evaluating evidence also involves evaluating sources such as books, periodicals, and television. We certainly want to know whether the source is credible or reliable, but there are other important considerations as well.

Perhaps the first question to ask of a source is whether it can be reasonably believed on the topic at hand. Thus, we should ask of any source of evidence:

Test 1:   Is the source of the evidence reliable?

Evidence can be derived from a variety of sources, and judgments about reliability will depend on the type of source we are evaluating. A reliable source is one whose qualifications to provide a particular kind of evidence are clear, or can be reasonably established.

Since many of the sources available to you for evidence are periodicals and books, the next two sections explore the reliability of such sources in more detail. A brief discussion of television programs as potential sources of evidence is also included.[4]

THINKING CRITICALLY ABOUT PERIODICALS AS SOURCES

Any trip to the library quickly reveals that you have available to you, in addition to the books, a wide range of periodicals. We may be uncertain about the quality of some of these periodicals, and perhaps especially about their quality as sources of evidence.

One type of periodical is the *scholarly journal*. Examples of scholarly journals are *JAMA: The Journal of the American Medical Association, Psychological Bulletin, Journal of Marriage and the Family, Sex Roles: A Journal of Research, Mind*, and *Communication Monographs*. These publications look sober and serious. They may feature tables, charts, statistics, and lengthy analyses of intellectual issues. They include few, if any, photographs, and little or no advertising. But their essays and studies are well documented, and typically include footnotes and bibliographies. The writers are scholars and researchers who are well qualified to be writing in their various fields. They have come through a long and rigorous period of training to achieve their status as experts on a subject.

The audience for scholarly publications usually consists of others in the same discipline. The language is scholarly and technical, and often difficult for the average reader to understand. These periodicals most commonly are published by professional and scholarly organizations, and their purpose is to report on original research or experimentation. Scholarly journals are often good sources of highly reliable evidence, but their scholarly approach and technical language may make them hard to use.

Another type of publication is the *general interest periodical*. Examples include *The Economist, The New York Times Magazine, Newsweek, Time, Psychology Today*, and *The Smithsonian*. These are attractively presented magazines, usually illustrated with many photos. The stories and reports are written by qualified authors—researchers, reporters, and scholars—though the writers may not cite their actual sources of evidence. In fact, the authors often consult the scholarly journals, just described, as well as government reports and the publications of foundations and institutions. General interest publications can provide very good evidence that is accessible to and readily understood by many readers.

Readers of these periodicals tend to be well educated; the language may be moderately technical; and the writing is of high quality. These periodicals are published by commercial publishers, professional organizations, and institutions. Their purposes are to provide information to a broad audience of interested readers, to make a profit, and sometimes to advocate a political perspective.

Another type of publication is the *popular magazine*. Examples include *Family Circle, Sports Illustrated, Parents, Reader's Digest*, and *Woman's Day*. These are attractive, slick-looking magazines that feature numerous graphics, and even more advertisements. Stories and reports in these magazines rarely cite sources, and the pieces are written by staff members, by freelance writers, and occasionally by a well-known person who may or may not be expert in the appropriate field. As a result, these magazines may not be good sources of evidence, although there are exceptional cases.

Popular magazines are aimed at a general audience, and no high level of education is assumed of the readers. The language is simple; articles are often short and may lack depth. Commercial publishers produce these periodicals, which are published for entertainment, to present information, to promote a point of view, and to make a profit—not necessarily in that order.

Finally, we are all aware of the *sensational press*, publications sold at supermarket check-out stands carrying headlines ranging from celebrity gossip such as "Burt and Lonnie's Marriage Breaking Up" to pure fiction such as "Family of Werewolves Found Living in Newark Suburb." Examples of these periodicals are *The Globe, The National Examiner, Star*, and *The National Enquirer*. Your library possibly does not house publications such as these, but you may encounter them other places. Although their style of presentation varies, they often use a newspaper format.

In most cases, writers for these publications make no effort to cite their sources at all, and the reports can amount to fabrication and the repetition of rumors, especially those detailing the lives of entertainment celebrities. Who actually wrote a given piece may be in question. These publications often employ a staff or freelance writers who are not clearly identified in the periodical itself. For all of these reasons, the sensational press should not be considered as a good source of evidence.

Who is the audience for the sensational press? These publications often have large circulations, but the readership must be considered to be those who are gullible or those who are simply seeking entertainment by reading reports they know are not necessarily accurate. The language employed is elementary and frequently is inflammatory or sensational: "Half-Man Half-Woman Makes Self Pregnant."

Who publishes these periodicals? Various commercial publishers whose goal is simply profit. If there is a goal beyond profit, it may be to arouse curiosity in and to entertain their readers.

THINKING CRITICALLY ABOUT BOOKS AS SOURCES

Books are another important source of evidence, and some guidelines for evaluating them can be useful. When evaluating a book as a source of evidence, here are some questions to ask.

1. *Who wrote the book?* The author's credentials or qualifications to be writing a book on the subject should be assessed. In evaluating the author's qualifications, you may want to ask about the author's experience, education, or position. Some books contain brief notes describing these characteristics. When you want additional information, check *Who's Who* or biographical dictionaries. Reference librarians in your library may be able to point you to additional sources of information about an author.

2. *When was this book published?* Just as good evidence should be recent, good books should reflect the most current information in the field. This is especially important in continually changing fields such as the sciences and the social sciences. Determining the recency of a book is usually as simple as checking the publication date; with reprinted books you may want to look for the earliest copyright date.

3. *Who is the book's publisher?* Well-known publishers are usually reliable. University publications likely contain reliable scholarship. Ask the reference librarian about publishers whose names you don't recognize. Beware of "vanity press" publishers, which will publish anyone's work provided the author pays for publication. You also should be skeptical of publications by organizations known to hold extreme views. And if no publisher is listed, watch out!

4. *For what kind of audience is the book written?* The more general, less educated the audience is, the simpler the book will be. This doesn't mean that the book is not good, but the evidence it presents may not give a complete picture of the situation. As with periodicals, books written for an educated audience usually provide the most thorough and best researched evidence.

5. *Does the author have an evident bias?* This question asks about the author's underlying assumptions, which may color his or her presentation or interpretation of information. Here you can use some of the recommendations discussed in the next section, on how to spot a political perspective in a source.

6. *What method of obtaining data or conducting research did the book's author use?* You may want to determine whether the book appears to have been carefully researched or whether it relies on anecdotes, rumors, assumptions, and biases. Did the writer conduct the research reported or use facts gathered by others? Are facts, statistics, and other data sufficiently documented? Good books let the readers know where their information, quotations, and statistics come from. Along the same line, check whether the book has an index and a bibliography. These elements generally indicate a scholarly approach to the topic.

7. *What do others think of the source?* To find an answer to this question, note whether the book is mentioned in other books on the topic. You also can find reviews of many books in a publication called *Book Review Digest*. Ask a librarian for help in finding this reference work if you cannot locate it.

THINKING CRITICALLY ABOUT
TELEVISION AS A SOURCE

Documentary-type programs such as *60 Minutes*, interview programs such as Phil Donahue's, and investigative reporting shows such as Geraldo Rivera's are fundamentally commercial programs. This means that they must be interesting in order to be watched and that they must compete successfully with situation comedies and sports programming. For these reasons, they tend to focus on human interest and individual stories rather than on careful analysis of controversial issues. The analysis they do provide may be brief and shallow. The hosts sometimes "lead" guests, even expert guests, to say what the host wants to be said. Thus, such sources of evidence should be used sparingly and cautiously, if you choose to use them at all. They should not stand as your sole source of evidence on a topic.

Some documentaries and interview programs on public television provide more detailed analysis of issues, because these programs are not required to hold viewers' interest long enough to get attention for commercials. As a result, these programs may provide you with good evidence on occasion.

When evaluating sources of evidence, reliability is not the only consideration. Even when dealing with a reliable source, trying to ascertain the political perspective from which the source writes or speaks is usually important. Even sound sources of evidence may be advocating a point of view when they appear to be reporting "events as they are." A critical reader or listener has to be aware of the influence of political perspective on the presentation and interpretation of evidence. This concern can be presented as a question:

Test 2:   What is the source's political perspective?

Although ascertaining a **source's political perspective** is not always easy, some clues can provide an indication. The following questions and techniques may be helpful in this regard.

SPOTTING A SOURCE'S POLITICAL PERSPECTIVE

One important question to ask of a source is what *assumptions* seem to be at work in the writing. What seems to be taken for granted by the author or speaker? What conclusions and evidence are treated as worthy of acceptance without examination? On the other hand, what evidence and conclusions are taken as worthy of repudiation—rejection without consideration? For instance, does the source seem to assume that almost any policy change is preferable to a new tax? If so, you may be reading a politically conservative source. Does the source seem to assume that almost any use of government money is better than defense spending? If so, the source may be politically liberal.

A second approach that is helpful in spotting a political perspective is to try to *imagine the event in question being reported in a different way*. When the Israeli government sent troops into Palestinian neighborhoods on the West Bank of the Jordan River, some journals reported it as the Israelis controlling a rebellion by Palestinians. These publications may have been expressing a preference for Israel's point of view in the matter. Other journals reported the same action as an Israeli government crackdown on legitimate Palestinian dissent, and thus may have reflected their sympathy with the Palestinians affected.

A third factor in determining a periodical's political perspective is to consider its *reputation and purpose*. This is especially helpful when dealing with periodicals that have a well-known editorial bias. For example, the *National Review* is widely recognized as a politically conservative journal, as is *Forbes*. On the other hand, *The New Republic* represents a politically liberal point of view, as does *Rolling Stone*—though not perhaps on the same issues.

A fourth consideration in spotting a political perspective is *how groups are described or treated*. For instance, what is the view of homeless people, or of the unemployed? Are they portrayed as victims of political decisions, or as people who lack initiative? Are immigrants discussed as welcome additions to our population who deserve our assistance, or as threats to the economy and to American citizens seeking scarce jobs?

Fifth, clues to the political perspective of a source are often provided by the *language and labels* used. What phrases are repeated? Are any emotionally loaded terms used, such as censorship, murder, or political repression? Are labels such as Communists, abortionists, bleeding hearts, or fundamentalists used to describe groups? A writer's efforts to discredit a group by the use of a label is often a good clue as to that writer's political orientation.

Though these five clues to political perspective are not always reliable, they sometimes can provide a sense of the writer's or speaker's point of view. Knowing that point of view can help you evaluate the source as a source of evidence.

WRAP UP

In addition to testing evidence, the sources of that evidence should be evaluated. The following tests have been suggested:

1. Is the source of the evidence reliable?
2. What is the source's political perspective?

Various specific questions are appropriate when evaluating periodicals, books, and television as sources of evidence. The recommended approaches can also help in ascertaining a source's political perspective.

Chapter Review

Some evidence is specific to particular kinds of arguments. Special tests are presented, in later chapters, for such evidence. This chapter has considered some tests of evidence and its sources, which are capable of general application. We also have discussed ways of evaluating two different types of testimony as evidence. In addition, we have looked in more detail at periodicals, books, and television programs as sources of evidence. Finally, ways of identifying a source's political perspective have been explored.

These tests of evidence and sources should be helpful in evaluating the evidence we read or hear advanced in arguments. In addition, these tests can assist you in thinking critically about the quality of evidence and sources you employ in your own arguments.

EXERCISES

A. Each of the following examples presents a kind of testimony that can be described using terms from this chapter. Considering three terms for each (example: expert, unbiased, individual), identify the kind of testimony being employed in each of the following examples. Context statements may help in making some determinations about the type of testimony being advanced.

1. *Context*: In deciding whether the following testimony would be considered expert or ordinary, determine whether the person is testifying on a matter that draws on his expert knowledge of banking.

   A bank president's son is accused of stealing a large amount of money from his father's bank. Before the bank's board of directors, the president testifies that his son stole the money from the bank at his direction.

2. *Context*: In deciding whether the following source is reluctant, biased, or unbiased, you probably will have to attribute to him a motive.

   Your brother, normally an honest and reliable individual, tells you he saw a flying saucer while camping in the mountains.

3. *Context*: Henry Kissinger was Secretary of State while Richard Nixon was President. How would this fact affect your judgment regarding the kind of source Kissinger would be in the following examples?

    a. Henry Kissinger, in an interview with a major news magazine, testifies that relations between the U.S. and other world powers *improved* dramatically during the Nixon years.

    b. Henry Kissinger, in an interview with a major news magazine, testifies that relations between the U.S. and other world powers *declined* dramatically during the Nixon years.

4. *Context*: For the following testimony to be found reliable in a courtroom setting, what should be true of the source?

    A psychologist brought to court by the prosecution testifies that John Hinkley was sane at the time he shot President Reagan.

5. *Question*: For the following concurrent, expert testimony to be found reliable, what must be true of the source?

    A local high school has had problems with students getting sick during classes. Some of the teachers suspect that a newly installed insulation material may be causing the sicknesses. Two environmental toxicologists hired by the school district, after sampling the air in the classrooms, testify that the insulation in the school building is safe and could not be causing the sicknesses.

6. A vice-presidential political candidate claims that his running mate is the best qualified person to serve as President.

7. *Context*: In several recent and well publicized cases, individuals have come forward to testify against their own companies. In such situations, reflected in the following examples, are the sources likely to be biased, unbiased, or reluctant?

    a. A technician working for a major airline testifies in court that the flight recorders from a plane owned by his company indicate that the crew did not extend the plane's flaps before take-off. He also testifies that this oversight could easily have caused the plane's crash in which nearly 200 people were killed.

    b. An engineer employed by the rocket manufacturer testifies that his company had been warned that the O rings in the Challenger booster engines would crack in extreme cold, and that these warnings had been ignored.

8. Several followers of the Maharishi testify that they have seen him heal people of terminal illnesses.

9. a. You testify in court that an eccentric millionaire, now deceased, signed a note leaving you $6 million.

b. Five independent handwriting experts hired by the estate testify in court that an eccentric millionaire, now deceased, signed a note leaving you $6 million.

10. A company advertises that "our tires are the best on the road today!"

B. Select a general interest periodical from among those housed in your library. Provide citations for three articles from three different issues of the journal. Based on your reading of three essays, locate the journal on the three scales below.

1. Conservative _____ _____ _____ _____ _____ _____ Radical

2. Mass Appeal _____ _____ _____ _____ _____ _____ Scholarly

3. Specialized _____ _____ _____ _____ _____ _____ General

Cite some evidence to support your judgment on each of the scales. Based on your analysis of this journal, write a brief description (one paragraph) to guide other library users.

C. Evaluate each of the following sources in relation to the assignments suggested.

1. You must write a short researched paper on spouse abuse. Evaluate these potential sources of evidence:

a. A videotaped *Donahue* show in which four battered women tell their stories.

b. An article titled "Don't Hit Me Anymore" in *Ladies Home Journal* (January 1988).

c. An article in *Psychology Today* titled "Till Murder do us Part" (July 1985).

d. An article in *Psychological Bulletin* titled "The Decision to Leave an Abusive Relationship: Empirical Evidence and Theoretical Issues" (September 1988).

2. You are writing about reverse discrimination as one effect of affirmative action laws. Evaluate the following potential sources of evidence:

a. A transcript of a *60 Minutes* segment about reverse discrimination.

b. An article titled "What Every Manager Should Know about Discrimination" in *Working Women* (November 1987).

c. An article in *National Review* titled "Does America Hate Whites?" (August 1, 1986).

    d. An article in *Economist* on reverse discrimination cases before the Supreme Court (January 28, 1989).

D. Find an example in the media of either expert or ordinary testimony being used as evidence. Apply the tests discussed in this chapter to your example, and suggest whether the testimony can be accepted as reasonable evidence in support of its conclusion.

ENDNOTES

1. Chaim Perelman and L. Olbrechts-Tyteca, *The New Rhetoric*, translated by John Wilkinson and Purcell Weaver, (Notre Dame, IN: University of Notre Dame Press, 1969), pp. 31-35.

2. See also Philip K. Tompkins' discussion of "intention" in *Communication as Action* (Belmont, CA: Wadsworth, 1982), pp. 64-66.

3. For a fascinating discussion of eyewitness testimony, and a review of some literature on the topic, see Elizabeth F. Loftus, "Eyewitnesses: Essential but Unreliable," *Psychology Today* (Feb. 1984), pp. 22-26.

4. Unpublished material developed by Professor Barbara Mezeske, Hope College, is a source for much of the discussion of periodicals and books as sources of evidence, and for exercises C1 and C2.

4 CONCLUSIONS AND THE STRUCTURE OF ARGUMENTS

Chapter Preview

FOUR TYPES OF CONCLUSIONS

Discussion that will help you identify four types of conclusions and determine how arguments should be structured to support each.

THE LANGUAGE OF POLICY DEBATE

Definition of some technical terms of policy debate.

Key Terms

factual conclusions	propositions of value	*prima facie*
propositions of fact	value claims	case
factual claims	value term	negative case
descriptive claims	criteria of evaluation	affirmative case
propositions of past fact	evidence	inherency of problem
causal claims	normative conclusions	adequacy of plan
interpretations	propositions of policy	practicality of plan
predictive conclusions	presumption	workable policy
evaluative conclusions	burden of proof	ethical policy
	status quo	

A ll arguments arrive at conclusions, but not all arguments arrive at the same kind of conclusion. Some types of conclusions require more support, or a different kind of support, than others do. Moreover, the structure we expect of an argument may depend on the kind of conclusion it arrives at.

❖ TYPES OF CONCLUSIONS

Four types of conclusions are common in public discourse. These are: factual, predictive, evaluative, and normative conclusions.

FACTUAL CONCLUSIONS

Factual conclusions are *conclusions that describe, characterize, or make causal claims*. They are sometimes called **propositions of fact** or **factual claims**. Under the same umbrella heading we include conclusions that advance descriptions (sometimes termed **descriptive claims**), those that make claims about past events (often called **propositions of past fact**), and those alleging that one event causes another (also called **causal claims**).

The following argument arrives at a factual conclusion:

A: After a careful review of the available evidence, the Warren Commission found that Lee Harvey Oswald acted alone in killing President John F. Kennedy. B: No subsequent evidence has come to light that conclusively refutes the Commission's findings. <u>Thus</u>, C: it is safe to conclude that Oswald did act alone in killing the President.

This argument's factual conclusion—in this case, a proposition of past fact—is statement C: "it is safe to conclude that Oswald did act alone in killing the President." The qualifier, "it is safe to conclude that," indicates the rather high degree of certainty attached to the conclusion by the individual making the argument. The conclusion makes the factual claim that Lee Harvey Oswald acted alone in killing President Kennedy, which is a claim about a past event.

You may be thinking that "Oswald acted alone in killing President John F. Kennedy" is not a fact, that it is only a theory, an opinion, or a hypothesis. In calling this a factual conclusion, *we are not saying the statement is actually true*. We are using the word "factual" in a way different from the way it is normally used. "Factual" only means that the conclusion is capable of certain verification as being either true or false, that it potentially could be established as either true or false to the satisfaction of a reasonable person. The fact that this argument does not itself advance such certain verification of its conclusion does not render the conclusion something other than factual. The claim is still either true or false and is potentially capable of verification.

Arguments that arrive at factual conclusions can have a simple structure. They often only advance their evidence and draw their conclusion from that evidence. Some arguments arriving at factual conclusions also include **interpretations** of their evidence. Interpretation of evidence is important when: (a) evidence is technical or difficult to understand, (b) evidence might be taken several ways, or (c) implications of the evidence might not be readily appreciated. In these cases, arguments arriving at factual conclusions may include interpretive statements that assist the reader or listener in understanding why the evidence supports the factual claim. But interpretations of evidence are themselves often argumentative; they may advance one among many possible interpretations.

Here's an example of interpretation of evidence advanced by Melinda Beck of *Newsweek*:

Americans collectively toss out 160 million tons [of garbage] each year—enough to spread 30 stories high over 1,000 football fields, enough to fill a bumper-to-bumper convoy of garbage trucks halfway to the moon.[1]

The amount of garbage Americans throw out each year and the seriousness of the resulting problem are easier to comprehend given Beck's interpretation of the evidence.

For an argument arriving at a factual claim to be reasonable, then, the evidence must be good, according to the criteria suggested in chapter 3, and the interpretation given this evidence must be clear, and better than other possible interpretations. To summarize, arguments arriving at factual claims should show the following structure, though these elements may not appear in this order:

1. They must advance the *factual claim* itself.

2. They must advance reasonable *evidence* in support of the factual claim.

3. If necessary, they should *interpret* their evidence.

The evidence in the example concerning Lee Harvey Oswald is advanced in statements A and B, and its interpretation is implied in the argument's conclusion: The Commission's finding and the absence of conclusive counter-evidence are interpreted as proving that Oswald acted alone in killing Kennedy. The factual conclusion itself appears as statement C.

TESTS OF ARGUMENTS ARRIVING AT FACTUAL CONCLUSIONS

The structure of arguments arriving at factual conclusions suggests that there are two general tests of such arguments. The first test considers the quality of the evidence:

Test 1:   Is good evidence presented in support of the claim?

Here the general tests of evidence introduced in chapter 3 are appropriate. We should ask if the evidence in the argument is internally and externally consistent, accessible, adequate, recent (if appropriate), and relevant to the conclusion. We might note here that, although internal consistency does not seem to be a problem, the evidence in our example is inconsistent with the opinions of several published authorities on Kennedy's assassination. This does not by itself mean the evidence is bad, but it should make us a little more cautious about accepting the evidence and its claim.

The second test suggested by the structure of arguments that arrive at factual conclusions has to do with interpreting the evidence. It asks:

Test 2:   Is this a reasonable interpretation of the available evidence?

Interpreting evidence is difficult and, in some cases, complex. As an initial consideration, however, we can at least ask if the interpretation advanced seems to fit the evidence advanced. If we have reason to doubt the interpretation, we should try to articulate the reasons for our reservations. Returning to the example argument, we might reasonably wonder whether the observation that "No subsequent evidence has come to light that conclusively refutes the Commission's findings" can reasonably be interpreted as supporting the conclusion that "it is safe to conclude that Oswald did act alone in killing the President." Even if the former claim is accurate, it does not rule out the possibility that evidence has come to light that *raises serious questions* about the Commission's findings regarding whether Oswald acted alone.

PREDICTIVE CONCLUSIONS

Predictive conclusions are *conclusions that make claims about the future*. The following argument arrives at a predictive conclusion:

A: The number of medical malpractice suits has skyrocketed in the past fifteen years, as has the cost of malpractice insurance. B: In some states obstetricians are refusing to deliver babies—this according to the American College of Obstetrics and Gynecology. C: More than 25 percent of doctors surveyed in New York reported that they would not enter the practice of medicine if given the choice today. D: In 1987 the American Medical Association reported that enrollments at medical schools have declined steadily for the past decade. <u>Such evidence clearly indicates that</u> E: America will soon be a nation with a severe shortage of doctors and medical care.

In this argument, statements A, B, C, and D are advanced as evidence. Statement E is the argument's predictive conclusion. As this example suggests, the general structure of arguments advancing predictive conclusions is similar to that for arguments advancing factual conclusions. Arguments that advance predictive conclusions ought to include the following elements:

1. A *claim regarding the future*.
2. *Evidence* supporting the claim.
3. A stated or implied *interpretation of the evidence* as supporting the predictive claim.

TESTS OF ARGUMENTS ARRIVING AT
PREDICTIVE CONCLUSIONS

Because of their special inference concerning the future, predictive conclusions are treated here as different from factual conclusions. The interpretation that certain evidence allows us to draw conclusions about the future is often more difficult to establish than is a claim about what was or is currently the case.

The general tests of arguments arriving at predictive conclusions are, first:

Test 1:   Is this good evidence?

Application of this test to an argument arriving at a predictive conclusion does not differ from its application to any other argument. The same general tests of evidence and sources discussed in chapter 3 would apply. For example, we might question the recency of the report from the American Medical Association. Are medical school enrollments still declining? If more recent evidence shows a reversal of this trend, the argument is weakened.

But, as was noted when discussing factual conclusions, much evidence is subject to various interpretations. Thus, the second test of arguments arriving at predictive conclusions asks:

*Test 2:   Does the evidence allow this interpretation
concerning future events?*

This is a difficult test to satisfy for any argument, because the predictive conclusion makes an unverifiable claim about the future. In short, no one knows what the future holds. Nevertheless, trying to predict the future is sometimes necessary, and some predictions are better supported than are others. Weather reports, economic forecasts, demographic predictions—each is an example of a situation in which predictive conclusions have to be advanced. Special pursuits and disciplines, such as meteorology and economics, have developed rules of inference for determining whether certain evidence allows for interpretation concerning reasonable predictions, and these rules would have to be referred to in cases of technical arguments. In everyday argument, such as in the example, we would at least want to be sure we accept that a prediction can be drawn from the evidence. Sometimes, asking if similar evidence has in the past allowed similar predictions to be made accurately is helpful.

EVALUATIVE CONCLUSIONS

Evaluative conclusions are *conclusions that render value judgments.* These are sometimes called **propositions of value** or **value claims**. An evaluative conclusion always will contain a **value term** such as good, bad, immoral, virtuous, vicious, attractive. The following argument arrives at an evaluative conclusion:

A: Despite the criticism leveled at Reagan recently, I con-tend that B: he was a good President. C: A President's quality can be judged by three criteria: the success of his economic policy, of his domestic policy, and of his foreign policy. D: Reagan's economic policy brought America back from the recession of the Carter years and spurred economic growth. E: His domestic policy eliminated wasteful spending on useless social programs. <u>Finally</u>, F: Reagan's foreign policy intimidated our enemies and reestablished confidence in America as the defender of the Free World.

This argument begins with a reservation, advanced in statement A. The evaluative conclusion is statement B, and the value term is "good." Statement C presents the **criteria** to be employed for judging a President good. Statements D, E, and F provide evidence that Reagan satisfied the criteria advanced in C.

The structure of this argument is characteristic of the expected structure of arguments arriving at evaluative conclusions. These arguments ought to contain the following elements, though not always in this order:

1. A conclusion that advances a *value term* applied to an object being evaluated.

2. A set of *criteria* that define the value.

3. *Evidence* showing that these criteria have been satisfied by the object being evaluated.

The value term in this example is "good," and it is applied to Ronald Reagan as President. The criteria advanced, which define a good President, and which serve as connectives in the argument, are: (a) success in economic policy, (b) success in domestic policy, and (c) success in foreign policy. The evidence, advanced in the last three sentences of the argument, is intended to satisfy the criteria in the argument.

TESTS OF ARGUMENTS ARRIVING AT EVALUATIVE CONCLUSIONS

From this general structure for arguments that arrive at evaluative conclusions, we can derive two general tests:

Test 1:   Do the criteria adequately define the value?

We should always ask whether we accept the criteria that are stated or implied in arguments arriving at evaluative conclusions. In this example, we might respond that the criteria ought to include some other factor, such as providing moral leadership. But even if we accept that the criteria advanced are adequate to define the value, we might object to the argument on other grounds.

In addition to advancing criteria, arguments arriving at evaluative conclusions must show by evidence that the criteria have been satisfied. Thus, the second test of such arguments asks:

Test 2:   Have the criteria been satisfied by the evidence?

In arguments arriving at evaluative conclusions, a strong link must be forged between the criteria defining the value, and the evidence advanced. Only on the basis of this link can the argument achieve the status of being reasonable. Obviously, if the evidence itself poses a problem, the argument has a hard time passing this test. If, however, the evidence looks reasonable, we must ask if it seems to satisfy the criteria.

In the example, both approaches are possible in answering the argument. We might respond that the evidence is no good, that it is not true that Reagan's economic policy ended the recession. We could argue that policies in place before Reagan took office had that effect. On the other hand, we might agree that Reagan did seriously cut domestic spending but that this was not a "success" in domestic policy. We could argue that the cuts were a disaster in domestic policy, eliminating vital programs for the poor. In the same fashion, we might agree with the evidence that Reagan's foreign policy did intimidate other world powers but that this cannot be considered a "successful" foreign policy. We might argue that a successful foreign policy ought to be based on diplomacy and tend toward peace rather than to be based on military might and tend toward international tension.

NORMATIVE CONCLUSIONS

Normative conclusions are *conclusions that urge action.* These are sometimes referred to as **propositions of policy**, especially when they concern laws, rules, or regulations. The following argument arrives at a normative conclusion:

A: The B-2 Stealth Bomber is extraordinarily expensive, having already cost in excess of $22 billion. Moreover, B: it does not serve any function not already served by existing bombers. Finally, C: the B-2 does not render Soviet air defenses obsolete, as has been claimed. Thus, D: the B-2 should be dropped from the current defense budget. E: Cutting the B-2 would allow for the development of other, more needed military hardware, and F: would eliminate an economic black hole from the budget.

The normative conclusion, statement D, is the final conclusion of the argument, and statements A, B, and C are advanced as evidence in its support. Statements E and F are claims about benefits that would attend the proposed action.

Notice that this argument describes a problem and then proposes a solution. This structure is typical of arguments that arrive at normative conclusions, involving the following elements:

1. A stated or implied *need* or *problem*.

2. A *plan* or *solution* to satisfy the need or solve the problem.

3. Claims regarding *benefits* of the proposed action.

TESTS OF ARGUMENTS ARRIVING AT NORMATIVE CONCLUSIONS

With this structure, four general tests of arguments arriving at normative conclusions are as follows:

Test 1:   Is the problem well established?

Before urging any action, it seems to make sense to have established some need for the action. In the example, the need is largely implied: Most people respond to a need to cut unnecessary expenses, and elimination of unnecessary government spending is suggested.

When propositions of policy are being debated, convincing others of the need for the new policy can be difficult, as people arguing for new laws often find out. The following discussion should help us understand why showing a need for action in policy controversies can be difficult.

❖ THE LANGUAGE OF POLICY DEBATE

A few technical terms of policy debate should be introduced and defined at this point. The **status quo**, or *the way things are now*, generally will prevail unless a pressing need for change can be shown. We sometimes say that the *status quo* has **presumption** over new ideas—that is, *an accepted idea or practice remains in place until it is adequately challenged*. Those challenging the *status quo*, or any other idea that has presumption, are said to have the **burden of proof** in a debate or controversy; they have *the obligation of advancing a prima facie case against the idea or course of action that currently has presumption.*[2]

An accepted idea or way of doing things (the *status quo*) has presumption (maintains its position) until a *prima facie* case has been advanced against it. **Prima facie** cases are *arguments sufficient to raise a reasonable question regarding the status quo, or any other widely accepted idea or course of action. Prima facie* does not mean a conclusive or irrefutable case against an idea or course of action, only one strong enough to raise a significant doubt regarding it. A **case** is *a group of arguments all advanced in support of the same general conclusion.* A **negative case** is *a case in support of the status quo*, whereas an **affirmative case** consists of *arguments urging a change in the status quo.*

From this discussion we can conclude that advocates of a negative case enjoy presumption until the affirmative advocates advance a *prima facie* case against the status quo. The negative side in a debate doesn't even have to respond until the affirmative side has raised a significant question regarding the way things are currently done. In addition, the affirmative case in a debate has *the obligation to show that a significant problem results directly from the current way of doing things.* This is sometimes referred to as showing the **inherency of the problem**—that is, that the problem is inherent to the *status quo,* and is not caused by extraneous circumstances.

Now that we have some understanding of the requirement to argue for a need or problem, we can consider the second test of arguments arriving at normative conclusions:

Test 2:   *Is the plan or solution well suited to satisfying the need or solving the problem?*

Just as in arguments arriving at evaluative conclusions, a link must be forged between criteria and the evidence that satisfies the criteria, so in arguments arriving at normative conclusions, a link must be forged between the problem and its solution. *Showing that the plan would be sufficient to solve the problem or address the need* is sometimes referred to as showing the plan's **adequacy**, and it is another obligation of the affirmative side in a policy debate.

In the example, the person arguing must show that the problems associated with the B-2 would likely be solved by dropping the plane and turning attention to other military projects. In any event, the person arguing an affirmative case must show that the plan or solution would satisfy the need or solve the problem.

Of course, if the plan being advocated is not practical, it is not reasonable. Thus, the third test of arguments arriving at normative conclusions is:

Test 3:   Is the plan or solution practical?

Showing the practicality of a plan is another obligation of anyone advocating an affirmative case. **Practicality** involves *establishing that a plan
can be put into place, and that significant obstacles in its way can be
overcome.* Suppose the recommendation is made that solving the AIDS
crisis simply involves testing everyone in the country for AIDS, then iso-
lating those who have the virus. This plan is probably not **workable**. To
test every American for AIDS would be nearly impossible. Imagine trying
to test every drug addict in every American city. It would be tremen-
dously expensive and extremely time-consuming to actually get a blood
sample from every American.

And a second issue probably should be discussed under practicality
as well. To be accepted as practical, a plan cannot violate widely accepted moral or ethical standards. Thus, a plan must be not only workable
but also **ethical**. It cannot violate important values or principles. Requiring everyone to supply some of his or her blood to the government for
testing would constitute a violation of privacy, and it would probably
amount to an illegal search as well. Many other ethical problems might
be associated with this plan.

Finally, a plan must be shown to avoid unintended consequences—
disadvantages that would attend the plan's implementation. For example,
would cutting the B-2 throw thousands of people out of work, thus dramatically affecting the economy in some parts of the nation? In presenting
a proposed plan of action, significant disadvantages must be addressed.
The question of the comparative advantages of various proposals is discussed further in chapter 8, in the section on pragmatic arguments.

If the plan could be shown to be practical, however, we would
have to ask another question of the argument:

*Test 4:   Are the benefits and value of the plan well
           established and convincing?*

The benefits of a plan are what "sell" it, or make it persuasive. If somehow our condition is improved by adopting a course of action, provided
that course of action is workable and ethical, we are likely to act. Establishing benefits involves advancing evidence that the benefits are: (a)
likely to attend the course of action, (b) significant, and perhaps (c) not
already associated with the *status quo*. In our example concerning the
B-2, the person arguing would have to establish that scrapping the project
would result in significant savings, no loss in military security, and money
better spent elsewhere. These benefits are significant and apparently are
not associated with keeping the B-2.

WRAP UP

Conclusions in longer arguments, especially ones ending in normative or policy recommendations, have an almost inevitable progression. Factual and evaluative conclusions are advanced in an effort to show the presence, seriousness, and inherency of a problem. Predictive conclusions may be advanced to show that the problem will get worse if it is not corrected. Normative conclusions are affirmed as a solution to the problem is recommended. Finally, factual, evaluative, and predictive conclusions may be advanced regarding the plan's practicality and the benefits likely to attend its adoption.

Chapter Review

Arguments may arrive at one or more of four types of conclusions: factual, predictive, evaluative, and normative. In addition, the kind of conclusion at which an argument ultimately arrives has implications for the expected structure of the argument. These structures suggest certain very general tests of arguments. Later chapters will present more specific tests that can be applied to the various types of arguments. Finally, arguments urging actions often involve a progression of some or all of the four types of conclusion.[3]

EXERCISES

A. For each of the following arguments, identify the type of conclusion being advanced:

1. Bob must have gone bowling, because he came home drunk.

2. The recent U.S. invasion of Panama was immoral, since it was a case of intervention in the internal affairs of a soveriegn nation.

3. Four out of five dentists recommend sugarless gum to their patients who chew gum, so you should chew sugarless gum.

4. Marx theorized that all societies would eventually become socialist, so we can expect America to become socialist.

5. Because the plant could have been knocked off the shelf only by you, by a ghost, or by an earthquake, we both know how the plant got knocked off the shelf.

6. You should not accept his ideas, because they are ridiculous.

7. All religions teach about the same thing, and so they should be regarded as equally legitimate.

8. Gambling is something that cannot be stopped. Therefore, gambling should be legalized.

9. It's only a story, so I don't have to prove it.

10. Because interest rates are going up, home sales can be expected to decline.

11. Military aid will not stop the flow of drugs from South American countries, since military aid does nothing to solve the problem of poverty in those countries.

12. Surrogacy is an acceptable practice. After all, in more than 500 cases of legal surrogacy, only three have resulted in lawsuits.

13. We should give Jones the new car because it would serve to motivate the other employees to work harder.

14. Public schools should conduct their classes only in English because education laws read, "Education should be provided in the common language of the people." "The common language" must be taken to mean the language common to the most people, and that's English.

15. Art is a worthless pursuit because you can't make a living at it.

B. Identify the following conclusions by type, and suggest the structure of an argument intended to support each.

1. Jones is the best salesperson on the team.

2. We should give Jones a promotion.

3. Requiring AIDS testing of everyone applying for life insurance would lower the price of life insurance.

4. AIDS testing should be required of everyone applying for life insurance policies.

5. The canyon ought to be preserved as a wilderness area.

6. The canyon ought to be developed into a public recreational area.

C. Find an argument that advocates a solution to a problem. Identify any conclusions advanced in the argument according to the four types discussed in this chapter. Indicate the sections of the argument that present the problem, the solution, and the solution's practicality and benefits.

D. In a longer argument arriving at a normative or policy conclusion, it is often the case that factual, predictive, and evaluative conclusions are advanced and supported along with the final normative conclusion. In the following example, identify any conclusions according to the four types discussed in the chapter, and note any evidence advanced in their support. Indicate which parts of the argument present the problem, the solution, and the practicality and benefits of the solution.

Toward a More Secure Social Security
Super IRAs
Gloria R. Moser

1. Social Security, enacted during a period of privation and hopelessness, was a blessing to millions. But the Social Security system has failed to adapt to the changing demands of our aging society, and it now amounts to a bad investment for most contributors. A study published by the National Chamber Foundation noted that even a low-income worker who pays in less than the maximum payroll tax during his career can expect a return of only 2.13 percent on that investment. A worker contributing the maximum payroll tax will lose about 1 percent of his or her investment.[1]

2. Beyond representing a bad investment, the Social Security system is based on an economic foundation which violates one of the most basic tenets of investment strategy. An investment must be a program of savings that shows significant growth over time. The money paid into social security today, however, is not saved; it is paid out in immediate benefits.

3. Though Social Security provides basic income security to millions of Americans, it does not provide an adequate standard of living. Government records show that even among social security recipients, many are trapped below or near the poverty line.

4. Current demographic shifts that show an increasing portion of the population over the age of sixty-five, combined with zero population growth, contribute to increased demands on the system. The National Advisory Council and the National Institute of Aging summarized these changes:

   People 65 years old and older constitute about 10 percent of the total population. Over the next 50 years, this figure is expected to be between 12 and 16 percent. If zero population growth is reached within the next 50 or 60 years, there will be 1 person over the age of 65 for every 1.5 persons under 20; the ratio is now 1 to 4.[2]

Thus, the Social Security system seems certain to crumble under its own weight.

5. In addition, workers are being asked to contribute an increasingly larger share of their income to the system to keep it afloat. Consider this:

During the first 13 years of its existence, Social Security enacted a maximum employer/employee contribution of $60 per year per worker. As recently as 1958 the maximum combined Social Security tax was only $189; by 1965 it was still only $348. Today it is $6,006, and by the end of the decade it will approach $8,000.[3]

6. We cannot afford this kind of expansion. Who can help but remember on November 5, 1982, when the Old Age and Survivors Insurance and Disability Insurance trust fund became insolvent and had to borrow to pay its benefits? Reforms are being attempted, but they do not offer a solution to the threat of future insolvency. Temporary budget surpluses, tax shifts, and short-term borrowing offer too little assistance to negate the trend toward economic disaster.

7. Clearly the Social Security system must be fundamentally changed, and "Super IRAs" offer a means of avoiding disaster before the Social Security system collapses.

8. "Super IRAs," proposed by Peter Ferrara of Cato Institute as an alternative to Social Security dependence, would give a dollar-for-dollar income tax credit to workers who establish IRAs. The worker would still contribute to Social Security at the current rate, to provide for the needs of the truly poor, but would forego some or all of his or her Social Security benefits. Social Security dependence will be phased down to the lowest possible level. We would at the same time phase-in the Super IRA incentive plan with its dollar-for-dollar income tax credit up to a pre-established "reasonable" limit.

9. As part of the phase in plan, workers will be able to contribute further amounts of their IRAs each year to purchase life insurance to ensure the well-being of their children and spouses in case of early death. In turn, the worker will forego Social Security benefits equal to those received under the Super IRA. The worker, as well as the employer, will still be obligated to contribute to the Social Security treasury as before.

10. This bill will encourage private investment in retirement security since the worker's retirement security is no longer dependent on

the inefficient Social Security system. Moreover, when the worker retires, he or she will receive reduced or no Social Security benefits, depending on his or her contribution to the IRA. Thus, Social Security payments would be limited to only those who are truly poor or who cling to the "security" of the government program, and the savings would be tremendous.

11. The plan is not without its critics. Some argue that IRAs are simply not as secure as the federal program is. But, by purchasing shares in a broad-based pool of stocks, the worker is "in a sense, buying a piece of the economy as a whole." Thus, "workers would bear no greater risk than the chance of collapse of the entire economy, a risk faced by Social Security as well."[4] Others claim the plan is too costly. But this plan is not costly in the long run. Though the initial start-up cost would run as high as $14.5 billion, Ferrara notes that "this loss would eventually be offset completely by reduced Social Security expenditures, as more and more workers retired relying to a large extent on Super IRAs rather than Social Security."[5]

12. Super IRAs offer potential to ensure security to our aging population while producing very small (if any) side effects. Clearly implementation of the bill is warranted. Therefore, the federal government should adopt a Super IRA savings incentive plan to replace the bulk of Social Security.

Notes

1. William Hoffer, "Taking Social Security Private," *Nations Business*, July 1986, p. 33.

2. S. Barakat and T. Mulinazzi, "Elderly Drivers: Problems and Needs for Research," *Transportation Quarterly* 41, (1987), p. 190.

3. Hoffer, p. 30.

4. Peter J. Ferarra, ed., *Social Security: Prospects for Real Reform* (San Francisco: Cato Institute, 1985), p. 200.

5. Ferrara, p. 197.

ENDNOTES

1. Melinda Beck, "Buried Alive," *Newsweek* (November 27, 1989), p. 67.

2. For a detailed discussion of the concepts of presumption and burden of proof, see Richard Whately, *Elements of Rhetoric*, edited by Douglas Ehninger

(Carbondale: Southern Illinois Press, 1963), pp. 112–132 (original work published 1828).

3. For further discussion of the various types of conclusions at which arguments arrive, and strategies for advocating each, see George W. Ziegelmueller, Jack Kay, and Charles A. Dause, *Argumentation: Inquiry and Advocacy*, 2d ed. (Englewood Cliffs, NJ: Prentice Hall, 1990), chapters 12 and 13; and Barbara Warnick and Edward S. Inch, *Critical Thinking and Communication* (New York: Macmillan, 1989), chapters 8 and 9.

5 ANALOGIES

A lobbyist for a national organization interested in firearms made the following argument to the school board of a major American city: "Students should be taught handgun safety in school. After all, cars are potentially lethal instruments, and we teach students how to drive safely in the public schools." In this argument the lobbyist compared a familiar and generally accepted educational goal—driver's education—with a less familiar educational goal he was advocating—firearms education.

Comparisons such as this, **analogies**, are one of the most frequently encountered forms of argument. Analogies are *arguments that compare things with which we are familiar, or about which there is some agreement, to things with which we are less familiar, or about which there is some question.* The goal of analogies is to urge a conclusion about the latter on the basis of what we know about the former. This chapter considers five kinds of analogies that are particularly common in everyday argumentation:

1. Literal analogies.

2. Contrasting analogies.

3. Argument *a fortiori,* or super-analogies.

4. Judicial analogies.

5. Figurative analogies.

❖ LITERAL ANALOGIES

Perhaps the most common analogy is the **literal analogy**, *an argument that directly compares two things from the same realm of experience.* Thus, literal analogies might compare a person to a person, a city to a city, or a product to another similar product. Each of the first four types of analogies listed—literal, contrasting, super-, and judicial—involves a literal comparison, a comparison of objects from the same realm of experience. Contrasting, super-, and judicial analogies involve unique features that require special consideration, to be discussed later in the chapter.

The evidence in literal analogies consists of similarities between *something with which we are already familiar, or about which there is general agreement*—the **evidence case**—and *something unfamiliar, or about which there is likely to be disagreement*—the **conclusion case**. They then proceed to draw a conclusion about the conclusion case.

Looking at a literal analogy will help to clarify the concepts just introduced. The following example involves a literal analogy. As you read it, try to identify the evidence case and the conclusion case, the points of similarity between them, and the argument's conclusion:

Central American nations are involved in civil wars, just as Vietnam was when we got involved there. We are now sending military advisors to assist government forces in fighting guerilla groups, just as we did in Vietnam. We are being pulled into a worsening military crisis with ever increasing commitments of troops and money, just as we were in Vietnam. In Vietnam we ended up in an unpopular military conflict with no clear goals and no hope of winning, and we're headed for that fate in Central America as well. So let's not make the same mistake we made in Vietnam. Let's get American forces out of Central America now!

In this example, Vietnam is treated as the evidence case—the case with which we are familiar, or about which there is general agreement—and Central America is the conclusion case. Several similarities between Vietnam and Central America are advanced in this argument. Notice that these similarities are selected from among dozens of potential points of comparison between the two places. The analogy draws our attention to only a few similarities that are relevant to the particular conclusion being urged. Analogies usually compare only a few relevant similarities between the evidence case and the conclusion case, to establish that the cases are similar in certain significant ways that support the conclusion. We can mark the similarities in this example by using the scanning technique and by treating each similarity as a single evidence statement:

A: Central American nations are involved in civil wars, just as Vietnam was when we got involved there. B: We are now sending military advisors to assist government forces in fighting guerilla groups, just as we did in Vietnam. C: We are being pulled into a worsening military crisis with ever increasing commitments of troops and money, just as we were in Vietnam.

We can now see more clearly the conclusion of the argument:

E: Let's not make the same mistake we made in Vietnam.
Let's get American forces out of Central America now!

Three similarities are advanced to support the conclusion that we should
get out of Central America.

But what about the other sentence in this argument, the one that
should have been marked D? Notice that it differs from statements A, B,
and C in an important way. It makes a fourth claim about Vietnam, and
it predicts that something similar will be true of Central America, which
has not yet been observed. Thus, this sentence is actually two statements,
which we will designate as D and D'. Statement D stands as further
evidence in the argument—an observation about Vietnam—whereas statement D' functions as an intermediate conclusion in the argument.

To show the relationship between the evidence case and the conclusion case in this argument, and the nature of the connective in literal
analogies, the argument can be set out in the following manner:

Evidence: Relevant Similarities

Evidence Case Vietnam	Conclusion Case Central America
A: Ongoing civil war	Ongoing civil war
B: Sent military advisors	Sent military advisors
C: Greater involvement	Greater involvement
D: Unpopular, costly conflict without clear goals and with no hope of winning	
	[therefore] D': Unpopular, costly conflict with no clear goals and with no hope of winning

so

Conclusion E: [We must] get American forces out of
Central America.

Perhaps now we can see more readily that literal analogies involve an unstated connective reason, which affirms that some similarities between two things allow us to draw conclusions about other similarities. Only such an assumption allows movement from the evidence in statements A, B, C, and D to the predictive intermediate conclusion D', and finally to the normative conclusion, statement E. A general formulation of this connective, which works for most literal analogies, might take the following form:

Connective: Some significant similarities between these
               two cases indicate other similarities as well.

We now can insert this connective into the form presented, giving it the designation F* to indicate that we have supplied it as a missing reason:

Evidence: Significant Similarities

Evidence Case	*Conclusion Case*
Vietnam	Central America
A: Ongoing civil war	Ongoing civil war
B: Sent military advisors	Sent military advisors
C: Greater involvement	Greater involvement
D: Unpopular, costly conflict without clear goals and with no hope of winning	

[therefore]
D': Unpopular, costly conflict with no clear goals and with no hope of winning

F*: Some significant similarities between these two cases these two cases indicate other similarities as well.

<u>so</u>

Conclusion E: [We must] get American forces out of
               Central America.

At this point it will be helpful to standardize and diagram this example using the method introduced in chapter 1:

A: Central American nations are involved in civil wars, just as Vietnam was when we got involved there.

B: [The United States is] now sending military advisors to assist government forces in fighting guerilla groups, just as we did in Vietnam.

C: [The United States is] being pulled into a worsening military crisis with ever increasing commitments of troops and money, just as we were in Vietnam.

D: In Vietnam [the United States] ended up in an unpopular military conflict with no clear goals and no hope of winning.

F*: [Some significant similarities between these two cases indicate other similarities as well.]

[therefore]

D': [The United States is] headed for that fate in Central America as well.

so

E: [We must] get American forces out of Central America now!

This standardization yields the following diagram, which shows the dependence of the evidence—A, B, C, and D—and the connective reason, F*:

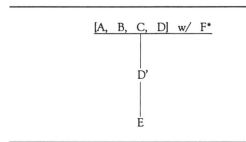

By standardizing the argument, we have set out its reasons, including the missing connective reason, and we have used a diagram to examine the argument's inferential structure. At this point we can test the argument's reasonableness. In making such decisions about arguments, some tests are useful. This text discusses tests for each type of argument it introduces. Before introducing the tests for literal analogies, the reasons for testing arguments will be discussed in more detail.

TESTING ARGUMENTS

Like other tests of arguments to be presented in this book, tests for making judgments about the reasonableness of literal analogies actually have three functions:

1. The tests can help to *assess the reasonableness* of arguments we read or hear. When deciding whether to accept or reject arguments, we can benefit from some critical tools. The following four tests provide some important critical guidelines for making such decisions about literal analogies. Other argument tests in this book are designed to provide similar guidelines for other kinds of arguments you are likely to encounter.

2. The same tests *provide possible refutations* of analogies, which can be employed whenever we find ourselves having to respond to someone else's arguments. At times you may need or wish to respond to a literal analogy. The four tests suggested provide you with means of making a response. Tests of other arguments in this text offer you refutational strategies for a variety of arguments.

3. The tests *assist composition* of your own arguments. In writing papers and speeches, we often employ analogies and other arguments. By testing arguments as we compose them, we have a better idea of how to structure our arguments, and of how to make them stronger or more convincing.

As you study the various argument tests in this and following chapters, recall that the tests assist you in making judgments about the reasonableness of arguments, provide you with refutational strategies for arguments, and can help you in developing stronger and clearer arguments of your own.

TESTS OF LITERAL ANALOGIES

The tests we will be suggesting for literal analogies are derived from their connective reason, which affirms that some significant similarities between two cases suggest other similarities, as well as from the structure of these arguments as comparisons. Though other tests may occur to you, the following four, at least, are important when deciding whether to accept or to reject literal analogies.

We will begin by testing the literal analogy's connective reason. We can call into question the assumption that connects evidence to conclusion in an analogy. In fact, the assumption that some similarities between two things can be taken to indicate other similarities between them is important to all analogies, and it should be tested in any analogy. Thus, we can formulate the first test of literal analogies as a question that might be asked of other analogies as well:

Test 1:   *Does the presence of some significant similarities between this evidence case and the conclusion case indicate the presence of other such similarities?*

To our example comparing Vietnam and Central America, we might respond that these similarities simply do not indicate any other similarities between American involvement in the two regions, or the danger of further American involvement in Central America. We might go so far as to respond that the similarities noted actually might be insignificant or irrelevant to discussions of American policies regarding Central America.

Some argument theorists suggest that the presence of certain similarities between two people, events, or objects never indicates that other similarities are present as well. As a result, they take the position that analogies are seldom or never reasonable arguments. Their point is well taken. After all, the two things being compared *are* different things, and what's true of the one may not tell us anything about the other. I do not agree with the view that analogies are never good arguments, but I ask you to keep in mind that they are based on a precarious connective reason. Therefore, analogies should always be used with some caution.

In some cases we may be willing to accept that significant and relevant similarities exist between the evidence and the conclusion cases in a literal analogy. But the relevant dissimilarities between the two may be more important than the noted similarities are. This brings us to the second test of literal analogies:

Test 2:   *Are the cases being compared dissimilar in some critical respect?*

A critical dissimilarity is one that in some important way bears on the conclusion of the argument. For instance, in responding to the Vietnam-Central America analogy, we might point out that Central America is much closer to the U.S. than is Vietnam. This dissimilarity in proximity, it could be argued, might make America's involvement in another nation's civil war reasonable and also might increase popular support for American involvement. In this way, a single important dissimilarity might effectively counteract numerous similarities advanced in the original argument.

Another possibility for answering or testing literal analogies is to question the accuracy of the evidence case as it is presented in the argument. Clearly, if the evidence case is presented inaccurately, the argument is weakened. Thus we might ask:

Test 3: Has the evidence case been described accurately?

Is the description of Vietnam in the example argument accurate, or has something been alleged that is not true to fact? An analogy is reasonable only to the extent that the evidence case is advanced accurately. We might respond to the analogy between Vietnam and Central America by claiming that Vietnam was not embroiled in a civil war when we got involved there, but that it had been invaded and we were simply helping an ally defend itself against an aggressor nation. In this way we would be challenging the accuracy of the evidence case's description.

In some cases we may be willing to accept a literal analogy as advanced but still find the argument to lead to a questionable conclusion. In these instances we may be aware that other comparisons are possible, which lead to quite different conclusions. Thus, we should ask of literal analogies:

Test 4: Are there any relevant counter-examples?

We might be willing to accept that some relevant and significant similarities exist between Vietnam and El Salvador, and that the situation in Vietnam has been described accurately. Still, we may not be willing to accept the conclusion of this analogy. Other similar cases in which American withdrawal of military forces would have been a mistake may occur to us. We might respond, for example, that the points made concerning Vietnam can be made with equal force about Korea, but that withdrawing from Korea would have been a mistake for the U.S. Korea then would stand for us as a relevant counter-example to Vietnam.

Once we have advanced a counter-example, we are developing an analogy argument of our own, which is subject to some of the same tests as other literal analogies. This observation points up the fact that the process of advancing and testing arguments is interactive and involves continuing critical scrutiny of our own arguments and others' arguments. If we are to be reasonable people, we should be willing to examine our own thinking and arguing with the same standards we apply to the arguments of others.

WRAP UP

Literal analogies are arguments that make direct comparisons between things from the same realm of experience. These comparisons depend on showing that relevant and significant similarities exist between the evidence and the conclusion cases. They also involve the connective assumption that some similarities between two cases justify concluding that other similarities will be present as well. The four tests of literal analogies focus on the assertion of similarity between the two cases, and on the crucial connective reason.

Other important analogies are covered in the following sections. Although each involves a comparison, like the literal analogy, unique qualities separate the various types from one another.

❖ CONTRASTING ANALOGIES

Some analogies deal with a relevant difference between the cases compared, as well as with relevant similarities. These **contrasting analogies** are *arguments that seek to show some striking difference between two otherwise similar things, and then to explain the difference*. Consider the following example:

A: That India has never been able to establish itself as a stable force in the world economy because of its crippling dependence on foreign aid is clear when one compares India to China. B: China and India were both poor countries after World War II. C: Both are Asian nations, and D: both were occupied during the war. E: Both have enormous populations. F: China did not receive aid from major powers in its efforts to rebuild, whereas F': India did receive aid from both America and Britain, and later also from the Soviet Union. Thus, G: China was forced to rebuild on its own, to rely on its own resources in people and materials, whereas India was not forced to do this rebuilding work. As a result, H: today China is a much stronger nation, whereas India continues to struggle with basic economic problems such as feeding its population, and establishing an economic base.

Like literal analogies, contrasting analogies compare things from the same realm of experience. But contrasting analogies arrive at conclusions, not about further similarities but, rather, about a critical dissimilarity between the evidence case and the conclusion case—the case about which the conclusion is drawn. In almost every instance, contrasting analogies advance an account of why two otherwise similar situations are different in some important respect. Often, the relevant dissimilarity—the point of contrast—is itself advanced as the reason for other important differences.

Because the contrasting analogy involves a different kind of inference from that drawn in a literal analogy, the connecting reason is also different. To show that difference, we will set out our example in a form similar to that used with the earlier analogy comparing Vietnam and Central America. The structure of contrasting analogies is only slightly different from that of literal analogies. We still find a comparison of what are taken to be similarities between the evidence and the conclusion cases, but we also find one or more relevant dissimilarities advanced. Differentiating the evidence and the conclusion cases in contrasting analogies can be difficult at times. The conclusion case is mentioned in the argument's conclusion, whereas the evidence case is the case that is not the focus of the argument's conclusion. Thus, in our example, the evidence case is China, because the argument seeks to draw a conclusion not about China but instead about India:

Evidence: Similarities and Differences

Evidence Case	*Conclusion Case*
China	India
B: China was poor	India was poor
C: China is Asian nation	India is Asian nation
D: China was occupied	India was occupied
E: China has enormous population	India has enormous population
F: China *did not* receive foreign aid	<u>whereas</u> F': India *did* receive foreign aid
<u>thus</u>	
G: China had to rebuild on its own, relying on its own resources <u>as a result</u>	India did not have to rebuild on its own

H: Today China is a stronger   India continues to
   nation   struggle
   [thus]
A: That India has never been able to establish itself as a
   stable force in the world economy because of its
   crippling dependence on foreign aid is clear when one
   compares India to China.

With the analogy presented in this form, it is easier to see that a connective reason is necessary to forge a link between the evidence presented in statements B through F' and intermediate conclusion G. The connective assumption seems to be some version of the following claim:

Connective: An important dissimilarity between two
              otherwise similar cases can account for further
              dissimilarities.

Inserting this connective into the example, following the same format, reveals the following inferential progression in this argument:

Evidence: Similarities and Differences

| *Evidence Case* | *Conclusion Case* |
| China | India |

B: China was poor   India was poor
C: China is Asian nation   India is Asian nation
D: China was occupied   India was occupied
E: China has enormous   India has enormous
   population   population
F: China *did not* receive
   foreign aid

                                    whereas
                          F': India *did* receive
                              foreign aid

I*: An important dissimilarity between two otherwise
    similar cases can account for further dissimilarities.
    thus

G: China had to rebuild on   India did not have to
    its own, relying on its   rebuild on its own
    own resources
    <u>as a result</u>
H: Today China is a stronger   India continues to
    nation   struggle
    [<u>thus</u>]
A: That India has never been able to establish itself as a
    stable force in the world economy because of its
    crippling dependence on foreign aid is clear when one
    compares India to China.

At this point we can provide the following diagram for the argument:

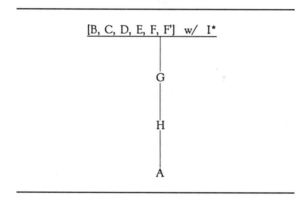

[B, C, D, E, F, F'] w/ I*
G
H
A

In this argument, the similarities between India and China are advanced as evidence, as is the point of contrast presented in statements F and F'. This evidence is connected to intermediate conclusion G by interaction of the evidence with connective reason I*. The assumption that an important difference between otherwise similar cases can account for further dissimilarities is what justifies drawing this conclusion.

Contrasting analogies develop by setting out similarities between two cases and then drawing attention to some striking or important dissimilarity. The example argument reveals the contrasting analogy's tendency to use the contrast between the two cases to account for further differences. The account is derived from the very point of contrast revealed by the comparison. Thus, in this example the main point of contrast is China's not receiving foreign aid and India's receiving aid. Foreign aid is taken to be the reason for India's problems, and its absence the source of China's strength—a further difference between the two cases.

TESTS OF CONTRASTING ANALOGIES

Like literal analogies, contrasting analogies compare two things from the same realm of experience. Thus, some of the same tests might be expected to apply to each type of argument. This is, in fact, the case. Because of its use of a contrast, however, the contrasting analogy demands a test unique to it, and we will introduce that test first.

You may have been thinking that points of contrast other than foreign aid between China and India might better account for the observed dissimilarities in their present conditions. This is a possibility that should be tested for in this and other contrasting analogies. Thus, the first test of a contrasting analogy asks:

> Test 1:   *Is there a contrast between the two cases that
> better accounts for the observed dissimilarities?*

If India's current situation is more likely a result of factors unrelated to foreign aid (e.g., its Hindu culture as contrasted with China's Confucian culture), the argument concerning foreign aid is undermined and perhaps collapses entirely. Unlike literal analogies, contrasting analogies *admit* critical dissimilarities between the evidence case and the conclusion case. But one dissimilarity—the one advanced in the argument's evidence—supports the argument's conclusion, whereas others not mentioned in the argument may call that conclusion into question. This test is similar to test 2 of literal analogies concerning a critical dissimilarity between the evidence and conclusion cases.

Like literal analogies, contrasting analogies are only as good as the accuracy of their evidence, which is drawn from both the evidence and the conclusion cases. Thus, the second test of contrasting analogies is similar to test 3 of literal analogies. We will apply the test to our example:

> Test 2:   *Is the evidence drawn from the two cases
> presented accurately?*

That China and India both are Asian nations with large populations are probably not assertions open to reasonable question. We might ask, however, whether it is true that China did not receive any foreign aid after World War II. In fact, China did receive some aid from the USSR after the war. If the description of China advanced as evidence is not accurate, the contrast between China and India breaks down, and the analogy is weakened.

Because counter-examples also may be employed in testing, answering, or composing contrasting analogies, the third test of these arguments is similar to test 4 of literal analogies:

Test 3:   Are there any relevant counter-examples?

In applying this test, we are searching for cases that involve a similar contrast but that suggest a different conclusion. For instance, we might point to a nation such as Japan, which, though devastated by the war, was helped by foreign aid to rebuild. Clearly, Japan has since flourished. Such a counter-example tends to diminish the strength of the original analogy, which targets foreign aid as the source of India's economic problems.

WRAP UP

Like literal analogies, contrasting analogies draw a comparison between two cases from the same realm of experience. Unlike literal analogies, however, contrasting analogies search for a point of contrast on the basis of which other dissimilarities between the two cases can be accounted for. But the contrast can be accepted as a reason for other differences only in the event that some other point of contrast does not offer a better account of differences between the cases, the argument's evidence is accurate, and good counter-examples are not available.

❖   ARGUMENT A *FORTIORI*: THE SUPER-ANALOGY

The literal analogy makes a direct comparison of two cases from the same realm of experience and affirms that what is true of one is or will be true of the other as well. Some analogies, however, urge that what is true of their evidence case is even more likely to be true of their conclusion case. Consider the following dialogue in which Jack is advancing an argument:

Bill: Well, Jack, Simpson sure liked the idea you presented to the committee. Do you think the boss will go for it?

Jack: I'm confident he will.

Bill: How can you be so sure?

Jack: A: Simpson likes to take risks, and the boss is even

more fond of taking risks than Simpson is.
B: Simpson liked the idea, <u>so</u> B': I'm confident the
boss is going to love it!

Jack's comments to Bill contain an analogy argument. The argument compares Simpson and the boss. Based on what he knows about Simpson (the evidence case), Jack concludes that his boss (the conclusion case) is *even more likely* to like his idea. This type of comparison traditionally has been labeled the **argument *a fortiori*,** and amounts to a what might be called a super-analogy.[1] **Super-analogies** are *analogies that affirm that what is true of their evidence case is even more likely to be true of their conclusion case*.

We can see the relationship between evidence case and conclusion case more clearly by setting out this argument as follows:

Evidence Case	*Conclusion Case*
A: Simpson likes risk	The boss likes risk *even more*
B: Simpson liked the idea	
	<u>so</u>
	B': The boss is *even more* likely to like the idea

To know exactly what belief, value, or assumption connects evidence and conclusion in super-analogies is somewhat difficult. In this example, it seems the stronger presence of a particular quality in the conclusion case than in the evidence case—the love of risk—is taken to indicate the stronger likelihood of some associated quality in the conclusion case. We will try to formulate this general assumption into a connective reason. The connective for a super-analogy, then, is probably some form of the following:

Connective: The even stronger presence of [quality x] in the conclusion than in the evidence case makes it *even more likely* that the associated [quality y] is present inthe conclusion case.

We can try putting this connective into our argument:

Evidence Case	*Conclusion Case*
A: Simpson likes risk	The boss likes risk *even more*
B: Simpson liked the idea	

C*: The even stronger presence of [love of risk] in the conclusion than in the evidence case makes it *even more likely* that the associated [liking of the idea] is present in the conclusion case.

so

B': The boss is *even more* likely to like the idea.

We can now suggest the following diagram for this argument:

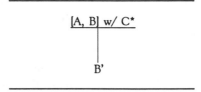

TESTS OF SUPER-ANALOGIES

Again, because of their similarity of structure with literal analogies, some tests of literal analogies are appropriate for super-analogies as well. For instance, the first test of super-analogies is also directed to the usually hidden connective reason:

> *Test 1:   Does the even stronger presence of some quality in the conclusion than in the evidence case make even more likely the presence of some associated quality in the conclusion case?*

The fact that Simpson liked Jack's idea, even if he liked it because of the risk factor, does not ensure or make more certain that the boss will like the idea, even if the boss is more inclined toward risk than Simpson is. That these two qualities are associated in Simpson does not by itself prove that they will be similarly associated in the boss, and even more strongly. The boss may like risk more than Simpson does, but may not like Bill's idea for other reasons.

Another test similar to that applied to literal analogies comes into play with super-analogies. We will still want to ask of these arguments:

Test 2:   Is there a critical dissimilarity between the evidence case and the conclusion case?

In the example concerning Jack's idea, Simpson possibly likes Jack and the boss does not. This dissimilarity certainly would be relevant to whether the boss will like Jack's idea, and particularly to the conclusion that he is even more likely to like the idea. Other critical dissimilarities are possible, of course.

Finally, as with the literal analogy, it should be asked of the argument *a fortiori*:

Test 3:   Is the evidence case described accurately?

In the example about Jack's idea, we would want to know not just whether Simpson actually liked the idea but also whether he liked it because it involved risk. If this is not the case—if, for example, he liked it because it would lead to his advancement in the company—Jack's argument is clearly rendered less reasonable.

WRAP UP

The argument *a fortiori*, or super-analogy, is an interesting analogy in which the conclusion case is affirmed as even more likely than the evidence case to possess some quality. As with the literal analogy, we should ask whether any important dissimilarities exist between the two cases, and whether the evidence case has been described accurately. In addition, we should consider whether the assumption expressed in the connective is justified.

❖ JUDICIAL ANALOGIES

Another common type of comparison argument possesses an interesting quality that requires special discussion. These analogies urge fair or equal treatment for similar cases. The treatment that one person, idea, or institution already has received—the evidence case—is taken as the standard for some other allegedly similar case—the conclusion case. Consider the following argument:

A: I have worked for the company for five years, and so has Jones. B: I have the same special training she has. C: I didn't get a promotion, <u>and</u> C': she did. D: I should get a promotion, too.

The **judicial analogy** is *a comparison argument that urges similar treatment for people, ideas, or institutions in similar circumstances.* The connective reason for such analogies is relatively easy to formulate:

Connective: Similar cases should be treated similarly.

The value expressed in this connective has been labeled "the rule of justice."[2]

To show the place of this connective in the judicial analogy, we can set out our example argument in the same form as we used for literal and contrasting analogies. Because Jones is the individual who already has been treated in a particular way, she serves as the evidence case in this argument. The person advancing the argument is the conclusion case:

Evidence Case	*Conclusion Case*
A: Jones worked for company for five years	I worked for company for five years
B: Jones has special training	I have same special training
C: Jones got a promotion	
	and
	C': I *did not* get a promotion
E*: Similar cases should be treated similarly.	
[therefore]	
D: I should get a promotion, too.	

Setting the argument out in this way suggests the following diagram:

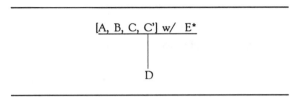

Statements A and B are evidence of the similarity of the two cases. Statements C and C' are also evidence, though of a different type; they show dissimilarity in the treatment of the two cases. When all of this evidence is combined with the connective, statement E*, it yields the conclusion, statement D. Of course, we may not be convinced by arguments such as these, or even find them to be reasonable in all instances. As with other analogies, tests for the judicial analogy should be applied.

TESTS OF JUDICIAL ANALOGIES

Like literal analogies, judicial analogies compare things from the same realm of experience. Like contrasting analogies, judicial analogies set up a contrast between their evidence case and their conclusion case. Because of these similarities, judicial analogies share some tests with literal and contrasting analogies. But the application of these tests to judicial analogies deserves comment.

The judicial analogy, perhaps more than other types of comparison arguments, depends on establishing close similarity between the cases being compared. The rule of justice demands that the cases be clearly similar. Thus, we can employ a test with judicial analogies that was first introduced with literal analogies:

Test 1:   Is there a critical dissimilarity between the evidence case and the conclusion case?

These two employees must actually represent similar cases to the company. Otherwise, the rule of justice does not apply to the cases being compared. For instance, if the disgruntled employee in the example was once reprimanded for unethical behavior, her case and Jones's case may be relevantly dissimilar to company executives who make decisions about promotions. If this is the case, the rule of justice would not come into play.

The employee advancing this argument possibly is not being accurate in her presentation of the evidence of similarity between her case and Jones's case. Thus, it should be asked:

*Test 2:   Is the evidence drawn from the evidence and
            conclusion cases presented accurately?*

We might want to ask, for example, if Jones indeed has the same level
of training as the angry employee does. If Jones has more training, or
better training, the argument is weakened. We also might ask if the two
employees actually have been with the company for the same amount
of time.

The rule of justice has a great deal of force in democratic societies.
Rights such as equal protection under the law, and practices such as
allowing candidates equal time to present their views in the media, are
grounded in a widely held acceptance of the rule of justice. When it can
be clearly established that two cases are in fact similar, the rule of justice
is a powerful principle.

In some instances, however, exceptions may reasonably be made
even to this rule. Thus, the third test of judicial analogies asks:

*Test 3:   Even if similar cases are being compared, is there
            a good reason for making an exception to the
            rule of justice in this case?*

Perhaps Jones is being singled out as part of an experiment in motivating
employees to work more efficiently. Jones has been given the promotion
to see how it will affect her productivity. This is not to say that other
employees will be happy with the exception, but it is to suggest that
cases exist in which legitimate exceptions to the rule of justice may be
allowed. Of course, it is important to ensure in such instances that the
exception being made is justifiable; an excuse for unfair treatment might
sound a lot like a "legitimate" exception to the rule.

THE JUDICIAL ANALOGY AND
DANGEROUS PRECEDENT

Because the judicial analogy is such a powerful form of reasoning, sometimes efforts are made to prevent the rule of justice from being invoked.
The **dangerous precedent** argument *affirms that once a particular
precedent has been established, similar cases will have to be treated
similarly, with serious negative consequences.* The following example
involves the argument from dangerous precedent:

Janet: You ought to let me take the exam next Tuesday
            rather than this Friday. I have two other exams
            on Friday.

Professor: Although I understand your predicament, I'm
             afraid I can't do that. It would mean letting
             other students take exams late any time they are
             under pressure. I then would have no way of
             enforcing examination dates, or any other
             deadlines, for that matter.

The professor in this example is arguing from dangerous precedent, and in so doing is anticipating that to grant Janet's request would allow other students to invoke the rule of justice. The resulting consequences would be negative for the professor, in that a large number of exceptions might have to be granted and the rule against extensions could become meaningless.

Of course, the dangerous precedent argument, like other arguments, can be tested for reasonableness. One test is particularly relevant to the argument from dangerous precedent:

Test 1:   Is the event in question really precedent-setting,
          or can it be treated as a legitimate exception to
          an otherwise binding rule?

Failing to recognize that most rules have legitimate exceptions is usually considered a mistake in reasoning, sometimes called the **fallacy of accident**. *Arguing that your case is, in fact, an exception to an otherwise binding rule* is often called **special pleading**. What we need to know is whether the exception in question is actually setting a dangerous precedent or whether the professor could perhaps make a legitimate exception in Janet's case without establishing a precedent for all future requests for deadline extensions. We would have to determine whether Janet's special pleading is justified.

WRAP UP

Judicial analogies urge similar treatment for people, ideas, or institutions in similar circumstances. When properly constructed, judicial analogies are powerful arguments. In a free society only the rare individual will openly challenge the rule of justice. Thus, arguments employing it, if they are well-constructed, are usually persuasive. To be reasonable, however, such analogies must actually compare similar cases, present their evidence accurately, and not involve a legitimate exception to the rule of justice.

❖ FIGURATIVE ANALOGIES

Whereas the analogies considered so far compare things from the same realm of experience, **figurative analogies** are *arguments that compare relationships among things from different realms of experience*. These analogies are sometimes called similes or metaphors.

Figurative analogies create a problem for the person employing them in argument. Many people do not accept figurative analogies as proof but only as devices for clarifying or illustrating a point, or for making writing more appealing. The problem discussed earlier regarding all analogies becomes particularly acute when employing figurative analogies. Since figurative analogies are often used in argument, however, and since they are both advanced and (perhaps mistakenly) accepted as proof, we have to have some understanding of them *as* arguments. Nevertheless, these analogies should not be relied on as the sole evidence supporting a conclusion.

The following argument involves a figurative analogy:

A: Pornography is a cancer in our land, and <u>thus</u>, B: like a cancer, it must be removed before it causes our society's death.

This is an argument from figurative analogy. But does it actually *prove* anything? Before answering this question, we must recognize that, unlike literal, contrasting, and judicial analogies, figurative analogies do not compare similarities between cases so much as *similar relationships between things*. To clarify this point, the example argument will be set out as two relationships. *The relationship with which we are familiar, and which is used as evidence in the argument*, will be termed the **evidence relationship**. *The relationship being urged in connection with the conclusion in a figurative analogy* will be termed the **conclusion relationship**. Our example, then, can be presented as the following relationships:

| **Evidence Relationship** | | **Conclusion Relationship** |
| *Cancer* is to the *body* | as | *pornography* is to the *society*. |

What, we have to ask at this point, is the intended relationship between cancer and the body? The argument suggests that in this relationship, if the former is not removed, it causes the death of the latter. What is affirmed, then, as the relationship between pornography and society? The same as that between cancer and the body. Thus, the conclusion is drawn that pornography, like cancer, must be quickly removed from the "body" it infects. Note that in this example the conclusion itself is not the same as the conclusion relationship.

We can see that, unlike literal analogies, which move from case to case, figurative analogies move from what is already known or accepted about one *relationship* to what will or should be accepted about another *relationship*. The connective that allows the move from the evidence of one relationship to a conclusion about an entirely different relationship is rather difficult to formulate. I suggest the following connective for figurative analogies:

Connective: Similar relationships between objects indicate
              that similar conclusions regarding each are
              appropriate.

We can try to insert this connective into a standardization of our example:

A: Pornography is a cancer in our land.
C*:   Similar relationships between objects indicate
      that similar conclusions regarding each are
      appropriate.
      <u>thus</u>
B: Like a cancer, [pornography] must be
      removed before it causes our society's death.

This standardization yields a simple diagram:

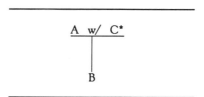

TESTS OF FIGURATIVE ANALOGIES

Since literal analogies and figurative analogies do not operate in the same manner, they are subject to different tests. First, because figurative analogies appear in arguments as both argument and illustration, and because these two functions are easily confused, we must ask what role a given figurative analogy is playing in a given argument. Thus, the first of four tests of figurative analogies is:

Test 1:   *Is the analogy advanced as illustration or argument?*

In the example, we have to ask whether the analogy is intended simply to illustrate what pornography is like, or whether it is being offered as an argument against pornography. The analogy in the example seems to be intended to do more than illustrate. It sounds as if it is being advanced to prove that pornography should be actively opposed. If the figurative analogy is advanced and understood as simply an illustration, and is intended to carry no rational weight, we may be willing to accept it without careful scrutiny. The actual argument is somewhere else, not in the analogy. But, if the figurative analogy is being advanced as an argument, it should be subjected to other tests.

Figurative analogies should not be used alone as arguments for or against a point of view. Their nature as arguments comparing unlike things precludes this possibility as reasonable. Thus, when a figurative analogy is being advanced as an argument, we should ask:

Test 2:   *Does the figurative analogy appear without other arguments or evidence?*

Rarely would we be willing to accept a figurative analogy alone as reasonable support for a conclusion. But the line between illustration and proof is often blurred when figurative analogies are involved, because they often are highly persuasive. If we can understand a point, we are more likely to think it has been proved. Still, when confronted with a persuasive figurative analogy, you should be sure that your judgment about the point in question is based on other types of arguments and evidence as well. Thus, in our example, we would not base our own decisions about pornography on a single comparison to cancer.

Further, we should ask whether the relationships between the two pairs of terms in the figurative analogy are, in fact, similar. This similarity is the only thing that gives the analogy any value as illustration or argument. We must be certain that we understand the relationship between the two terms of the evidence relationship and also that we find a similar relationship to hold between the two terms of the conclusion relationship. Thus, the third test of figurative analogies asks:

Test 3:   Is the evidence relationship actually similar to
the conclusion relationship?

The relationship between cancer and the body is one in which unchecked growth of the cancer eventually will destroy the life of the body. Therefore, if we accept the analogy, we must also accept that unchecked growth of pornography eventually will destroy a society. We also must presumably accept that the presence of any pornography in society is as unacceptable as the presence of any cancer in the body. We also would likely be accepting that pornography grows like cancer—rapidly and inexorably. If we are inclined to reject any or all of these intended relational similarities, we are saying that the figurative analogy fails this third test.

In a debate situation an opponent's figurative analogy, whether it is advanced as illustration or proof, often can be altered so as to support a contrary or even an absurd conclusion. This refutational possibility is expressed in the fourth test of figurative arguments:

Test 4:   Can the analogy be altered to support a contrary
or an absurd conclusion?

Sometimes figurative analogies contain the elements of their own refutation. Extending the analogy to the point where it supports a conclusion contrary to that being urged may be possible. Thus, one might respond to the cancer/pornography analogy by arguing that, to remain healthy, even the human body needs some foreign invaders, perhaps not cancer, but certain bacteria. Attempting to eradicate all the invaders in our own bodies would be foolish, would destroy health, and the same is true of "invaders" in society, such as pornography. Perhaps, like certain bacteria, we need these invaders to promote societal health. Or we might argue that if our society has cancer, we must accept the fact, working not to "cure" ourselves, as there is no known cure but, instead, to control the cancer. Thus, rather than eradicate pornography, we should control or regulate it.

Another refutational possibility inherent to figurative analogies involves extending the analogy to the point where the conclusions it allows are plainly absurd. Thus, it would be possible to respond to the cancer/pornography analogy by urging that, if pornography is like cancer, it is a cancer people seek out and pay for—such a strange disease, we might argue, that people pay to have it inflicted upon them. Shall we now expect that people will begin paying to be afflicted with cancer?

WRAP UP

Figurative analogies compare the relationships between two pairs of terms, each pair drawn from a different realm of experience. Because they compare items that are clearly not similar, some theorists question whether these arguments are ever reasonable. They are used as arguments, however, so we should try to understand how they work.

We should ask whether a figurative analogy is being advanced as illustration or argument. If it is being employed as an argument, we should ask whether other arguments are advanced in support of the same point. In testing figurative analogies, we should agree that the relationships on each side of the analogy are, in fact, similar. Finally, even a good figurative analogy sometimes can be altered in a debate setting to support a contrary or even an absurd conclusion.[3]

Chapter Review

Analogies are among the most frequently encountered arguments in public controversies. Thus, we should have some understanding of the different types of analogies, their structure, and the tests to which they are susceptible. Five types of analogies are: literal, contrasting, *a fortiori*, judicial, and figurative.

All analogies depend on establishing similarities between the things compared. Thus, each is especially susceptible to refutation by showing some critical dissimilarity between the evidence and the conclusion cases or relationships. Other tests appropriate to each type also have been discussed. Because all analogies depend on relatively vulnerable connectives, these arguments are best used in conjunction with other arguments and evidence. Nevertheless, when carefully employed, analogies can be persuasive and reasonable arguments.[4]

EXERCISES

A. In each of the following examples, state which type of analogy is being developed. Identify the evidence case, conclusion case, and conclusion for each argument. Apply the appropriate tests to each example, and explain where and why it might contain weaknesses.

1. The chemists in research and development are objecting to our request that they develop a new nerve gas. They say they're con-

cerned about what it might be used for. That's crazy! I don't ask the mechanic's opinion about where and how I drive my car when I take it in for repairs.

2. "No body can be healthful without exercise, neither natural body nor politic; and certainly, to a kingdom or estate, a just and honorable war is the true exercise. A civil war, indeed, is like the heat of a fever; but a foreign war is like the heat of exercise, and serveth to keep the body in health; for in a slothful peace, both courages will effeminate and manners corrupt." (Francis Bacon, *The True Greatness of Kingdoms*)

3. Just because someone believes strongly in something doesn't make it true or right. If a nurse puts carbolic acid instead of silver nitrate in a baby's eyes, the baby will go blind no matter how sincere the nurse was in thinking it was silver nitrate. In the same way, sincerely believing that abortion is morally permissible doesn't change the fact that it is morally repugnant.

4. *Context*: After the bombing of the American Embassy in Beirut, charges were leveled at the Reagan administration of failing to provide for the security of American personnel in Lebanon. William F. Buckley, Jr., rejects the reasoning of these critics by developing an analogy to another recent event, the attempted assassination of the President himself:

   "If Reagan himself runs the chance of being shot at the Hilton Hotel in Washington, D.C., a couple of miles from the center of the military-industrial complex of the most powerful nation in the world, then one must suppose our ambassador in the most heatedly uncontrolled part of the world is also going to run risks." (William F. Buckley, Jr., *Detroit Free Press*, September 28, 1984)

5. If the Democrats could not defeat the Republicans with an incumbent, moderate President—Jimmy Carter—they have absolutely no chance of winning this election by running a dark horse, ultra-liberal governor.

6. Why should he be exempted from paying the parking ticket just because he is a judge? I had to pay for mine, and he should have to pay for his!

7. Mills University and State University attract students from similar backgrounds, and the entering freshmen at each institution have about the same SAT scores. Why do Mills students, then, always have an easier time landing good jobs after graduation? I think it is because of the extensive internship programs at Mills—some-

thing almost entirely lacking at State. Therefore, State should institute such an internship program.

8. Last year pro players hit 50 percent of their two-point shots, as did college players. Pro players, however, hit only 28 percent of their three-point shots, whereas college players in leagues experimenting with the three-point rule hit 39 percent of the longer shots. The three-point line in the pros is drawn at 23'9" from the hoop. The three-point line proposed for college teams is drawn on a tangent from the top of the foul circle, nearly 4 feet closer to the basket. Clearly the three-point line proposed for college teams is too close to the basket.

9. There is no significant difference between maternity and paternity. Thus, in surrogacy, the female gamete donor should be afforded the same rights as the male gamete donor.

10. It is not at all surprising that the average American has difficulty understanding the tax code. Even Albert Einstein found the 1040 form mystifying.

11. Mr. T wondered why people were questioning his interest in being a preacher: "They wouldn't question Pope John Paul II's interest in being a preacher, would they?"

12. *Question*: Is the following argument more accurately identified as a literal analogy or a judicial analogy? Explain your answer.

    Airline pilots perform a task in which a single error can spell disaster, much like physicians. The knowledge pilots must appropriate is constantly changing—again, much like doctors. Pilots, however, must requalify periodically to keep their licenses. Physicians can practice indefinitely without requalifying. Surely, to require such requalification of doctors is just as important.

13. "Gang members should not be allowed to come to school. The situation is no different from students coming to school with measles. If a student is involved in a gang, we should be able to say, 'You stay away from the school,' just as we are allowed to say to students who contract the measles." (High-school principal in Chicago)

14. Lower-income Americans pay fewer visits to hospitals and doctors' offices than do lower-income Canadians. The health of these Americans is also worse than that of poorer members of Canadian society. The only important difference between the two medical

systems is that the American system is much more expensive for the consumer, and thus is often unavailable to the poor.

15. Some people who argue for the legalization of drugs contend that we would be able to control the use of drugs if they were legalized. We can't even control the use of alcohol. How in the world are we supposed to be able to control the use of legalized drugs?

B. The following historical examples suggest that figurative analogies have had a powerful impact in some important controversies. Identify the evidence relationship and the conclusion relationship for each of the following figurative analogies.[5]

1. *Context*: In his "Cooper Union Address," Lincoln argued that the Democrats—his opponents—were making an utterly unreasonable claim concerning why the voters should not elect a Republican to the office of President. At the Republican National Convention of 1860, Lincoln delivered the famous speech from which this figurative analogy is drawn. What is the picture presented in the evidence relationship? What is the exact relationship between the two people in the picture? To what groups does Lincoln compare these two people in his conclusion relationship?:

"But you will not abide the election of a Republican President! In that supposed event, you say, you will destroy the Union; and then, you say, the great crime of having destroyed it will be upon us! That is cool. A highwayman holds a pistol to my ear, and mutters through his teeth, 'Stand and deliver, or I shall kill you, and then you will be a murderer!' To be sure, what the robber demanded of me—my money—was my own; and I had a clear right to keep it; but it was no more my own than my vote is my own; and the threat of death to me, to extort my vote, can scarcely be distinguished in principle." (Abraham Lincoln, "Cooper Union Address")

2. *Context*: Henry David Thoreau, an ardent foe of slavery, made the following comparison of that institution to another endeavor. What is he saying slavery is like? What relationship is present on the evidence side as well as on the conclusion side of this figurative analogy?

"Much has been said about American slavery, but I think that we do not even realize what slavery is. If I were seriously to propose to Congress to make mankind into sausages, I have no doubt that most of the members would smile at my proposition, and if any believed me to be in earnest, they would think that I proposed something much worse than Congress had ever done. But if any of them will tell me that to make a man into a sausage would be much worse—would be any worse—than to make him into a slave—than it was to enact the Fugitive Slave Law—I will accuse him of foolishness, of intellectual incapacity, of making a distinction without a difference. The one is just as sensible proposition as the other." (Henry David Thoreau, "Fourth of July Oration")

3. *Context*: Americans take for granted that their Constitution reflects good ideas about the governance of a democracy. When it was first proposed, however, the document elicited tremendous debate. James Madison, along with Alexander Hamilton and John Jay, argued vehemently for the Constitution in a series of pieces known collectively as *The Federalist Papers*. Here, Madison develops a figurative analogy to urge adoption of the new Constitution that, he argues, may not be perfect but is clearly preferable to the Articles of Confederation. What two evidence relationships does he develop, and what is the relationship that is similar in each? What, then, is the conclusion relationship?

"It is a matter both of wonder and regret that those who raise so many objections against the new Constitution should never call to mind the defects of that which is to be exchanged for it. It is not necessary that the former should be perfect: it is sufficient that the latter is more imperfect. No man would refuse to give brass for silver or gold, because the latter had some alloy in it. No man would refuse to quit a shattered and tottering habitation for a firm and commodious building because the latter had not a porch to it, or because some of the rooms might be a little larger or smaller, or the ceiling a little higher or lower than his fancy would have planned them." (James Madison, *Federalist Paper* 38)

4. *Context*: Demosthenes, perhaps the greatest orator of ancient Greece, urges the Athenian Senate to fight Philip of Macedon as if the Senate had some idea about how to fight. To make his point, Demosthenes presents the following analogy, which develops around the Athenians' fondness for watching boxing matches between untrained foreign captives and trained Athenian boxers. It's no secret who usually won these bouts, and why. What evidence relationship does he develop in this argument? What is the conclusion relationship? What is the ironic twist that gives the argument its own "punch"?

"The citizens of Athens, however, possessed as they are of the greatest power of all in ships, fighting men, cavalry and monetary resources, have never to this day made a right use of any of them. The war against Philip exactly resembles the methods of an untaught foreigner in the boxing ring. If he is hit, he hugs the place, and if you hit him somewhere else, there go his hands again. He has not learnt, and is not prepared to defend himself or look to his front. So it is with the policy of Athens. If news comes of Philip in the Chersonese, an expedition there is voted; if it is Thermopylae, it is sent there. Wherever he goes, we hurry up and down at his instance, controlled by his strategy without any constructive military plan of our own, without foresight to anticipate news of what is happening or has happened." (Demosthenes, *Philippic* I)

C. Identify the similarities advanced between evidence case and conclusion case in the following examples. Suggest some potential relevant dissimilarities for each.

1. Mr. Smith should receive a Cadillac as a company car, since Mr. Jones received one. Both are good salespeople, and both have been with the company for fifteen years.

2. If Bush maintains a firm resolve about our right to be in the Persian Gulf, the Soviets will back down. This is what occurred in Cuba in the 1960s: firm resolve on the part of a strong President, and the Soviets caved in.

3. San Francisco will be hit by a quake in the near future. Geologic activity around the city is similar to that around Los Angeles before the big 1971 quake. We also see changes in the ocean and atmosphere in San Francisco that are close to changes noted just prior to the Los Angeles quake.

ENDNOTES

1. See also Aristotle, *Rhetoric*, translated by W. Rhys Roberts (New York: Modern Library, 1954), p. 144.

2. For a discussion of the rule of justice, see Chaim Perelman and L. Olbrechts-Tyteca, *The New Rhetoric*, translated by John Wilkinson and Purcell Weaver (Notre Dame: University of Notre Dame Press, 1968), pp. 218-220. Perelman writes, "The rule of justice requires giving identical treatment to beings or situations of the same kind" (p. 218).

3. If you would like to read more about figurative analogies and how they work, see I. A. Richards, *The Philosophy of Rhetoric* (Oxford: Oxford University Press, 1979), chapters V and VI (original work published 1936).

4. Some contemporary rhetorical theorists believe that the ability to form analogies, and perhaps especially figurative analogies, is fundamental to all reasoning. For a helpful discussion of this idea in the works of Ernesto Grassi, see Sonja K. Foss, Karen A. Foss, and Robert Trapp, *Contemporary Perspective on Rhetoric* (Prospect Heights, IL: Waveland Press, 1985), pp. 135–140.

5. I would like to thank Professor Michael Leff for suggesting these examples.

6 GENERALIZING ARGUMENTS

Chapter Preview

GENERALIZATIONS

Discussion of four common kinds of generalizations, along with tests for each. Also coverage of the language and concepts of basic statistics.

Key Terms

sample	bias	skewed sample
generalizations	self-selection bias	predictive
descriptive	survey research	generalizations
generalizations	mean	normative
population	mode	generalizations
inductive reasoning	median	argument from example
deductive reasoning	relative sample size	atypical example
property	absolute sample size	inadequate sample
extent	stratified sample	
inductive leap	sub-populations	

A quality control superintendent for a major automobile manufacturer is responsible for testing parts that arrive at the warehouse for installation in new cars. Because every part in a shipment cannot be tested, samples are selected from boxes as they are off-loaded. One shipment was clearly unacceptable on the basis of this sampling procedure. A worker reported to the superintendent, "We've tested fifteen units in the load of 500 that arrived last night, and five of them were defective. I say we send back the whole shipment."

The reasoning process involved in this worker's testing of parts shipments is called generalizing, and arguments based on this process are the topic of this chapter. These arguments move from evidence, called a **sample**—*observed members of a group*—to conclusions, called **generalizations**—*statements about an entire group or class of things based on a sample. The group, or class from which the sample was drawn and to which the generalization is meant to apply* is called the population.

Most generalization arguments can be categorized under one of four headings:

1. Descriptive generalizations.
2. Predictive generalizations.
3. Normative generalizations.
4. The argument from example.

We will begin with the most basic generalization arguments, descriptive generalizations, which will provide a basis for discussing other types of generalizations.

❖ DESCRIPTIVE GENERALIZATIONS

Descriptive generalizations are *arguments that describe an entire population after observing some members of that population. Reasoning that moves from particular observations to general conclusions* is sometimes referred to as **inductive reasoning** or simply **induction**. *Reasoning that moves from general principles to particular applications of these* is often called **deductive reasoning**. All generalizations involve inductive reasoning. Consider the following example:

A: The first two mechanical pencils I took from this box worked well. So, B: the other eight pencils in the box probably work well, too.

This argument moves from an observation of two members of the category, "the mechanical pencils in this box," to a conclusion about the population, "the other eight pencils in the box." The argument also involves a **property**, *a quality that is transferred from the sample to the population*. Statement A expresses the sample in this argument. Because the sample represents those members of the group that actually have been observed, it always stands as the *evidence* in a generalization argument:

Sample: A: The first two mechanical pencils I took
(evidence)   from this box worked well.

Statement B expresses the generalization itself, a statement that applies the property to the population. The **extent** of the generalization is *that portion of the population to which the generalization applies the property*. In our example, the extent is "the other eight pencils in the box," because the generalization affirms that they are all likely to work well.

Identifying the extent of any generalization we are advancing, or being asked to accept, is important. The extent of a generalization can be found in the generalizing statement itself. Does the generalization claim something about 39 percent of the target population, "most" of the target population, a third of the target population? Until we know the extent of the generalization, we cannot know how well the sample supports the generalization. The portion of the sample in which the property is observed should show a close correspondence with the extent of the generalization. That is, if the sample shows a property to be present in 33 percent of observed subjects, the generalizing statement ought to state that approximately one-third of the population may be expected to exhibit the same property.

In the statement of the extent of a generalization, there are three problems to watch for. First, the generalizing statement provides no extent, which leaves you unable to know the specific nature of the generalizing claim. Second, vague terms such as "most" and "nearly all" make it difficult to know what claim is being advanced. Third, some obvious discrepancy might be present between the property in the sample and what is being claimed about the extent of the property in the population. In these instances we may want further clarification of the extent of the generalization.

Because the generalization itself is a conclusion based on the evidence of the sample, it always will stand as one of the argument's conclusions:

Generalization: B: The other eight pencils in the box
(conclusion)   probably work well, too.

The property being transferred from the sample to the population in this example is:

Property: The property of working well.

Being able to identify the property transferred from the sample to the population is critical in any generalization. Knowing exactly what population is being generalized about before accepting a generalization argument is also vital. Generalizations often fail to adequately define their population. Accepting an argument that claims to make generalizations about some group is not reasonable if we are not certain about who or what makes up that group. To identify the population, we must *look at the generalization statement itself*. The sample may not indicate the population, only the group from which the sample was selected. In some arguments the generalization statement applies to a group broader than that actually sampled.

In generalization arguments there is a substantial leap from evidence to conclusion. This is sometimes referred to as the **inductive leap**. What assumption allows movement of this property from sample (evidence) to generalization (conclusion)? The person arguing must be assuming that the sample represents the entire population. In fact, some version of this assumption is present in all generalization arguments. The assumption is usually an unstated connective, which we can express as follows:

Connective: The sample represents the population.

We can now show the place of this connective in the example by standardizing it:

Sample:	A:	The first two mechanical pencils in that box worked well.
(evidence)		
Connective:	C*:	The sample represents the population. [so]
Generalization:	B:	The other eight pencils in the box are probably OK as well.

The generalization we have been looking at is simple, based on casual sampling. Some generalizations, however, involve more sophisticated, statistically based sampling. The following is an example of a statistical generalization:

A: In a random telephone survey of 2,500 registered voters interviewed, 39 percent expressed a favorable attitude toward the current administration's economic policies, whereas 53 percent expressed dissatisfaction with the President's policies. Thus, B: a majority of voting Americans oppose this administration's economic policies.

The sample in this generalization was gathered using a survey. When attitudes are being sampled using *survey research*, those gathering the sample must be careful to guard against **bias** entering the sample. Bias in survey research is *a factor that would encourage only some persons to respond to the survey, or would encourage those responding to answer in a particular way*. Thus, in doing this survey of political attitudes, the questions would have to have been phrased in such a way that they did not encourage a particular response. For instance, the question about attitudes regarding the administration's economic policies could not be phrased: "Many people have expressed dissatisfaction with the current administration's economic policies. What do you think of these policies?" Nor should it be phrased, "What is your attitude regarding the current administration's wasteful economic policies?"

Similarly, a mailed survey of car owners regarding their satisfaction with a certain car model might introduce a **self-selection bias**, which means that some factor in the surveying process encourages only some members of the population to respond. That is, the people who are most dissatisfied with their cars, and perhaps those who are highly satisfied, are the most likely to respond to the survey. Those without strong feelings about the car simply may not return a mailed survey, thus preventing the possibility of a representative sample. In such a case, a telephone survey might be preferable to a mailed one.[1]

In the political survey example the property being transferred from the sample of 2,500 registered voters to the target population of voting Americans is:

Property: The property of opposing the administration's economic policies.

In this example, knowing the meaning of the property is not as easy as it was in the example of the pencils. We may feel confident that we understand clearly the property of "working well" when discussing mechanical pencils. What is meant by "opposing the administration's economic policies," however, is less clear. We don't know, for example, the nature and strength of that opposition. These points are not clear from the argument itself. Does this mean that a majority of Americans are simply dissatisfied with the policies, or are willing to vote against the administration in the next election, or are likely to take some other action? Thus, the property remains a bit vague as presented.

The extent of this generalization in the telephone survey is expressed in the phrase "a majority," indicating that the property is being transferred to this portion of the population on the basis of the sample. Because "majority" is vague (it can mean anywhere from 51% to 99%) the actual extent of the generalization is not clear. But, because we know the actual percentage of the sample that opposed the administration's policies, lack of clarity about extent is not as serious in this argument as it might be otherwise.

Even though a more sophisticated kind of sampling and much larger numbers in the sample and population are involved, this argument uses exactly the same connective reason as did the earlier example of the pencils. We can show the place of this assumption in a standardization of the argument:

Sample: A: Of the 2,500 voters surveyed, 39% favor,
(evidence)   and 53% oppose, the current
                    administration's economic policies.
Connective: C*: The sample represents the population.
                    therefore
Generalization: B: A majority of American voters oppose the
(conclusion)   current administration's economic policies.

Notice that reasons A and C* are dependent; the evidence and connective must work together to produce the conclusion. Neither one by itself will allow the generalization to be drawn. This dependence would have to be represented in any diagram of the argument:

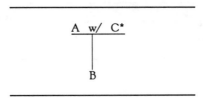

All generalization arguments involve an inferential unit like the one just presented, because all involve a sample (evidence), the dependent connective reason affirming that the sample is representative of the population, and the generalization itself. As this last example reveals, the property in a generalization argument may be an attitude.

DESCRIPTIVE GENERALIZATIONS AND BASIC STATISTICS

Suppose that the survey on which the previous example is based included the following item:

Which response best represents your reaction to the following statement?

In general, I oppose the current administration's economic policies.

1. Strongly agree
2. Agree
3. No opinion
4. Disagree
5. Strongly disagree

The results of the survey are as follows:

1. 535
2. 790
3. 99
4. 210
5. 866

The results of the survey indicate that 53 percent of the subjects, or 1,325 people, responded that number 1 or number 2 best represented their reaction to the statement, thus indicating that they disagree with the current administration's economic policies. Therefore, the generalization as we have it may be statistically accurate.

Knowing the actual responses, however, tells a little more than how a majority responded. For instance, we can see that the **mode** in this survey, *the most common response or the number occurring most frequently in a sample*, was number 5, strongly disagree, which was marked 866 times. This response may indicate that people disagreeing with the statement tend to have stronger opinions than do the people agreeing with it, an important fact in political polling, because people with strong opinions tend to take actions—such as voting.

The actual responses also reveal that a relatively small number of people had no opinion about the statement, perhaps indicating sharp divisions within the voting public on this issue. Thus, though the original claim that "a majority of voters oppose the current administration's economic policies" may be a statistically correct report of the results of the survey, it may not be an enlightening interpretation, or one that would lead to accurate predictions about voting behavior.

Basic statistical knowledge can assist our understanding of other common descriptive generalizations as well. For example, we often hear descriptive generalizations such as:

A survey of 500 employed residents of the city, about 1% of the total working population, indicates that the mean income for working people in the city is between $25,000 and $30,000 annually, well above the national average of $19,500.

Mean is simply another word for *the average, or the sum of a set of figures divided by the number of figures in the set*. For this example, the mean is determined by dividing the sum of the incomes of the members of the sample by the number of those surveyed, 500. Sometimes the mean can be misleading, especially because many people think mean, or especially average, means "typical" or "usual." The mean income figure reported in the example would seem to indicate that the residents of the city are doing well financially. Then again, it may not indicate this at all. Using income ranges rather than actual income figures, the survey showed the following approximate distribution of incomes:

$ 8,000–10,000	105
10,000–15,000	217
15,000–20,000	27
20,000–25,000	16
25,000–30,000	11
30,000–40,000	22
40,000–60,000	15
60,000–75,000	54
75,000–100,000	31
100,000 and above	2

Looking at these statistics, on the basis of which a descriptive generalization about average incomes for working people is advanced, we can see that the generalization itself may be misleading. The mode in this survey is an income of $15,000 to $17,000 annually, well below the reported mean of $25,000 to $30,000. More important, however, the mean does not reveal much about the actual distribution of incomes in the city.

Here, the median income would be a useful figure. The **median** is *the middle figure in a group of figures, the one that exactly divides the top half from the bottom half*. It is easy to see from these figures that well over half of the people surveyed, 322, or 64.4%, earn less than $15,000 annually, $10,000 to $15,000 less than the reported mean. It is also easy to see that very few people in the survey, 11, or 2.2%, actually earn the mean income. Thus, the mean, or average, income is clearly not a typical or usual income.

Moreover, the survey results reveal that 87 people, or about 17.4% of the sample, earn more than $60,000, about one-fourth the number that earn $15,000 or less. Using median incomes for each income category (the median in the $10,000 to $15,000 category is $12,500), however, the combined income for the 87 people making $60,000 or more is 150% to 200% more than the combined incomes of the 322 people making $15,000 or less. That is, about one-fourth the number of workers are earning about twice the total income. In addition, the combined income of the 217 people making between $10,000 and $15,000 annually is the same as the combined income of the 31 people who make $75,000 to $100,000. Thus, though seven times as many people are in the $10,000 to $15,000 range, their combined income is no more than the 31 in the $75,000 to $100,000 range.

Therefore, though the mean income in the city may be between $25,000 and $30,000 annually, this figure tells us little about the financial situation of the city's workers, and certainly does not tell us what a "typical" income in the city is. A typical income in this city, revealed more clearly in the median (more than 250 people make $15,000 or less) and mode (the 217 people making $10,000 to $15,000) than in the mean, is well below the reported national average of $19,500, although the report suggests the opposite. The survey results actually show a city in which a few people make relatively high salaries and a lot of people make very little.

These two examples suggest that statistical descriptive generalizations clearly have to be approached with caution. Whenever possible, it is a good idea to get a look at the actual figures from which the generalization was derived. If the actual figures are not available, obtaining the mean, median, and mode is useful. To accept means reported on their own requires great caution. Additional tests of generalizations can also help to ensure that our acceptance of such arguments is reasonable.[2]

TESTS OF GENERALIZATION ARGUMENTS

Generalizations are reasonable only to the extent that the assertion expressed in the connective reason—*the sample represents the population*—is accurate. This assertion alone allows the projection of a property from sample to population. Generalization arguments often move well beyond their evidence (the sample) to their conclusions (the generalization), and they do this strictly on the basis of this characteristic connective reason. Thus, this connective, if accurate, justifies the *inductive leap* spoken of earlier. If the assumption is inaccurate, the argument itself cannot be reasonable.

An example may help to illustrate how important the connective assumption is in generalization arguments, and how risky the inductive leap may be. We take for granted that political pollsters draw generalizations about 80,000,000 voters on the basis of a sample of a 3,000 or 4,000 of those voters. The sample, therefore, consists of a small fraction of 1% of the actual population. On the other hand, to contact all of the voters in the country would not be possible. Thus, careful efforts are made to ensure that the sample represents the population, since this surprising movement beyond the actual evidence of the sample is made possible only by the connective reason we have been discussing. If the sample does not represent the population in polls such as these, the poll will be unreliable. Again, this movement beyond the actual evidence—and the assumption on which it is based—is what makes generalizations both useful and risky.

The discipline of statistics seeks to provide rules for assuring that samples are representative of populations. Careful sampling procedures are developed which assist both natural and social scientists to sample members of populations in such a way that an accurate picture of that population can be achieved without looking at every member of the population. In this chapter I will be discussing only a few of the basic tests of generalizations. These basic tests can help you determine whether the connective in a given generalization is justified.

Several tests are useful in analyzing all generalization arguments. We will discuss these tests now, later adding any special tests appropriate to other types of generalizations when we discuss those types. Since all generalizations depend on the connective "the sample represents the population," the accuracy of this claim must be tested first.

Because a sample cannot be representative if it is too small, the first test of generalizations asks:

Test 1:   Is the sample of sufficient size to represent the population?

For a sample to be representative, it must not involve too few members of the population. How many is enough to provide an accurate picture of the population? That question belongs properly to the discipline of statistics, and a thorough answer is beyond the scope of this text. Nevertheless, we can point out the importance of two aspects of size—relative and absolute.

The **relative size of a sample** is *the sample's size in relation to the total number of members in the population*. The **absolute size of a sample** is simply *the total number of individuals in the sample*. Let's look again at an earlier example:

A: The first two mechanical pencils I took from this box worked well. <u>So</u>, B: the other eight pencils in the box probably work well, too.

The absolute size of the sample in this example is 2. The relative size is expressed in the ratio 2/10.

Sufficient sample size depends on a number of factors. Two of the more important are:

1. The size of the population.
2. The likelihood that members of the population will resemble each other.

Thus, the observation that two mechanical pencils from a box of ten worked well may be a sample of sufficient size to support the generalization "the pencils in this box work well." But observing that the first two people encountered in Paris were unfriendly is not a sample of sufficient size to support the generalization that "Parisians are unfriendly." There are simply too many Parisians, and they are not likely to be similar enough for such a small sample to support a generalization about them all.

Furthermore, a sample of sufficient size still may not accurately represent a population. It may reflect some bias because of the way in which the sample was gathered. To guard against this possibility, and to detect it when it has occurred, a second question to be asked of the sample is:

Test 2:   Is the sample random?

A random sample is *a sample in which every member of the population had an equal opportunity of being selected for the sample*. Imagine that you are going to survey student attitudes regarding the Bush Presidency on a campus with 16,178 students. To collect the sample, you are drawing names from a box containing the names of every student on campus. The first name selected has a 1/16,178 chance of being selected. For the sample to be random, that first name selected has to be returned to the box before the second name is drawn. Otherwise the second name has a slightly better chance—1/16,177—of being drawn. Notice that "random" used in this sense does not mean unplanned or accidental.

When testing the representativeness of a sample, a third consideration should be added to size and randomness. To be representative, a sample should reflect the diverse elements within a population. This is particularly important when the population is heterogeneous, when its members are diverse. *A sample that adequately reflects the groups within the population* is called a **stratified sample**. Thus, the third test of generalizations asks another question about the sample:

Test 3:   Is the sample stratified?

This test asks if **sub-populations** within the population show up in the sample in proportion to their occurrence in the population generally. For example, if I would want to know how many people in a given town were concerned about developing alternative energy sources, a sample of interviews conducted at local college and university campuses would not be sufficiently stratified across sub-populations in the town. *A sample that over-represents some elements of the population, and thus under-represents others*, is said to be **skewed**. Thus, my sample in this case would be skewed because university and college students are more likely than other groups in the general population to think alternative energy sources should be developed. I could correct this by interviewing people in various locations–factories, office buildings, retirement centers–with a concern for getting the most accurate picture possible of sub-groups of the population and their attitudes on alternative energy sources.

In the earlier example concerning attitudes toward the administration's economic policies, we would want to know what groups within American society were represented in the sample, and in what numbers, before we could be certain that the sample was stratified. If the sample is to be truly representative of the population, the sample and the population should be similarly stratified.

WRAP UP

Generalizations are arguments that move from observations about a few members of a group to a conclusion about the entire group. A property is transferred from the sample to some portion of the population on the basis of an inductive leap beyond the evidence of the sample. This inference beyond the evidence depends on a connective affirming that the sample represents the population. This inductive leap is both useful and risky, and it must be tested carefully. All generalization arguments are subject to three tests of representativeness: tests of size, randomness, and stratification.

❖ PREDICTIVE GENERALIZATIONS

Predictive generalizations go beyond simply describing some population. Though predictive generalizations almost always include an initial description of some population, they are characterized by an additional *generalization that affirms the property will also be present in the population in the future*. The following example involves a predictive generalization:

A: 62% of 500 undergraduates surveyed at California State University campuses said they voted for the Republican candidate for governor in the last election; 58% said they backed the Republican candidate for Congress. Thus, B: it seems that the conservatism that has marked the voting habits of Americans in the past several elections will continue into the next century as students mature and move into the political mainstream.

In this argument a claim is made about how students will vote in the future, based on their current student voting behavior. This effort to predict behavior based on what is currently true of a population involves greater risk than does simple description. Understanding the precise nature of this additional risk involves the realization that the connective for predictive generalizations is more involved than the one employed in descriptive generalizations.

The connective in predictive generalizations involves the same claim that serves as a connective for descriptive generalizations:

Connective: a. The sample represents the population.

Predictive generalizations usually involve a stated or an implied descriptive generalization, which requires the presence of this connective reason. In the example the descriptive generalization that students are conservative is implied. This generalization is drawn on the basis of the sample of 500 students, but it is never actually stated in the argument. Nevertheless, this descriptive generalization would have to be reasonable for the argument itself to be reasonable.

The predictive part of the predictive generalization requires a second assumption, which allows the prediction to be made:

b. What is true of the population now will be true of it in the future.

Every predictive generalization relies on this two-part connective and assumes that it is accurate. The presence of this connective is what distinguishes the predictive generalization from other types of generalizations.

To see how this two-part connective reason links its evidence to its conclusion, we can standardize our example:

Evidence: (sample)	A:	62% of 500 undergraduates surveyed at California State University campuses said they voted for the Republican candidate for governor in the last election; 58% said they backed the Republican candidate for Congress.
Connective:	C*:	a. The sample represents the population <u>and</u> b. what is true of the population now will be true of it in the future. <u>therefore</u>
	B:	The conservative trend in the country will continue as students mature and move into political mainstream.

This standardization suggests the following diagram, which reflects both parts of the connective:

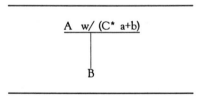

The diagram emphasizes the importance of both elements in the connective to drawing the predictive conclusion.

The connective for predictive generalizations, as we have noted, is the two-part claim that the sample represents the population, and also that what is true of the population now will be true of it in the future. All predictive generalizations involve this additional claim, which makes predictive generalizations more difficult than descriptive generalizations to support. To prove that things will be the same in the future as they are now, is more difficult than simply to describe what is currently true of a group.

Clearly, the predictive generalization goes a step beyond the descriptive generalization. It involves an inductive leap, not just from sample to population but also from present to future. The connective reveals this fact as well, because it involves two claims rather than just the single claim that the sample represents the population.

Since the three tests discussed in connection with descriptive generalizations apply to all generalizations, the same tests ought to be applied to predictive generalizations. But we need another test to be sure that the second claim of the connective reason—that what is true of the population now will be true of it in the future—is justified. Thus, predictive generalizations involve a fourth test in addition to the tests of sample size, randomness, and stratification already discussed:

Test 4:   Will what is true now of the population likely be true in the future?

Let's apply this test to the example involving the university students and voting patterns. If we would want to defend this predictive generalization, we could argue that these students will continue to vote for quite a while, and that their voting habits are not likely to change. This, we might allege, is a good reason for believing that the connective premise for predictive generalizations is justified in the case of this argument. Of course, someone could counter that voting habits change as people mature, and that our connective premise thus is not justified, that what is true now of the population of students is not likely to be true of them in the future. Because it is widely recognized that political thinking and voting behavior can and do change as we age, the prediction may be uncertain in this argument.

WRAP UP

Predictive generalizations operate in essentially the same way as descriptive generalizations and, thus, are subject to the same three tests. But they do involve a more elaborate connective which affirms that what is true of the population at the time of observation will continue to be true of it in the future. This risky assumption should be tested when predictive generalizations are advanced.

❖ NORMATIVE GENERALIZATIONS

Normative generalizations are *generalizations that urge an action on the basis of similar action observed in a sample.* Like predictive generalizations, normative generalizations nearly always involve an initial descriptive generalization. Consider the following example:

A: Recent studies indicate that half of Americans who smoked five years ago have quit smoking. So, B: if you smoke, quit. If you don't smoke, don't start.

This is a normative generalization because it urges an action strictly on the basis of a generalization about the actions of some people in a sample. Thus, the argument seems to assume, in addition to the claim that the sample represents the population, that what some have done, others should do.

Like predictive generalizations, normative generalizations involve a descriptive generalization, although it may be unstated. In the example, the population of people who smoked is generalized to on the basis of a sample that is not specified. Also like predictive generalizations, normative generalizations move beyond this descriptive generalization. They urge an action on the basis of the descriptive generalization. Thus, they also involve a connective with two parts:

Connective: a. The sample represents the population
               and
              b. what has been done by some should be done by others.

We can see the function of this connective reason by setting out the example argument in a standardized form:

Evidence: A: Half of those sampled who smoked
(sample)   five years ago have quit smoking.
Connective: C*: a. The sample represents the
                      population
                      and
                   b. what has been done by some
                      should be done by others.
                      therefore
Conclusion: B: You should quit smoking, or not start.
(generalization)

The diagram for this argument, like the diagram for the predictive generalization example, reflects the dependence of the sample and the two-part connective:

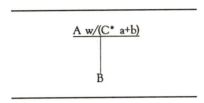

As with the predictive generalization, the normative generalization has a connecting premise which involves two claims. The second claim is that what is done by some members of the population should be done by others. Because the first claim, expressed as (C* a), is the same as that made in the connective reason of descriptive generalizations—that the sample represents the population—*the tests of sample size, randomness, and stratification also should be applied to normative generalizations.* But the second claim expressed as (C* b), requires an additional test, expressed in the following question:

Test 4:   Should what is done by some be done by all?

This question suggests that normative generalizations, like predicitive ones, can be hard to justify. Perhaps this is because they depend on a value that is easily called into question. Although we are certainly aware of factors such as peer pressure and the urge not to be different, the fact that some people are doing a thing is not usually considered a good reason for others to do the same thing.

In some cases, a reasonable connection may exist between the actions of others and our own actions. The value of some actions may be suggested or confirmed by the involvement of a large number of people, which is perhaps clear from the anti-smoking argument. The fact that so many people have decided to stop smoking may be a good reason for others to do the same. Actions with clear social benefits also may be found reasonable simply on the basis of many people affirming the action. For instance, the fact that many people refrain from littering may be a good reason for me not to litter. The most frequently encountered normative generalizations are those advanced in advertisements, for example:

> More than a million people have tried our new skin conditioning process—shouldn't you?

In advertisements, the normative generalization suggests that the preference of a large number of people for a product establishes the product's effectiveness or quality. Here we should be especially aware of the hidden element in the connective—that what has been done by some should be done by others. The fact that a million people have tried a product may only be proof of an effective advertising campaign. Normative generalizations rely on a rather precarious connective. This may prompt us to wonder whether, for example, the fact that polls show that a lot of people will vote for a given candidate is, by itself, a good reason for casting our own vote for that candidate.

WRAP UP

Like predictive generalizations, normative generalizations involve a complex connective, which really makes two claims. The first claim is the one common to all generalizations—that the sample represents the population. This claim must be evaluated according to the tests of size, randomness, and stratification. The normative part of the claim—that what has been done by some also should be done by others—which gives these arguments their identity, also requires careful testing.

❖ THE ARGUMENT FROM EXAMPLE

One type of generalization argument deserves special attention. The **argument from example** is *a generalization from a sample of one or a very small number of identified members of a population.* Consider the following example:

> A: The case of the U.S.S. Stark, which was completely incapacitated by a single Exocet missile from an Iranian fighter, <u>amply demonstrates that</u> B: small naval ships with lightweight hulls are highly vulnerable to high-tech weaponry.

This argument reveals a typical situation for the argument from example. When gathering a sample would be impractical, and when a single case ought to be enough to prove a general claim, the argument from example can be expected. You usually can tell that you are dealing with an argument from example when the member or members of the sample are actually named.

The indicator and qualifier, "amply demonstrates that," is emphasized. Its use reveals that the person arguing thinks that one case ought to be sufficient to support the generalization. This is usually true when we argue from example. We are assuming that a single, clearly representative example provides enough evidence to support a generalization. Thus, the connective for the argument from example is:

Connective: The example(s), as should be clear, represents the population.

Standardized, the same argument would appear as:

Evidence: A : The Stark was completely incapacitated
(sample)   by a single Exocet missile.
Connective: C*: The example, as should be clear,
                   represents the population.
Conclusion: B: Small naval ships with lightweight
(generalization)   hulls are highly vulnerable to high-tech
                   weaponry.

On occasion, two or three examples may be advanced in support of a generalization. The linguistic cue that someone is arguing from example is *the tendency to name or identify the examples*. This seldom occurs in other types of generalizations, in which members of the sample usually are represented numerically and are not named.

TESTS OF THE ARGUMENT FROM EXAMPLE

The example advanced possibly is not generally accepted as true to fact, or maybe it has been misinterpreted. If any doubt exists about the accuracy of the example or of its interpretation in an argument, it is important to ask:

Test 1:   Is the example presented and interpreted accurately?

An example is of no use if it can be shown that it is not true to fact. The example also is weakened if an example that is basically true to fact has been distorted or misinterpreted. In our example, the case of the Stark probably has been presented accurately and has not been misinterpreted. After this incident many experts concluded that the destruction of the Stark showed at least that ships such as this are vulnerable to missile attack. The similar fate of the H.M.S. Sheffield during the Falklands crisis tended to support this conclusion.

But suppose that we read a report of a virus in the same family as the AIDS virus but which can be transmitted by casual contact. This example might be misinterpreted as allowing the generalization that all viruses in this family can be transmitted by casual contact. Such a generalization would represent a significant misinterpretation of the example.

If we are satisfied that the example is true to fact and has not been misinterpreted, we can proceed to the second test of example arguments. The argument from example, as we know, generalizes from one or a few examples. But the example(s) is affirmed to be so clearly representative of the population that no further instances are thought necessary. Thus, the tests of representativeness that ask about size, randomness, and stratification of the sample are not relevant to the argument from example. Instead, we will want to substitute the following test, which recognizes the unusual nature of the argument from example:

Test 2:   Does the example represent the population?

Arguments from example can be refuted if the example can be shown to be **atypical** or **inadequate**. Thus, if what happened to the Stark can be shown to be unusual, which would mean advancing examples in which similar ships were not vulnerable to high-tech weaponry, the argument would be weakened. Similarly, if the Stark example is opposed as inadequate to prove the point—if other cases are demanded in confirmation of the generalization—the argument also may be weakened. In this particular case of the argument from example, a single incident does seem adequate to show that this type of ship is vulnerable to such weapons.

Finally, an example argument can be answered with another example argument. The third test of this argument, then, asks:

Test 3:   Is a significant counter-example available?

If an example were available of a ship similar to the Stark, which had absorbed a similar missile attack without significant damage, we would be able to answer the example argument. In legal settings, advocates often seek to answer precedent-establishing example decisions advanced by opponents, with their own example decisions that establish some other precedent.

WRAP UP

In some instances a large sample is not possible or is not necessary to support a generalization. Thus, some generalization arguments involve samples of one or a very few members of a population. These arguments from example can be reasonable provided that the example is clearly representative of the population.

Chapter Review

Generalizing arguments move from consideration of a sample to a generalization about a population. Therefore, they all depend on the sample accurately representing the population. This dependence is reflected in the connective of each generalizing argument discussed in this chapter: the descriptive, the predictive, and the normative generalization, and the argument from example. The tests of size, randomness, and stratification have been suggested as means of evaluating the claim to representativeness inherent to generalizations. Special tests also have been suggested for assessing the special claims of the predictive and the normative generalization, as well as that of the argument from example.

EXERCISES

A. Identify the following generalizations by type. For each, provide (a) the sample, (b) the population, (c) the property.

1. The members of that fraternity are real anmimals! I've gone out with three of those guys, and they've all been rude and aggressive. I'd advise you not to go out with Steve.

2. The death of University of Maryland basketball star Len Bias should be enough to prove to anyone's satisfaction that cocaine use is life-threatening.

3. A telephone survey of 500 Democrats who voted in the last election indicates that at least 15 percent of those surveyed were inclined to switch to the Republican party. Thus, we can expect a major defection to the Republican party in the next election.

4. The examples of India, Ethiopia, and Panama prove that massive foreign aid does not improve conditions in developing nations.

5. In the past five years we have seen a 35 percent increase in the number of people involved in some form of regular, aerobic exercise—this according to reports by 150 physicians in thirty states concerning more than 5,000 patients. Any of you over the age of twenty still wondering whether you should be doing aerobic exercise should follow the lead of these health-conscious people.

6. Most Americans favor U.S. involvement in the Middle East. In a recent poll of 250 people living in or around Chicago, 63 percent of those surveyed favor such involvement.

7. The failure of Reaganomics reveals that economic programs prohibiting massive tax increases are doomed to failure.

8. A survey of 1,500 graduating high-school seniors indicates that the space program is an important item on their political agendas. Thus, we can expect support for the space program to remain strong as we enter the twenty-first century.

9. We surveyed 450 people at a suburban train depot at rush hour, and 54 percent reported that inadequate public transportation was for them an important political issue. Thus, most Americans find the current state of public transportation to be an issue vital to the upcoming elections.

10. Our paper's thorough coverage of the war on drugs reveals our commitment to providing you with the very best news coverage of the most important stories of our day.

B. Suggest why the sample in each of the following generalization arguments might not be representative of the population.

1. We surveyed 450 people at a suburban train depot at rush hour, and 54 percent reported that inadequate public transportation was for them an important political issue. Thus, most Americans find the current state of public transportation to be an issue vital to the upcoming elections.

2. Age differences are insignificant to the success of a marriage. Why, I know a couple in which the wife is seventy-two and the husband is nineteen, and they are perfectly happy.

3. A survey of 1,500 graduating high-school seniors indicates that the space program is an important item on their political agendas. Thus, we can expect support for the space program to remain strong as we enter the twenty-first century.

4. Increasingly, American teachers are unhappy with their work. Of 112 veteran teachers interviewed, 87 said they found teaching less rewarding and more stressful than when they entered the occupation.

5. Clearex took care of my acne, and it can do the same for you!

C. Scan, standardize, and diagram the following generalizing arguments. Supply the missing connective for each in your standardization.

1. Most Americans favor U.S. involvement in the Middle East. A recent poll of 250 people living in or around Chicago revealed that 63 percent of those surveyed favor such involvement.

2. The examples of India, Ethiopia, and Panama prove that massive foreign aid does not improve conditions in developing nations.

3. A telephone survey of 500 Democrats who voted in the last election indicates that at least 15 percent of those surveyed were inclined to switch to the Republican party. Thus, we can expect a major defection to the Republican party in the next election.

4. According to fifty record store owners in the L.A. area, record-buyers are buying Rick Lane's latest release in record numbers! Get "To Your Heart," and find out why!

5. Professional investment analysts will continue to face hard times, as fewer and fewer people will seek the advice of professionals about investments. Responses from 377 members of the 90,000 member American Investors Association suggest that about 70 percent already do their own investment research, never consulting a professional.

D. Explain how bias may attend gathering a representative sample in the following example:

We are requesting that you complete the enclosed survey which will provide Citizens Against Drugs with important information about how Americans feel about drug use and random drug testing in the workplace. Before you fill out the survey, however, you should realize that more than 14,000,000 Americans have admitted using drugs this month alone, and 1 in 6 admit they use drugs at work! Transportation workers, health workers, and employees of the food industries all use drugs at work on a regular basis, and they are getting away with it! Please take five or six minutes to give us your opinion about this dangerous situation.

E. Find an example of a generalization argument in a magazine or newspaper. In your example, identify the sample, population, property, and extent. Employing the tests of representativeness, explain whether your example is a reasonable generalization.

ENDNOTES

1. For a more detailed discussion of sampling methods, see Mary John Smith, *Contemporary Communication Research Methods* (Belmont, CA: Wadsworth Publishing Company, 1988), chapter 5.

2. Many helpful texts are available for a more comprehensive introduction to statistical reasoning. See, for example, Frederick Williams, *Reasoning with Statistics*, 3d ed. (New York: Holt, Rinehart and Winston, 1986).

7 CAUSAL ARGUMENTS

Chapter Preview

CAUSAL ARGUMENTS

A presentation of several arguments that try to establish a causal relationship among events. Also, definition of terms and discussion of concepts common to causal reasoning.

Key Terms

causal arguments
conditional arguments
conditional statements
antecedent
consequent
affirming the
  antecedent
modus ponens
denying the
  consequent

modus tollens
sufficient condition
necessary condition
argument from cause
argument from sign
hypothesis arguments
observation
corroborating evidence
plausibility reasons
causal generalization

arguing from
  correlation alone
arguing *post hoc*
argument from
  direction
slippery slope argument
domino theory

A student complained, "Every time I stay up late before an exam, I fail it. I'm going to start going to bed early before exams, even if I don't feel I've studied enough." This student's comments denote a causal argument. She observes that staying up late before exams is followed by her failing exams. On the basis of this observation, she concludes that staying up late *causes* poor performance on exams. The type of reasoning engaged in here is one of several kinds of causal argument.

Causal arguments are *arguments that seek to establish cause-effect relationships between events*. Arguments such as these may seek or allege cause in a class of events, a single event, or a series of related events. This chapter covers four common causal arguments:

1. Conditional arguments.

2. Hypothesis arguments.

3. Causal generalizations.

4. The argument from direction.

❖ CONDITIONAL ARGUMENTS

Conditional arguments are *arguments that affirm a causal relationship between two events by means of a connective which appears in the "if . . . then . . ." form, or some equivalent*. These arguments are traditionally referred to as hypothetical syllogisms or conditional syllogisms. *The if . . . then statements in conditional arguments* are called **conditional statements**. The inferential structure of conditional arguments is common to many causal arguments, so considering these arguments before going on to other types of causal arguments may be helpful. Consider the following example:

If that thing over there is a cat, then it will sleep all day.

This conditional statement has two parts. *The "if" clause in a conditional statement* is called the **antecedent**, and *the "then" clause in a conditional statement* is called the **consequent**. We can apply these terms to our example:

---

conditional statement
(connective)

antecedent   *consequent*
If that thing over there is a cat, *then* it will sleep all day.

The *evidence* in a conditional argument—also called the second premise or minor premise—makes a claim about either the antecedent or the consequent of the conditional statement. The evidence can either affirm or deny the antecedent of the consequent. For example:

---

example a

	antecedent
Conditional:	<u>If</u> that thing over there is a cat,
(connective)	**consequent**
	<u>then</u> it will sleep all day.
Second premise:	It is a cat
(evidence)	
	<u>therefore</u>
Conclusion:	it will sleep all day.

Notice that the evidence refers back to the antecedent: "If that thing over there is a cat." Notice also that the evidence *affirms* the antecedent; *it says it is or will be true*. **Affirming the antecedent** in the evidence (sometimes referred to by the Latin name, ***modus ponens***) is one way of making a reasonable inference from the reasons of a conditional argument.

Recall from chapter 2, however, that a reasonable inference is only one requirement of a reasonable argument. It also must exhibit good reasons (support) and linguistic consistency. Thus, in saying that affirming the antecedent in the evidence results in a reasonable inference, we are not saying that this by itself makes it a reasonable argument. Before we could decide to accept the argument, we would have to accept the conditional statement and the evidence as true or accurate and believe that the terms in the argument were being used consistently throughout.

Let's alter the example a bit:

example b

	antecedent
Conditional:	<u>If</u> that thing over there is a cat,
(connective)	*consequent*
	<u>then</u> it will sleep all day.
Evidence:	It does not sleep all day.
	<u>Therefore</u>
Conclusion:	it is not a cat.

In this example the evidence or second premise takes us back to the consequent of the conditional statement. Moreover, it does not affirm the consequent but instead *denies* it or says it is not or will not be true. This is the only other valid inference for conditional arguments—**denying the consequent** in the evidence (sometimes referred to by the Latin name, **modus tollens**).

We now can set out the two rules of good inference for conditional arguments:

1. It is reasonable to affirm the antecedent.

2. It is reasonable to deny the consequent.

Again, these rules have to do only with inference, or the move from reasons to conclusion. They do not tell us anything about whether the evidence and connective are themselves acceptable (support), or whether key terms have been used consistently (linguistic consistency).

When dealing with conditional arguments, affirming the antecedent and denying the consequent are both reasonable inferences. Faulty conditional arguments tend either to deny the antecedent or to affirm the consequent. Let's look at examples of each of these errors:

example c

	antecedent
Conditional:	<u>If</u> that thing over there is a cat,
(connective)	*consequent*
	<u>then</u> it will sleep all day.
Evidence:	It is not a cat.
	<u>Therefore</u>
Conclusion:	it will not sleep all day.

---

example d

	antecedent
Conditional:	<u>If</u> that thing over there is a cat,
(connective)	*consequent*
	<u>then</u> it will sleep all day.
Evidence:	It does sleep all day.
	<u>Therefore</u>
Conclusion:	it is a cat.

Study the four variations on this example until the differences among them are clear. Only the first two, which affirm the antecedent and deny the consequent, represent reasonable inferences. If you are wondering why, the answer has to do with what the statement "If that thing over there is a cat, then it sleeps all day" is saying. Notice that it can be translated, "All cats sleep all day." It cannot be translated, however, "Only cats sleep all day." When we affirm a consequent or deny an antecedent, we are reading the statement as if it says, "Only cats sleep all day," which it doesn't. That's the answer to the question, though some study of the examples may be needed to understand *why* it's the answer.

There are a few special cases of conditional statements. Conditional statements that include the word "unless" should be read as if "unless" meant "if not." This also means that whatever follows "unless" is the antecedent. Thus, the conditional statement:

---

antecedent

The paper will continue to be delivered <u>unless you cancel it</u>

---

can be translated into the conditional statement:

If you do *not* cancel the paper, it will continue to be delivered.

"Unless" affects only the antecedent of the conditional statement.

Conditional statements that include "only if" should be read, "If not . . . then not. . . ." Both the antecedent and the consequent are rendered negative by the phrasing "if not . . . then not." For example:

The professor will respond *only if* you ask him

can be translated into the conditional statement:

If you do *not* ask him, then the professor will *not* respond.

Notice that the clause following "if" is the antecedent whether it appears first or last in the statement.

Following from what we have already said about "if . . . then" and "only if . . ." statements, we also can say something about statements that include the phrase "if and only if. . . ." In effect, such statements make two claims: They set up both a positive and a negative condition. For example, the statement:

The professor will respond if and only if you ask him

can be translated as the two statements:

If you ask him, *then* the professor will respond

and

If you do *not* ask him, *then* the professor will *not* respond.

For this reason, "If and only if" statements can have evidence statements that affirm or deny antecedent or consequent. There are, in effect, no inferentially unreasonable "if and only if" arguments.

Be sure to note that the antecedent is whatever follows the word "if," and the consequent is whatever follows the word "then." The first part of the conditional may be the consequent, as in this example:

Bob will get drunk if he goes bowling.

The antecedent here is "if he goes bowling," even though this clause appears second in the conditional statement.

An affirmation also may appear as a negative statement, as in the following argument, which affirms its antecedent:

If Bob does *not* go bowling, then he will not get drunk. Bob will *not* go bowling (affirms the clause "If Bob does *not* go bowling"); therefore, he will not get drunk.

Similarly, a denial may be stated positively:

If Bob did not go bowling, then he did not get drunk. Bob *did* get drunk (denies the clause "he did not get drunk"), therefore he did go bowling.

NECESSARY AND SUFFICIENT CONDITIONS

Conditional statements express conditional relationships between two events. These conditional relationships are of two types. The first, a **sufficient condition**, is *a condition under which some other event will occur*. The second, a **necessary condition**, is *a condition without which some other event cannot occur*. Consider this example:

If (a) the animal is a whale, then (b) it is a mammal.

Notice that this conditional statement says that (a)—being a whale—is a *sufficient condition* for (b)—being a mammal. If (a) is the case, then (b) must also be the case. This is another way of saying that affirming the antecedent of a conditional statement is reasonable.

Determining whether one event is a sufficient condition for another is possible simply by asking this question:

---

1. If (a) is the case, does this mean that (b) is also the case?

If the answer to this question is yes, then (a) is a sufficient condition for (b). If the answer to the question is no, then (a) is not a sufficient condition for (b). Because the answer to the first question is yes, when applied to our example, then it must be true that (a)—being a whale—is a sufficient but not a necessary condition for (b)—being a mammal.

We have now noted that to say, "If it is a whale, then it is a mammal," is also to say, "Being a whale is a sufficient condition for being a mammal." The same relationship may be expressed in a third way: "All whales are mammals." This leaves us with three ways of stating essentially the same relationship between two things:

1. (a) is a sufficient condition for (b).

2. If (a), then (b).

3. All (a) are (b).

Now, what about the *necessary condition* relationship? Recall that to deny the consequent of a conditional argument is inferentially valid. Thus, returning to our example, we can reason this way:

If (a) it is a whale, then (b) it is a mammal.
It is not (b) a mammal.
<u>Therefore</u>
it is not (a) a whale.

That is, if (b)—being a mammal—is not the case, then (a)—being a whale—is also not the case. This means that (b) is a necessary condition for (a), a condition without which (a) will not occur.

Another way to determine that (b) is a necessary condition for (a) in this example is to ask:

---

2. If (b) is *not* the case, does this mean that (a) is also *not* the case?

Because the answer to this question is yes, then (b) is a necessary condition for (a).

Recall that another way of saying "If not . . . then not . . ." is to use the words, "only if." Thus, we have a third way of expressing that (b) is a necessary condition for (a) in our example:

It is (a) a whale, only if (b) it is a mammal.

So three ways of expressing the necessary condition relationship are:

1. (b) is a necessary condition for (a).
2. If not (b), then not (a).
3. (a) only if (b).

Of course, two events may not have any conditional relationship to one another. For example:

(a) Being male and (b) being a college student.

If you are male, does this mean you are not a college student? No. If you *are not* male, does this mean you are not a college student? No. In this example, (a) is neither a necessary nor a sufficient condition for (b), even though males may be college students.

ARGUMENTS FROM CAUSE AND SIGN

Some causal arguments closely resemble conditional arguments. **Arguments from cause** are *arguments that proceed from the presence of the cause to a conclusion regarding the likelihood of some attendant effect.* We might say arguments from cause move from the presence of the antecedent to a conclusion about the presence of the consequent. For example:

We know that when food supplies are short in the southern part of that country, the residents flee to the North. Food supplies are now quite short in the South, so we can expect a crush of refugees to the North within the month.

This argument proceeds from the evidence of the presence of a cause—shortage of food—to a conclusion about the imminent effect—the movement of people to the North.

An argument that moves from the presence of an effect to conclusions about the presence of a cause is referred to as an **argument from sign**. We can reverse the evidence and conclusion in the example and create an argument from sign:

People in the South of that nation are fleeing to the North. Therefore, there must be a shortage of food in the South.

You may have noticed that the argument from sign amounts to affirming the consequent of a conditional statement. Thus, the conclusion of such an argument might be doubtful or even false. This is true in cases in which an effect only imperfectly indicates the presence of a cause, and such arguments may be termed *arguments from fallible sign*. But, when an argument involves an effect that always indicates the presence of a particular cause, we have what may be called an *argument from infallible sign*.

WRAP UP

Conditional arguments are causal arguments that employ an "if . . . then . . ." statement, or some equivalent, as their connective. The clause following "if" expresses the antecedent, and the clause following "then" is the consequent. It is inferentially reasonable to affirm the antecedent in the evidence of a conditional argument, or to deny the consequent. Necessary conditions are conditions without which some other event will not occur. Sufficient conditions are conditions under which some other event will occur.

Closely related to the conditional argument are the arguments from cause and sign. Arguments from cause move from the presence of a cause to the presence of some effect. Arguments from sign move from the evidence of an effect to a conclusion about the likelihood of a cause.

❖ HYPOTHESIS ARGUMENTS

Hypothesis arguments *seek to establish the cause of a particular event or set of circumstances*. The scientist in the laboratory or the detective piecing together evidence to solve a crime are both seeking to formulate a hypothesis that will adequately explain a single set of observed facts or events. Though the investigations of the scientist or the detective may be complex, the basic structure of their reasoning is relatively simple.

Let's look at an example of hypothesis reasoning:

A: The past ten years have witnessed an alarming increase in the number of homeless people in America. Why have their numbers risen so dramatically? B: The causes can be found in a weak economy and an uncaring administration. C: The economic recession has created a shortage of afford- able housing and jobs. D: An uncaring administration has re- duced federal funding for mental care facilities. E: Too few jobs, too little housing, and insufficient mental health care will always result in an increase in the number of people out on the streets.

This reasoning exhibits the elements of a hypothesis argument. Notice that there is an **observation**—*facts, circumstances or events, the cause of which is in question*. The observation in this hypothesis argument is contained in statement A:

A: The past ten years have witnessed an alarming increase in the number of homeless people in America.

The event for which an explanation is needed, then, is the increase in the number of homeless people in America. Notice that this event has the quality of being unusual. Had the number of homeless people re- mained constant at a relatively low level, possibly no cause for such an occurrence would have been sought. Thus, hypothesis arguments begin with some fact or event that is unusual enough to raise an implied ques- tion. In the example, the question is actually stated:

A: Why [has the number of homeless] risen so dramatically?

Statement B is *the explanation advanced to account for the unusual event*:

B: The causes can be found in a weak economy and an uncaring administration.

This explanatory statement is itself the **hypothesis,** and is therefore one conclusion of the argument. It also can be thought of as the initial answer to the implied question. Hypothesis arguments always involve some statement that advances a possible cause of the unusual event or fact, though they may move beyond this initial conclusion to draw other conclusions.

Statements C and D are **corroborating evidence,** *additional observations that tend to support the hypothesis*:

C: The economic recession has created a shortage of affordable housing and jobs. D: An uncaring administration has reduced federal funding for mental care facilities.

These statements offer evidence supporting the hypothesis. Most hypothesis arguments contain corroborating evidence.

This evidence, however, must be linked to the hypothesis by some connective. **Plausibility reasons** are *generalizations or assumptions that link corroborating evidence to a hypothesis*. Often these connective reasons are unstated in the argument, and the reader may have to supply them. In this example, the plausibility reasons are advanced in statement E:

E: Too few jobs, too little housing, and insufficient mental health care will always result in an increase in the number of people out on the streets.

This connective links the evidence in statements C and D to the hypothesis advanced in statement B.

To summarize, then, hypothesis arguments usually involve the following elements:

1. *An observation*: Facts, circumstances, or perhaps a set of events, which require a causal explanation.

2. *A question*: A statement or at least an implication, of a question of the type: What cause brought about these effects?

3. *The hypothesis*: A statement that advances an explanation of the observations. This statement can be thought of as an answer to the question (2, above). This explaining statement is itself the hypothesis and is a conclusion of the hypothesis argument.

4. *Corroborating evidence*: Additional observations in the situation that tend to support the hypothesis.

5. *Plausibility reasons*: Generalizations or assumptions that link the corroborating evidence to the hypothesis.

The same example can be set out with these parts labeled:

Observation:	A: The past ten years have witnessed an alarming increase in the number of homeless people in America.
Question:	A?: Why have their numbers risen so dramatically?
Corroborating evidence:	C: The economic recession has created a shortage of affordable housing and jobs. <u>and</u> D: An uncaring administration has reduced federal funding for mental care facilities.
Plausibility reasons:	E: Too few jobs, too little housing, and insufficient mental health care will always result in an increase in the number of people out on the streets. [thus]
Hypothesis:	B: The causes [of the alarming increase in homelessness] can be found in a weak economy and an uncaring administration.

A diagram of this argument appears as:

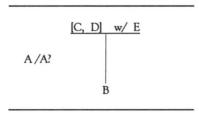

Statement A and the question A? are set to one side in the diagram to indicate that they are the controlling concern for the entire argument.

FORMULATING AND TESTING HYPOTHESES

Familiarity with the reasoning process by which hypotheses are formulated and tested is valuable, as it is common to many problem-solving situations and scientific inquiry.[1] The following example illustrates the general process:

We were perplexed by how humpback whales were able to remember such long songs, ones that change so frequently. We knew already that whale songs contain repeated phrases and sounds at predictable intervals. It occurred to us that perhaps, like humans, whales use rhymes to aid memory. Were this the case, longer songs, being harder to remember, would show a greater frequency of such rhyming patterns. We tested this idea by counting the frequency of the repeated patterns in longer songs and comparing these to the frequency in shorter songs. Sure enough, the longer songs did show a higher frequency of repetition, which tended to confirm our original thinking: that whales use rhyming to remember their long, intricate, and constantly changing songs.

This example includes the observation that whales are able to remember long and complicated songs, which raises the question: How are they able to remember the songs? In seeking to answer this question, the first step of inquiry is to:

1. *Generate a plausible hypothesis.* Generating a hypothesis involves formulating a statement in which possible causes are clearly set out in connection with the observed effect. In

this case the effect of the whales' ability to remember their songs is connected to a possible cause in the statement of a hypothesis:

Perhaps whales use rhymes to aid memory.

Some initial evidence, of course, indicates that this hypothesis is plausible. Still, the guess the hypothesis contains must be tested before it can be accepted as reasonable. This involves moving to the second step in the process of formulating and testing hypotheses.

2. *Generate the consequences of the hypothesis on the assumption of its accuracy.* For this step, we would assume that the hypothesis we were considering was accurate. Then we would ask: If it's accurate, what would we expect to find? In some respects, we are now treating a hypothesis as the antecedent in a conditional statement. For example:

If whales use rhymes to remember their songs, then the frequency of the repeated patterns in longer songs will be greater than the frequency of repetition in shorter songs.

---

3. *Compare actual observations to the generated consequences.* In accordance with this step, the investigators:

---

tested this idea by counting the frequency of the repeated patterns in longer songs and comparing these to the frequency in shorter songs.

---

4. *Accept, modify, or reject the hypothesis.* The researchers in the example decided to accept their hypothesis without modifying it, because the match between what they expected if their hypothesis were true was close to what they actually observed:

Sure enough, the longer songs did show a higher frequency of repetition, which tended to confirm our original thinking:

that whales use rhyming to remember their long, intricate, and constantly changing songs.

If the decision is made to modify or reject the hypothesis, the process of generating and testing hypotheses starts over again.[2]

ASSESSING RIVAL HYPOTHESES

Frequently, more than one hypothesis is advanced to explain an observation. A process similar to the one described for formulating and testing hypotheses can be used to test rival hypotheses, such as the ones advanced in the following example:

Anthropologists Roy Wilcox and Raymond Bannister believe they have solved the mystery of the sudden disappearance of the Qualapi civilization of Indonesia 2,000 years ago. Wilcox and Bannister theorized that the Qualapi people were victims, not of a rival tribe as had been believed previously, but of a relatively minor, local volcanic eruption. They were perplexed by the absence of evidence of conquest among Qualapi ruins. There was no substantial evidence of a large battle, such as remains of weapons, skeletons exhibiting broken bones; no evidence of another culture's immediate appearance in the region; and no mass graves.

   Their own theory was confirmed by a stratum of volcanic ash throughout an isolated region known to have been inhabited by the Qualapis, as well as by evidence in crop remnants of destruction by light-deprivation and cold weather, and skeletal evidence that the Qualapis died out over a period of two to three years. The volcanic ash could only have been the result of an eruption, and it is also possible that the same ash filtered rays from sunlight crucial to crops and for two years created nearly arctic conditions in a previously tropical region.

Professors Wilcox and Bannister apparently began with two rival hypotheses before them:

   a. The Qualapis were destroyed by a rival tribe.

   b. The Qualapis were destroyed by a volcanic eruption.

They proceeded to test the first hypothesis by following step 2, as previously set forth. Generating the expected consequences of destruction by a rival tribe, they arrived at the following:

If the Qualapis had been killed by some other tribe, <u>then</u>:
  a. there will be remains of weapons.
  b. there will be skeletons exhibiting broken bones.
  c. there will be evidence of another culture's immediate appearance in the Qualapi region.
  d. there will be mass graves.

At this point Bannister and Wilcox had some idea what a "real world" example of a tribe's defeat by another tribe would look like. They proceeded to compare this expectation with what has actually been observed, step 3 in the process. The expected evidence was not found:

There was no substantial evidence of a large battle, such as remains of weapons, skeletons exhibiting broken bones; no evidence of another culture's immediate appearance in the region; and no mass graves.

Finding no such evidence, they rejected the first hypothesis. Then, the process began again by generating hypothesis b as step 1 of the process:

The Qualapis were the victims of an isolated volcanic eruption.

Following step 2, effects were generated:

If an isolated volcanic eruption, <u>then</u>:
  a. there would be a stratum of volcanic ash throughout the region.
  b. there would be evidence in crop remnants of destruction by light-deprivation and cold weather.
  c. there would be skeletal evidence that the Qualapis died out over a relatively brief period.

According to step 3, these consequences then were compared to actual evidence:

Their own theory was confirmed by a stratum of volcanic ash throughout an isolated region known to have been inhabited by the Qualapis, as well as by evidence in crop remnants of destruction by light-deprivation and cold weather, and skeletal evidence that the Qualapis died out over a period of two to three years.

This corroborating evidence is also accompanied by plausibility reasons:

The volcanic ash could only have been the result of an eruption, and it is also possible that the same ash filtered rays from sunlight crucial to crops and for two years created nearly arctic conditions in a previously tropical region.

As a result of this process, Wilcox and Bannister felt confident to proceed to accept their hypothesis in step 4.[3]

COMBINING HYPOTHESIS ARGUMENTS WITH OTHER ARGUMENTS

To encounter a hypothesis argument advanced in combination with some other form of argument is not unusual. For instance, if a generalization raises a question of cause, a hypothesis may be advanced to explain the observation. As an example:

A: A random survey of 2,000 new car buyers in the U.S. indicates that during the past six months the sale of small European and Japanese cars has decreased nearly 40 percent. Clearly, B: Americans are buying fewer small imports. C: But why? D: The director of this study concluded, "It is obvious that Americans have outgrown their fascination for the small car, and that E: manufacturers should concentrate their efforts on the production of full-sized sedans."

In this example a generalization is advanced in statement B based on the evidence of a sample expressed in statement A. Statement C expresses the question that arises from statement B, and statement D advances a hypothesis to answer the question. Statement E is a further normative conclusion. Hypothesis arguments are encountered frequently in combination with other forms of argument.

TESTS OF HYPOTHESIS ARGUMENTS

If you are being asked to accept a hypothesis, several tests are available to ensure that your acceptance is reasonable. In some respects, these tests are implied in the method of assessing hypotheses as presented. We can apply the tests to the hypothesis advanced in the example concerning the disappearance of the Qualapi.

Perhaps the first and most obvious question to ask of any hypothesis is whether it adequately explains the observation. Thus, we can ask:

Test 1:   Does the hypothesis account adequately for the observation and its attending evidence?

This first test should filter out hypotheses that are clearly inadequate or insufficient. For example, someone might advance a hypothesis such as, "The Qualapis were contacted by extraterrestrial beings who convinced them to move to a different planet." This hypothesis, though perhaps convincing to some people, is probably not adequate to account for substantial evidence—such as geological evidence—available to anyone caring to investigate the disappearance of the Qualapi. The extraterrestrial being hypothesis would have to be found inadequate to explain the observation of the Qualapis' disappearance and its attending evidence.

On the other hand, if medical evidence were to indicate the presence of epidemic disease among the Qualapi at the precise time of their disappearance, we might have reservations about accepting the volcano hypothesis until it had been modified so as to account for that evidence. Wilcox and Bannister might argue that the diseases indicated by the new medical evidence would be expected only when food was scarce and climatic conditions harsh. The test of adequacy, like step 4 in the assessment scheme set out, suggests the possibility of rejecting a clearly inadequate hypothesis or modifying a plausible hypothesis.

Confirming or rejecting a hypothesis often involves suggesting the presence or absence of a causal agent in the alleged cause. Hypothesis arguments ought to involve an agent that could act to bring about the observed effects. The second test of hypothesis arguments focuses the question of adequacy on the specifc concern for a causal agent by asking:

Test 2:   Does the hypothesis involve a causal agent
sufficient to bring about the effects?

In the example concerning the Qualapi people, an effort is made to explain how the volcanic eruption involved agents sufficient to bring about the observed effects—the filtering action of the volcanic ash, and the subsequent cold weather and loss of crops. The absence of a clear causal agent in a hypothesis does not necessarily lead to its immediate rejection. Sometimes a cause is accurately identified before an agent can be adduced. In such cases, however, a search usually is undertaken to find the agent so as to confirm the hypothesis.

Hypotheses that clearly seem to lack a causal agent may be rejected as unreasonable. Thus, if anyone were seriously to propose that the Qualapi disappeared because their enemies pronounced a curse on them, the hypothesis could reasonably be rejected either as lacking an agent or as incapable of confirmation on the point of agency. There is no way of confirming such a hypothesis.

Other tests also can help in making a reasonable decision about whether to accept a hypothesis. If we knew that hypotheses similar to the one under consideration had been confirmed in similar cases, we would have some reason for believing that the hypothesis we are testing is accurate. The third test of hypothesis arguments is:

Test 3:   Has a similar hypothesis been shown accurate in
any similar cases?

For our example we should attempt to identify other instances in which a civilization has been wiped out by similar volcanic activity and its consequences. The difficulty with confirming this hypothesis on the basis of similar cases is implied in the argument itself: Apparently the local nature of the eruption makes it an unusual event, one that might not have many analogies in geological history.

This point raises a caution that we should acknowledge: Some events are genuinely unique and may require what amount to unique hypotheses. Some recent experiments with superconducting materials, for example, have involved unique hypotheses, and creating new elements in superconducting supercolliders also may be attended by similarly unique hypotheses. In cases such as these, the test of similar cases/similar hypotheses may not be applicable. This test is more useful for confirming a plausible hypothesis than it is for rejecting a weak one.

Recommending an alternative hypothesis to the one being considered is always possible. Accordingly, we will want to ask of hypothesis arguments:

Test 4:   Does an alternative hypothesis better explain the observed events?

This test asks whether another explanation of the observed events might be better than the hypothesis under consideration. In the case of the Qualapis, the hypothesis that they were wiped out by disease might better account for their disappearance than the hypothesis that a volcano was responsible for their mysterious demise. If the alternative hypothesis were to be advanced, it also would have to pass the tests outlined.

These four tests—*adequacy, agency, similar cases/similar hypotheses,* and *alternative hypothesis*—should be applied to any hypothesis argument. We should be careful about accepting a hypothesis argument that does not pass all four tests. As was noted, however, when genuinely unique events are being investigated, it may be necessary to forego the third test, because no analogous cases would be available with which to compare it.

WRAP UP

Hypothesis arguments argue a cause for a particular event. They usually involve an observation that implies a question. The hypothesis is advanced as a conclusion, and other evidence—plausibility reasons—also are often advanced in an effort to support the hypothesis. The hypothesis argument suggests a method of inquiry for resolving questions concerning cause. A hypothesis is generated, along with its likely consequences if true. These consequences are compared to actual observations, and the hypothesis is accepted, modified, or rejected accordingly. In a similar fashion, rival hypotheses to explain the same event can be tested. Hypothesis arguments often are used in conjunction with other types of argument, particularly when some previous argument raises a question about the cause of an event. Finally, hypothesis arguments can be tested by inquiring about adequacy to explain, agency, similar cases, and the presence of stronger alternative hypotheses.

❖ CAUSAL GENERALIZATIONS

The **causal generalization** is *an argument that alleges a causal relationship between two categories of events.* Consider the following example:

One hundred participants in a study at the University of California, Berkeley, took 500 mg. of vitamin C each day for one year. These subjects had one-half as many colds as members of a control group who did not take any vitamin C supplements. Thus, vitamin C seems to have a significant effect in reducing the incidence of colds.

As in generalizing arguments, discussed in chapter 6, causal generalizations involve a sample, a population, a generalization about a population, and a projected property. But these arguments go beyond describing a population to allege a causal connection between two categories or classes of event, one of which is treated as cause, the other as effect. In the example, the two causally related categories of event are:

Cause: taking vitamin C
Effect: getting fewer colds

Like predictive and normative generalizations, the causal generalization does more than simply describe. For this reason, it involves a connective reason with two parts:

Connective: a. The sample is representative of the population
             and
             b. these two events are causally related.

Standardized, then, our example argument would look like this:

Sample: One hundred participants in a study at the University of California, Berkeley, who took 500 mg. of vitamin C each day for one year had one-half as many colds as members of a control group who did not take vitamin C supplements.

Connective: a. The sample is representative of the population

<u>and</u>
b. these two events are causally related.
<u>thus</u>

Conclusion: Taking vitamin C reduces the incidence of colds.

TESTS OF CAUSAL GENERALIZATIONS

As noted previously, the connective in causal generalizations makes two claims, and each of these must be tested. The first of these claims—that the sample is representative of the population—should be tested by applying the three tests for generalizations discussed in chapter 6: Is the sample of sufficient sample *size*? Is the sample *random*? Is the sample well *stratified*?

The second claim expressed in the connective of a causal generalization—that these two events are causally related—requires its own tests. The first of these asks:

Test 1:   Are the two events correlated?

This test asks whether the two events occur together with some regularity. In the example, we would need to confirm that vitamin C use and reduced incidence of colds occurred together with some frequency in the study. *Arguing from correlation alone*, however, is to affirm a causal link between events solely on the basis of their occurrence together and is usually a mistake. Statisticians employ the maxim "correlation is not causation" to express this caution against reasoning from correlation alone to cause. The following example helps to illustrate the problem with arguing from correlation alone:

In the summer, increased consumption of ice cream and an increased incidence of people going barefoot are strongly correlated. In fact, during the summer the incidence of the two events can be seen to increase and decrease in remarkable correlation. Thus, one of these events must cause the other.

Failure to identify the common cause of two correlated events represents one of the pitfalls of reasoning from correlation alone. In this example a third factor is correlated both with consumption of ice cream and with people going barefoot. This third factor, hot weather, is the likely cause of both of the other two events, and for this reason eating ice cream and going barefoot are correlated.

Of course, we often reason accurately from correlation alone. To observe that thunder and lightning occur together with remarkable consistency, and then to decide that one must therefore cause the other, is to draw an accurate conclusion. But bear in mind that correlation arguments often lead to inaccurate conclusions, so we should approach them with caution.

To correlation must be added a concern for succession if we are to establish a causal link between two categories of event. We will want to ask:

Test 2:   Do cause and effect exhibit succession?

This test seeks to ensure that the alleged cause in fact occurs *before* the alleged effect. Effects cannot precede their causes. For the vitamin C example, satisfying this test would require showing that vitamin C use (the alleged cause) precedes a reduced incidence of colds (the alleged effect). If the reduction in incidence of colds in the study group could be traced back to a time before the group started taking vitamin C, the causal claim would be undermined.

Arguing from succession alone is also a risky way of reasoning. This mistake is so common that it has a special name: **arguing *post hoc*.** This name comes from the Latin expression *post hoc ergo propter hoc*, which means "after this therefore because of it." As with correlation, succession alone should not be taken as proof of causation. For example:

Examination of the in-flight recorder revealed that one of the pilots was whistling loudly three minutes before the crash. Could it be that a whistling pilot can cause such accidents?[4]

Like reasoning from correlation alone, reasoning from succession alone can lead to failure to identify a potential common cause of both events, or it may suggest a causal relationship between two events that exhibit only coincidental succession.

Correlation and succession together get us closer to being able to establish cause. When we both see two events occurring together with some frequency and we note that one of the events seems always to precede the other, we can begin to make a case that one event causes the other. But one critical observation about the alleged cause still must be made. Thus, the third question we have to ask to establish a causal link between two categories of event is:

Test 3:   Is there evident agency in the alleged cause that could bring about the observed effect?

This test asks whether we can identify a factor in the cause that could act (serve as agent) to bring about the effect in question. In our first example, then, we should at least advance a reasonable hypothesis concerning the means by which vitamin C prevents colds. What is it about vitamin C that acts on the body so as to increase resistance to colds? Although the researchers who designed this study may not be able to point directly to the causal agent, they are at least obliged to advance a hypothesis, or educated guess, concerning a possible or likely causal agent in vitamin C that could prevent colds. Only when the tests of correlation and succession have been satisfied, and a plausible agent has been suggested, can we begin to have some confidence that the claim to causality has been established in a causal generalization argument.

WRAP UP

Causal generalizations affirm a causal relationship between two categories of events. In this way they combine features of generalization arguments and of hypothesis arguments. Therefore, causal generalizations should be tested like other generalization arguments. In addition, we should ask about the correlation and succession of cause and effect categories, as well as about the potential presence of a causal agent in the causal category. Arguing from either correlation or succession alone are common errors in causal reasoning.

❖   THE ARGUMENT FROM DIRECTION

We are all familiar with the argument from direction, having used it ourselves and having experienced its use against us. Here is an example:

> Laws that require the registration of guns are the first step toward dictatorship. Once guns are registered, no gun owner will be safe from the threat of confiscation. When guns are taken from private citizens, there will be absolutely no defense against a government intent on denying other freedoms—or liberty in general.

This is an example of the **argument from direction**, *an argument affirming that some "first step" in a series of causally related events will lead to an inevitable and undesirable consequence.*[5] These arguments involve as evidence the claim that some set of events is causally linked, which we can call the *progression*. These arguments nearly always are used to caution against some action, and so seem to involve the connective:

Connective: The result of the progression is inevitable and
                undesirable.

The conclusion of the argument from direction is almost always normative, urging that the first step in the progression not be taken. It is this aspect of the argument that has led to its being labeled the **slippery slope argument.**

We often encounter the argument from direction in political controversy. For example, you may have heard some variation of the following argument:

A: We must prevent the fall of El Salvador to Communist insurgents. B: If El Salvador falls to the Communists, then Honduras will follow, and after it Guatemala, Panama, and Costa Rica. Soon even Mexico would fall under Communist influence. C: Are we interested in having a Communist nation on our very borders?

We can put this argument in standard form:

Progression: B: If El Salvador falls to the Communists,
(evidence)   then Honduras will follow, and after
                    it Guatemala, Panama, and Costa
                    Rica. Soon even Mexico would fall
                    under Communist influence.
Connective: C: We certainly do not want a
                    Communist country on our border.
                    (The result of the progression is both
                    inevitable and undesirable.)
                    <u>so</u>

Conclusion: A: We must prevent the fall of El Salvador
                       to Communist insurgents.

When it appears in political discussions, as it does in this example, the argument from direction is sometimes called the **domino theory**.

In sum, the argument from direction involves the affirmation that some action is the first step in an inevitable causal progression leading to an undesirable result. This affirmation serves to connect evidence and conclusion in direction arguments, and so is a connective for these arguments. The argument's conclusion usually urges that the first step in the progression be avoided.

TESTS OF THE ARGUMENT FROM DIRECTION

Two closely related tests can be applied to the argument from direction. Because the argument from direction depends on the assumption that some causal progression will occur, we can ask:

*Test 1:   Are steps in the alleged progression likely to
            occur as suggested?*

The argument from direction may be thought of as a series of linked conditional arguments. So the argument could be presented in the form: "If A then B, and if B then C, and if C then D. D is undesirable, so don't allow A to occur." The argument from direction, then, involves a series of causal claims, each of which can be questioned. The direction argument *can be challenged at every point in the progression*. If any part of the progression is not likely to occur, there is no longer a reason to avoid the first step in the progression, and the argument is rendered unreasonable.

Applying this test to the example, we could ask whether the fall of El Salvador would actually result in the fall of Honduras, if the fall of Honduras would be likely to bring about the fall of Guatemala, and so on. An even more effective tack would be to present evidence showing that some link in the progression is actually *unlikely*. In this way we turn the test into a strategy of refutation. Thus, if it could be shown that Honduras could withstand the presence of a Communist neighbor, the argument would be stopped at the first step in the progression.

Perhaps an alleged progression is difficult to challenge, or for some other reason we are not inclined to answer an argument from direction in this way. We can still question the assumption that the result of the progression is undesirable. The second test of the argument from direction asks:

*Test 2:   Is the alleged consequence of the progression
actually inevitable and undesirable?*

In certain cases we may wish to admit the possibility that the progression
will occur as predicted, but we deny that the consequences are undesirable. This test could be applied to our example. We might respond to
the argument by allowing that the progression is possible—that El Salvador
falling to the Communists might indeed increase the possibility of some
bordering nation or nations also becoming Communist. But we might
object that this does not mean that Mexico eventually would become
Communist, or even that a Communist Mexico would be a wholly undesirable consequence.

WRAP UP

The argument from direction—the slippery slope argument—suggests that
some series of events is causally connected, and that the occurrence of
the first event in the sequence will bring about the others as well. In
most cases a serious and undesirable result is forecast, along with a warn-
ing that the first step must be avoided. In testing these arguments, we
must ask whether the progression is actually likely to occur as suggested,
and if the result, even if we admit the possibility of the progression,
would be undesirable.

Chapter Review

Some arguments seek to establish a causal relationship between events.
Four causal arguments are: the conditional argument, the hypothesis argument, the causal generalization, and the argument from direction.

Conditional arguments affirm a conditional relationship between
two events, using an "if . . . then . . ." statement, or some equivalent.
These arguments are governed by rather precise rules of inference. Sufficient and necessary conditions are another way of expressing the kinds
of relationships suggested by conditional arguments. And arguments from
cause and sign are causal arguments that move either from the presence
of a cause to the likelihood of an effect or from the presence of an effect
to the likelihood of a cause.

Hypothesis arguments seek the cause of a single event or set of
circumstances. Thus, they involve an observation that implies a question.
The hypothesis itself is advanced as an answer to the question, as a cause

for the observed events. These arguments often include further evidence that tends to corroborate the hypothesis, and plausibility reasons that link the evidence to the hypothesis.

Like hypothesis arguments, causal generalizations seek the cause of an event or observation. Like generalizations, however, these arguments affirm a cause for a whole class of event by looking at a sample. They are tested like other generalizations, but with the addition of tests that assess their causal claim.

Arguments from direction affirm an inevitable causal connection in a series of events. These arguments usually urge that the result of the progression from some "first step" to its ultimate consequence is both inevitable and undesirable. Therefore, the first step is to be avoided.

The causal arguments discussed in this chapter are encountered in many arenas of public and private discourse. Therefore, we should try to understand their structure and the means by which each can be evaluated.

EXERCISES

A. For each of the following conditional arguments, identify the conditional statement, the evidence, and the conclusion. Put the conditional statement in its "if . . . then . . ." form if necessary. State whether the evidence is affirming or denying antecedent or consequent and whether the argument is thus valid or invalid.

1. If our administrators were well trained, then our schools would be among the best. Our schools are not among the best, so our administrators must not be well trained.

2. No major political change in this nation will come about unless the people vote. The people are beginning to vote, so we can expect to see major political change.

3. The government said it would intervene only if the region had problems. The region had problems, so we intervened.

4. If this is a genuine Picasso, it will exhibit his careful attention to form. It does exhibit careful attention to form, so it must be a genuine work of the master.

5. Your children will obey you if you raise them properly. You are raising them properly, so I'm sure they will obey you.

6. If Anderson cooperates, then he will be given a reduced sentence. But I happen to know that Anderson will not cooperate, so he will not be given a reduced sentence.

7. If capital punishment actually deters crime, then we can expect to see the number of murders climb when the death penalty is abolished. And this is just what we see: The murder rate increased in Michigan and California after those states voted to do away with capital punishment. Thus, we can see that capital punishment is a deterrent to murder.

B. For each of the following hypothesis arguments, identify the observations and suggest the question that arises out of them. Identify the hypothesis and any corroborating evidence advanced in its support. Suggest what the plausibility reasons for each might be, if they are not provided in the argument. Suggest one possible weakness or response for each argument, based on the appropriate tests.

1. Friday's accident was the first crash of a B-1 bomber. Surviving crew members say they observed a large flock of birds in the vicinity of the aircraft just before it crashed. It is speculated that the birds were sucked into the powerful engines of the bomber, causing it to crash.

2. The Arbuckle triplets were separated from one another at birth, raised by different families in different parts of the country. At their first reunion here on Sunday, it was discovered that each wears his hair in the same style, each smokes the same brand of cigarette, and each works as an auto mechanic. This is further proof that twins and triplets share the same life force.

3. Sheila got sick right after eating that fish. It must have been contaminated.

4. We find in the U.S. that the last 100 years have brought an increase in the literacy rate, improved standards of living, economic growth, and better health care for all. We also find great growth in population. My belief is that the latter, population growth, is the cause of these other improvements. Why? Because more people means more minds working to solve social problems.

5. When I went out this morning, I discovered that the dog was missing. I think he must have been scared off by the thunder last night. There is a hole in the fence large enough for him to crawl through, and he has escaped there before. The thunder was very loud, and he is quite frightened of loud noises.

C. Identify the following causal arguments by type. Suggest a test or tests that might reveal a weakness in each. If the argument stands as a reasonable one, explain why. Provide answers for any additional questions.

1. The pleasure derived from smoking marijuana eventually diminishes. This leads to a desire for harder drugs that can produce that first "high." Because the same gradual diminution of effect will accompany every new drug, the search for a new high goes on and on. Eventually the "social" user of marijuana finds himself addicted to heroin or "crack." So the best advice I can give you is: Don't smoke that first joint.

2. *Context*: In 1978, San Francisco city councilman Dan White, a former policeman, sneaked past a metal detector into San Francisco City Hall, entered the office of Mayor George Moscone, and shot him to death. White then walked down the hall into the office of city councilman Harvey Milk and shot him to death. White was known to have been angry with both men. In the course of his trial for murder, White's attorney succeeded in securing him a reduced charge on the basis of the following argument, which the press dubbed "the Twinky defense."

   Dan White went into a frenzy every time he ate junk foods such as Twinkies. Because his urge for these foods was uncontrollable, and because the resulting frenzy was also uncontrollable, he cannot be held responsible for killing Mr. Milk and Mayor Moscone.

3. Giving loans to Third World countries leaves them with a crippling debt, which they can never pay off. The effort to pay off interest on the debt leads to further borrowing and deeper debt. The lending nations are left with bad debts, and their own economies suffer as a result. Thus, it would be better not to make loans to Third World countries.

4. Lowering the speed limit saves lives as well as fuel. Studies conducted in fourteen states that have reduced speed limits to 55 mph on all highways show an average reduction in highway fatalities of 2 percent for every mile-per-hour of speed reduction. We should urge those states that are considering raising their speed limits to 65 mph to carefully consider this evidence.

5. Failing to recognize the gestational mother in a surrogacy case dehumanizes her. This leads to a situation in which contract takes precedence over human rights. Eventually, legal motherhood will depend on payment and contractual agreements alone. Thus, if surrogacy is to be allowed, the gestational mother's rights must be carefully protected.

6. Japan and England have tough gun control laws. The homicide rate in both countries is quite low. Thus, strict gun control laws can lead to a decrease in violent crime.

7. We cannot afford to be politically neutral, because neutrality leads to ambivalence, and ambivalence eventually gives way to confusion.

8. *Question*: Is the following an example of causal generalization or of the hypothesis argument? Explain your answer.

   The behavior of two hyperactive children in the class improved dramatically immediately after the new lighting system was installed. This proves that this lighting system is effective for behavior control in classroom settings.

9. Heavy rainfall last April resulted in 8,000,000 gallons of raw sewage being spilled into the Grand River from the Grand Rapids sewage treatment facility. Doctors in Grand Rapids report that, since the spill, they have seen a sharp increase in giardia—a bacterial infection that causes intestinal distress. Many doctors have suggested that new cases of the disease have resulted from people swimming in the contaminated river.

10. Suggestions that we make small cuts in medical assistance programs may seem benign but are really dangerous. Small cuts will pave the way for larger cuts in medical assistance to the poor, and finally will lead to the elimination of all federal medical assistance to poor people. If these cuts are unopposed, the administration will take it as a sign to eliminate all programs that help the needy.

11. Strong evidence now exists that buying your son or daughter a computer will improve his or her performance in school. Six hundred students were involved in a study at two large Detroit area high schools. Those with personal computers had a mean grade point average of 3.7, whereas those without personal computers had a mean grade point average of 2.3.

12. It is not abortion itself that I oppose but, rather, the principle it introduces. It seems to legitimize the notion that a society can terminate unwanted human life. This principle, once accepted, can be extended and applied to a wide variety of potentially "unwanted" human life. The aged, the terminally ill, the handicapped—in another time, perhaps even members of a despised race or religious faith—all of these people are at risk.

D. In the following example, rival hypotheses are advanced to explain the same phenomenon. What are the hypotheses? How might they be tested to determine which one is more reasonable?

A strange image appears on the Ables' TV screen at unpredictable times, and it began during the New Age convention in Whitewine, California. "I was watching TV with my family Sunday night," Gill Able said Wednesday. "I switched on the news to see about the harmonic convergence thing when a bright light came out and this odd image appeared. In the last few days she has become brighter and more defined. She is definitely an angel bringing us a message of peace and unity." Frank Lee, owner of Whitewine Electronics saw the television Tuesday and quickly identified the problem. In fact, he has duplicated it in his shop for anyone who wants to see it. "There was a bad circuit board in the set. I have seen the problem lots of times before," said Mr. Lee.

E. Find one example of a causal argument in something you have read or heard. Identify the argument according to the types discussed in this chapter. Employing the appropriate tests, suggest whether the argument does a good job of establishing causation.

ENDNOTES

1. Steps in this section suggested by Monroe C. Beardsley, *Thinking Straight*, 4th ed. (Englewood Cliffs, NJ: Prentice Hall, 1975), pp. 97–104.

2. For a more technical and detailed discussion of hypothesis formulation and testing, see Mary John Smith, *Contemporary Communication Research Methods* (Belmont, CA: Wadsworth Publishing Company, 1988), especially chapter 2.

3. M. Neil Browne and Stuart M. Kelley offer a helpful discussion of why we may select a wrong hypothesis, in their book *Asking the Right Questions*, 3d ed. (Englewood Cliffs, NJ: Prentice Hall, 1990), chapter 8.

4. Example suggested by Trudy Govier, *A Practical Study of Argument* (Belmont, CA: Wadsworth, 1985), p. 314.

5. The term "argument from direction" is from Chaim Perelman and L. Olbrechts-Tyteca, *The New Rhetoric*, translated by John Wilkinson and Purcell Weaver (Notre Dame, IN: University of Notre Dame Press, 1969), pp. 281–286.

8 CATEGORY ARGUMENTS

Chapter Preview

CATEGORY ARGUMENTS

A discussion of arguments that draw conclusions about people, objects, actions, or ideas after placing them in categories.

LANGUAGE IN ARGUMENT

A consideration of several important issues of clear and effective language use in argumentation.

Key Terms

category arguments	argumentative context	pragmatic argument
argumentative definitions	common usage	comparative advantages
euphemisms	etymology	argument from principle
ambiguity	paradigm case	argument from quantity
equivocation	definition by intent	argument from quality
	definition by authority	

T his week you can save up to 40 percent on all major appliances. So hurry to Appliance City for our big clearance sale!" Advertising claims such as this one often employ **category arguments,** *arguments that place objects, ideas, people, or actions into a group about which judgments can be or have been made.* In this example the action of buying an appliance at a reduced price is placed in the category of "actions that offer us some benefit"—in this case, saving money. Similarly, a politician might defend an illegal act by arguing, "I wasn't breaking the law; I was acting in the interest of national security." By defining the act in question as belonging to the category "acts that are in the interest of national security" rather than to the category "illegal acts," this politician is also advancing a category argument.

The category arguments discussed in this chapter are:

1. Argumentative definitions.
2. Pragmatic arguments.
3. Arguments from principle.
4. Arguments from quantity.
5. Arguments from quality.

❖ ARGUMENTATIVE DEFINITIONS

We advance definitions in argumentative contexts for various reasons, the most common of which is to clarify the meaning of an important term. For example, in the process of interpreting a legal document, we might hear or read the following definition:

> The term "parent" in this document refers to the biological parents or legally recognized guardians of a child.

Though such efforts at simple clarification are common, some definitions seek to do more than clarify or illuminate. Definitions can be advanced in an effort to support a particular conclusion. Definitions such as this can be termed **argumentative definitions,** *definitions developed in the effort to strengthen an argument or support a conclusion.*

In a debate over custody of a child, we might encounter an argumentative definition such as the following:

A: Parents are those who nurture and care for a child, those who look out for a child's best interests, those who love the child. B: Though they are not his biological parents, the

Joneses have visited John, brought him gifts, shown consistent concern for his well-being. <u>Thus</u>, C: the Joneses, not
the Smiths, are John's true parents, and they should have
custody of him.

Definitions establish criteria that express beliefs, values, or assumptions
about some class of things. Thus, a definition can function as a connective
in an argument if it can be shown that some person, object, or action
satisfies the criteria set out in the definition. In these arguments, observations about individuals who belong in the defined category function
as evidence. When a definition is not a standard definition, or one that
would achieve agreement among parties to a controversy, we may be
dealing with an argumentative definition.

In the following example, the term "parent" is defined in a way so
as to support the conclusion being drawn. Notice how the definition is
not a generally accepted one, and that its acceptance would tend to
support the conclusion being drawn by the person arguing. Notice also
how the definition establishes criteria for being a parent, and how the
evidence seeks to show how the Joneses have satisfied these criteria:

Evidence:	B: The Joneses have visited John, brought him gifts, shown consistent concern for his well-being.
Definition: (connective)	A: Parents are those who (a) nurture and care for a child, (b) those who look out for a child's best interests, (c) those who love the child. <u>thus</u>
Conclusion:	C: The Joneses, not the Smiths, are John's true parents, and they ought to have custody of him.

This example shows us a typical argumentative definition at work. Such
definition arguments usually involve three steps:

1. A category or class of things is defined by setting out criteria
   that reveal certain beliefs, values, or assumptions about the
   category in question.

2. A person, object, idea, or action is placed in the defined category on the basis of its having satisfied the criteria of the definition.

3. The new member of the category is asserted to have the qualities of other members of that category.

Thus, the effort is made here to define the category "parent," place the Joneses in the category and attribute to them the usual qualities of parents—in particular the right to custody of their children.

Any time a similar effort is made, we can say that an argumentative definition is being advanced. Let's look at another example:

Mr. Wren has admitted threatening the clerk with a can of mace, but did he thereby commit a crime using a handgun? He certainly did, if we understand a handgun to be a hand-held object that emits a projectile capable of causing significant physical harm.

Here is a case of argumentative definition. The individual arguing intends to expand the category described by the word "handgun" to include cans of mace. Once this is done, mace can be given other qualities of members of that category—namely the quality of specific legal sanctions being connected with their use in the commission of a crime.

EUPHEMISMS

Some cases of argumentative definition are *efforts to replace a harsh, condemning, or emotionally charged term with a less objectionable and less accurate one*. These argumentative definitions are referred to as **euphemisms**. For example:

The executive described his willingness to persuade elderly people to invest in his failing savings and loan institution, and then to use their money to speculate in real estate, as "bad judgment."

Since "fraud" is a condemning phrase to describe the executive's action, it is redefined using the euphemism "bad judgment." Euphemisms are quite common in political discourse and should be recognized for what they are—a kind of argumentative definition.

AMBIGUITY AND EQUIVOCATION

In chapter 2, linguistic consistency was advanced as one of three criteria for reasonable arguments (the other two being support and validity). Linguistic consistency refers to the requirement that all key terms in an argument maintain a clear and consistent meaning throughout the argument. The following discussions of ambiguity and equivocation suggest the causes of unclear and inconsistent definitions or meanings, as well as some solutions to these problems.

A problem closely related to definition in argument arises when a key term is not carefully defined, and as a result has two or more meanings. *More than one meaning of a word or phrase in a single context* is called **ambiguity**. For example, a headline reads:

Local school needs to be aired.

The term "aired" is ambiguous here, because it can mean at least three different things. It might mean that local schools are experiencing needs that are to be discussed or expressed—aired. Or the sentence might be taken to mean that the local schools are stuffy and should be aired out— aired. "Aired" also might mean, in this context, broadcast. The headline was intended to communicate the first of these three possibilities, but in some respects all three meanings were communicated, potentially causing a problem in understanding.

Ambiguity in a key term in an argument can be identified and resolved by rephrasing the term or phrase in question so as to reveal its various meanings. In doing this, rephrasing should not use the ambiguous term itself; otherwise the ambiguity will persist. Suppose the following statement were to appear in an argument:

Christians believe in a personal God.

In this statement, the key term, "personal," is ambiguous. The ambiguity can be identified and perhaps resolved by rephrasing the statement so as to reveal the possible meanings of "personal" in this context. For example, the following rephrasings might be advanced:

Meaning 1:	Christians believe that God exists as a person.
Meaning 2:	Christians believe that God relates to people individually.
Meaning 3:	Christians believe that God's nature is determined by individual people as they see fit.

At this point we have at least revealed the ambiguity in the term "personal." Clarification of the ambiguity would require the person making the statement to select one of the three meanings as the one intended in the statement or to recommend some other meaning.

Ambiguity is similar to the problem of **equivocation**, *a key term changing meaning in the course of an argument*. When a key term is equivocal in an argument, the argument cannot satisfy the criterion of linguistic consistency. For example, watch what happens to the meaning of the word "nothing" in the following facetious argument:

Nothing is better than a good education. On the other hand, a ham sandwich is better than nothing. So it seems logical to conclude that a ham sandwich is better than a good education.

If you were to check the inference in this argument against the rules of logic for syllogisms, you would find it to be inferentially reasonable. Moreover, the reasons are true enough, although we might disagree with the first sentence. (You could substitute anything you wished for "education" and still have essentially the same problem.) How, then, can the conclusion be so far off?

The answer is that the term "nothing" has two quite different meanings here; it is equivocal. In its first occurrence it means something like:

Meaning 1:   Not anything you can think of.

In its second occurrence it means something like:

Meaning 2:   Not having anything at all.

By rephrasing the two occurrences of the equivocal term, we can demonstrate and perhaps resolve the equivocation. This is important, because *as long as an argument exhibits equivocation in an important term or phrase, it cannot be accepted as a reasonable argument.* Clearly, the first meaning of "nothing" does not work if we substitute it for the word "nothing" in the second sentence. This argument is unreasonable because its terms are not used consistently throughout. This is a problem to watch for in all arguments, although it is particularly troublesome in category arguments.

As we have seen, the method of identifying and resolving equivocation is similar to that used with ambiguity. It is important to provide a synonymous term or phrase for the equivocal term in each of its appearances in the argument. It then should be possible to show that the synonyms are different and are not interchangeable in the argument. The following argument contains an equivocal term:

Natural foods are good for you. Ice cream is a natural food, and so are hot dogs, potato chips, chocolate, and french fries. So these things must be good for you.

The possible equivocation here could be pointed out by suggesting that the word "natural" in the first sentence means something like:

Meaning 1:   Wholesome, unrefined, uncontaminated by
              synthetic preservatives.

The word "natural" in the second sentence probably means something like:

Meaning 2:   Made from ingredients originating in nature.

Because the two meanings cannot be substituted for one another in the argument, the term "natural" is probably equivocal here. As with ambiguity, we should watch for equivocation in all arguments, and particularly in category arguments.

TESTS OF ARGUMENTATIVE DEFINITIONS

Argumentative definitions are subject to several tests. First, argumentative definitions are usually an effort to circumvent some more generally accepted definition of a term. The "new" definition must come from somewhere, so it makes sense to ask:

Test 1:   *Is the source of the definition in question appropriate?*

When we suspect that an argumentative definition is being advanced, this should be pointed out in some convincing way. Often it involves showing that the definition develops from some way of defining terms that is not appropriate to the context. Let's look again at the definition of "parent" from our earlier example:

Parents are those who nurture and care for a child, those who look out for a child's best interests, those who love the child.

Where does this definition of "parent" come from? It might be objected to as being either a personal definition or a narrowly cultural one. To define "parent" in this way may be to express a personal, cultural, or group preference.

Definitions that can be shown to be derived from narrow or subjective sources often can be answered with alternative definitions from a more appropriate source. This brings us to the second test of argumentative definitions:

Test 2:   *Can a more appropriate alternative definition be advanced?*

There are several possibilities for developing alternative definitions to a definition we wish to challenge. **Argumentative context** is critical to determinations regarding the appropriateness of definitions. What will or ought to be accepted as the best definition of a term in an argument will be governed by the context within which the argument develops. Is the context legal, where definitions must be consistent with the intent of the law or the intent of the law's framers? Is the setting political or religious, wherein standard usage may be an appropriate source of definitions? The most appropriate definition will be the one that best suits the argumentative context. With this principle in mind, we will explore some standard sources of definition: **common usage, etymology, paradigm case, intent,** and **authority**.

1. *Common usage*, or what a term means in everyday language, is one source of definitions. The word "parent" in common usage usually refers to the biological or adoptive relationship of one person to another, with overtones of responsibility for that person, and perhaps legal guardianship. Because common usage is one source of definitions that is recognized as appropriate in a number of contexts, and usually as more appropriate than personal preference, arguing that an alternative definition is in keeping with common usage might be effective in this case.

In the example involving a definition of handgun, we probably would want to point out that in common usage "gun" usually refers to a weapon that emits a solid projectile at high velocity and is capable of doing great physical harm. Under this common definition of the term, mace would not be considered a gun or a handgun. Even though the new definition relies on common usage, it tends to advance the case of the defense and therefore is itself argumentative. This means that the new definition also will be susceptible to the tests being discussed in this section.

2. *Etymology*, or the origin of the word, is another source of definitions that is appropriate to some contexts. In the case of "parent," the word originated with the Latin verb *parere*, which means "to give birth to." Thus, the definition in the argument—"one who nurtures or cares for"—violates the origin of the word, or its etymology. Etymology doesn't always help in defending a definition, though. The etymology of the word "gun" is not likely to help in answering the argument about mace; the etymology is highly complex. But the history of the word does suggest that "gun" properly refers to an explosive device that propels a projectile. Brief etymologies often can be found in dictionary entries prior to presentation of the definition itself. Dictionaries such as the *Oxford English Dictionary* and Ernest Weekley's *An Etymological Dictionary of the English Language* provide extensive etymological information on English words.

3. A *paradigm case*, or "good example," also can provide a basis for developing a definition of a class or category. Paradigm cases are representative cases of the thing in question—one typical member of the category which represents the entire category. Thus, in the case of "parent," we might propose that our own relationship with our parents is paradigmatic of the parent-child relationship, or that an opponent's or an audience member's relationship with his or her parents is paradigmatic. To the extent that our example case is recognized as typical, our definition may be accepted as more appropriate than the one being contested.

4. *Intent* is another source of legitimate definitions. Particularly important in cases in which a document or law is being interpreted, it refers to the intent of a document's authors. Thus, assuming the argument about custody comes out of a controversy in which a law is being interpreted, we might ask what the intent of the authors of the law was regarding the term "parent." We might suggest that their intent in defining "parent" for the sake of resolving custody disputes was not to identify those persons who tend to love or care for a child but, rather, those persons who have a legitimate claim to legal custody of the child.

The same approach could be taken with the definition of "handgun" in the law in question. The persons framing the law (and similar laws) likely had in mind to discourage criminals from using handguns, and thus to limit the number of injuries and homicides associated with robberies. They did not likely have in mind to limit the use of mace, water pistols filled with bleach, or cans of insecticide.

5. *Authority* can serve as a source of definitions. Various kinds of authorities may be consulted for definitions. Some persons' expert knowledge qualifies them to advance definitions of terms within their field of expertise. Works such as dictionaries also might be considered authoritative for definitions. Thus, if in the opinion of a legal authority on custody, "parent," when used in custody laws, means those persons who ought to have legal responsibility for a child on the basis of a biological or an adoptive relationship, then that definition might be advanced as more legitimate than the one being contested. In similar fashion, if a legal dictionary defines "handgun" as a handheld object emitting a solid projectile and capable of

causing great bodily injury or death, this definition might be advanced as more appropriate than the one that would render a can of mace a handgun.

These five sources of definitions—common usage, etymology, paradigm case, intent, and authority—all might provide appropriate definitions for arguments. Remember that context will be a controlling concern in deciding which type of definition to develop.

WRAP UP

Some terms in an argument are defined in a manner agreeable to both parties. Others, however, may be defined so as to advance one case or the other. Argumentative definitions have to be identified in criticizing or constructing arguments. The meanings of key terms should be a matter of agreement among disagreeing parties, and meanings should remain consistent throughout an argument so that conclusions can be arrived at reasonably. Euphemisms are efforts to substitute an innocuous term for a potentially offensive one, and these amount to an argumentative definition. Ambiguity and equivocation—multiple meanings of a key term in a single context or in different contexts—are also definitional issues. Finally, definitions can be derived in a number of ways, the most appropriate being determined by the argumentative context. Definitions can be derived from common usage, etymology, paradigm case, intent, and authority.

❖ PRAGMATIC ARGUMENTS

The **pragmatic argument** *recommends or discourages a course of action on the basis of its consequences*. If an action is being recommended, the connective reason for the pragmatic argument is some version of one of the **following**:

Connective 1:   Actions that result in good consequences should be pursued.

The following is an example of the pragmatic argument employing this connecting assumption:

A: We should sell the Saudis the five radar planes <u>because</u>
B: this is greatly to our economic advantage.

Standardized, the argument looks like this:

		<u>because</u>
Evidence:	B:	[Selling radar planes to the Saudis] is greatly to our economic advantage.
		[<u>and</u>]
Connective:	C*:	Actions that result in good consequences should be pursued.
Conclusion:	A:	We should sell the Saudis the five radar planes.

This argument affirms that something should be done because it has good economic consequences, and in that way is pragmatic. The argument works by placing the action of selling the Saudis the radar planes into the category of "actions that result in good consequences" and assumes that actions such as these should be pursued. The pragmatic argument is perhaps the most common argument in deliberative discourse.

Connective 2:	Actions that result in bad consequences should be avoided.

Pragmatic arguments also may discourage action on the basis of bad consequences. For example:

A: Legalizing marijuana would make it available to people who might not have used an illegal substance. <u>Thus,</u> B: the number of actual drug users would increase, along with all of the problems associated with substance abuse. <u>Although</u> C: it represents a difficult matter of enforcement, D: marijuana should not be legalized.

This pragmatic argument takes as evidence the bad consequences of legalizing marijuana and draws the conclusion that "marijuana should not be legalized." It gets from evidence to conclusion on the basis of the connective, "Actions that result in bad consequences should be avoided." Standardized, then, the argument looks like this:

Evidence: A: Legalizing marijuana would make it
                   available to people who might not have
                   used an illegal substance.
                   <u>thus</u>
                B: The number of actual drug users would
                   increase, along with all of the problems
                   associated with substance abuse.
Connective: E*: Actions that result in bad consequences
                   should be avoided.
                   <u>although</u>
Reservation: C: [Legalizing marijuana] represents a
                   difficult matter of enforcement.
Conclusion: D: Marijuana should not be legalized.

This standardization results in the following diagram:

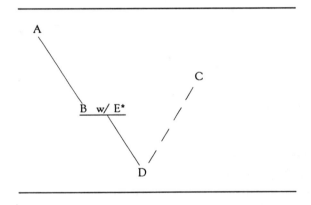

TESTS OF THE PRAGMATIC ARGUMENT

Since pragmatic arguments develop on the basis of alleged good or bad consequences, it is always possible to ask whether the consequences will actually develop from the action. Thus, the first test of the pragmatic argument can be phrased:

Test 1:   Is this action likely to have these consequences?

In the case of this example, we could challenge the assertion that selling weapons to the Saudis is to our economic advantage, that it will have good economic consequences. Perhaps selling them weapons would harm trade with Israel, and thus would be to our economic disadvantage. Likewise, it would be possible to question whether legalizing marijuana would actually have the bad consequences alleged in the second example argument. Perhaps the bad consequences from legalization are not likely to occur, or possibly have been exaggerated.

If the consequences from an action are obvious, or for some other reason we are not inclined to question them, possibilities for testing or answering the pragmatic argument remain. A second test would compare the advantages of a recommended action to those arising from some other course of action. It asks:

Test 2:   Would some other action be more advantageous?

We might respond to our example argument that not selling the radar planes to the Saudis would tend to increase the likelihood of trade with several other Arab nations. This would be economically even more advantageous than increasing trade with the Saudis alone. Thus, on a comparison of two actions, one is held to be more pragmatic than the other. This test suggests the strategy known as **comparative advantages**, or comparing the advantages of one course of action to those of another. This strategy frequently is used in controversies in which alternative solutions to a problem are being considered.

Finally, pragmatic arguments often conceal or ignore a principle or value that is at stake if the suggested action is pursued. Thus, a third test of pragmatic arguments asks:

Test 3:   Does the proposed course of action violate some important principle or value?

We might ask whether selling arms to the Saudis violates an agreement between the U.S. and Israel. If it does, the action could be seen as violating an important principle: the principle of abiding by our agreements with other nations. Pragmatic arguments often can be answered by appealing to a principle that would be violated by the proposed action. The tension between these two types of reasoning is common in policy controversies and will be discussed further in the next section.

WRAP UP

Pragmatic arguments are one of the most commonly encountered infer-ential forms, especially in policy debates or in arguments arriving at nor-mative conclusions. They urge, quite simply, that we ought to do the things that benefit us and avoid the things that don't. So strong is our self-interest that these arguments would almost always prevail were it not for the next type of argument to be considered.

❖   ARGUMENTS FROM PRINCIPLE

This last test of pragmatic arguments brings us to **arguments from prin-ciple**, *arguments affirming that we should take those actions that are in keeping with a value or principle, or should avoid those actions that violate accepted values or principles*. The following argument from principle might be advanced in response to the previous example:

A: The sale of radar planes to the Saudis represents a threat to our friends in Israel. B: We have a duty to assist our friends, and not to act in such a way as to threaten their se-curity. <u>Therefore</u>, C: I oppose the proposed action.

This argument affirms that selling the radar planes to the Saudis does not fall into the category of actions that are in keeping with our principles. It concludes that the action therefore should not be pursued.

Arguments from principle may appeal to values such as those for freedom, justice, or equality. They also may appeal to duties or obliga-tions, such as the duty to care for one's family or the obligation to care for the environment. Some arguments from principle derive from rights such as the right of free speech or the right to vote.

Regardless of the type of principle being advocated, arguments from principle seem to employ a connective that affirms the principle in ques-tion as applicable in the situation at hand. We can formulate this con-nective generally as asserting that:

Connective: The principle in question ought to be adhered to.

We can insert this connective into our example and standardize it as follows:

Evidence: A: The sale of radar planes to the Saudis
                  represents a threat to our friends in Israel.
Connective: B: We have a duty to assist our friends, and
                  not to act in such a way as to threaten
                  their security [the principle in question—
                  our duty to assist our friends—ought to
                  be adhered to].
                  therefore
Conclusion: C: I oppose the proposed action.

In this particular example, the principle is actually stated.

TESTS OF THE ARGUMENT FROM PRINCIPLE

The argument from principle is often very powerful, because principles, like rights, values, and duties, are important to life in a democratic society. But these arguments still ought to be tested to ensure their reasonableness. We have to ensure that an appropriate principle is being considered. The first test of the argument from principle asks:

*Test 1:   Is the principle in question relevant to the issue
            at hand?*

Applied to the example, this test asks whether the principle of helping our friends is relevant to the issue of selling arms. Clearly, the person advancing the argument thinks the principle *is* relevant. But possibly the proposed action poses no threat to Israel, or maybe not selling the planes to the Saudis does not in any way assist Israel. If either of these situations were the case, the principle in question would not really come into play.

Perhaps we agree that the principle in question is relevant to the issue being resolved. Then the question arises as to whether the proposal being advanced actually represents a violation of, or adherence to, the principle before us. Thus, we can ask:

*Test 2:   Is the proposed action in keeping with the
            principle in question?*

We might respond to the example that the proposal is in keeping with our duty to assist our allies, the Israelis, because the Saudis are a moderate force in the region and will balance the more radical forces opposed to

Israel. In this way we would be arguing that the action being proposed, though it does not appear to be, is actually in keeping with the principle in question.

Often the response to an argument from principle is a pragmatic argument. In such cases the respondent is affirming that pragmatic considerations actually outweigh the principle in question. The test being employed in those instances can be stated as follows:

Test 3:   *Do pragmatic considerations outweigh adherence
          to the principle?*

We might contend that, even though we do not wish to threaten Israel's security, it is more important to try to reduce tensions in the region—a good consequence of selling Saudis the radar planes—than to be scrupulous about adhering to the principle of honoring friendships. Again, many policy arguments involve the affirmation that the consequences of an action outweigh adherence to a principle. This tension between pragmatic and principle arguments is common in policy debates.

WRAP UP

The argument from principle often is advanced in response to a pragmatic argument. It affirms that some principle—a right, a duty, a value, or an obligation—ought to be honored or adhered to. Because such principles are important to life in a free society, the argument from principle is often a potent one, and an effective response to the pragmatic argument.

❖ ARGUMENTS FROM QUANTITY

Another pair of category arguments are commonly opposed to one another—arguments from quantity and from quality.[1] The **argument from quantity** *expresses a preference for things characterized by great number, abundance, longevity, and the like, or a disregard for things not exhibiting such characteristics*. The following is an argument from quantity:

A: Senator Jones should be the party's candidate <u>because</u> B:
he has been in government longer than any other candidate,
having served thirty-three years in the House and Senate.

The argument suggests that Senator Jones is preferable to other candidates on the basis of greater experience—literally a greater number of years in the Senate. This preference for quantity can be expressed in a connective linking the evidence of quantity to some conclusion. Thus, this argument, like other quantity arguments, involves a connective something like:

Connective: That which exhibits quantity is desirable or significant.

Standardizing our example, then, we have:

---

	because
Evidence:	B: Senator Jones has been in government longer than any other candidate, having served thirty-three years in the House and Senate.
	[and]
Connective:	C*: That which exhibits quantity is desirable or significant.
Conclusion:	A: Senator Jones should be the party's candidate.

TESTS OF THE ARGUMENT FROM QUANTITY

The argument from quantity is easy to understand. It simply affirms that things that exhibit quantity are desirable or significant and things that do not are not. Therefore, this argument can be answered by simply showing that some other thing exhibits even greater quantity than the thing being recommended. We can formulate this test into a question:

Test 1: Does something else exhibit even greater quantity than the thing in question?

Applying this test to our example, we might ask: Does Senator Philips have even more years of experience than Senator Jones? Suppose the answer is yes. Then, if quantity is the controlling concern, Philips, not Jones, should be the candidate. If quantity is the sole concern, that which exhibits the greatest quantity will be found the most desirable.

If we cannot argue that something else has greater quantity than the thing in question, or we are not inclined to, possibilities still exist for testing or answering this argument. We must ensure that quantity is really the most important consideration in this case. The second test of the argument from quantity asks:

Test 2:   Is some other consideration more important than quantity in this case?

It is possible to object that a principle is at stake in the recommendation. For example, perhaps Senator Jones has been indicted for some ethical offense. In this event, his appointment to an important committee might pose a problem of principle. Or perhaps we can show that some quality is of greater significance than sheer quantity. Senator Anderson may be a skilled legislator, even though she just recently was elected to the Senate. We might argue that legislative skill is a more important criterion of one's suitability for candidacy than is length of service.

❖ ARGUMENTS FROM QUALITY

This last test of the argument from quantity brings us to the **argument from quality,** *an argument that expresses a preference for the unique, the beautiful, the rare, the good, and so on.* The following is an argument from quality:

A: Congresswoman Anderson is the best candidate for President, <u>since</u> B: she has those rare qualities of leadership that we always look for in a President—courage, determination, wisdom.

Any argument that appeals to that which is beautiful, rare, unique, or in some other qualitative way desirable is operating on the basis of quality considerations. These arguments seem to involve some form of the connective:

Connective: That which exhibits the quality in question is desirable.

Our example can be standardized:

since
B: Congresswoman Anderson has those rare qualities of
leadership we always look for in a President—courage,
determination, wisdom.
and
C*: That which exhibits the qualities in question is desirable.
A: Congresswoman Anderson is the best candidate for
President.

TESTS OF THE ARGUMENT FROM QUALITY

Like the argument from quantity, which it resembles and often opposes,
the argument from quality can be tested by asking whether the quality
in question is actually present in the thing under consideration. We can
express this test as the question:

*Test 1:   Does the thing in question really possess the
quality in question?*

Does Congresswoman Anderson really possess courage, determination,
and wisdom, or does something in her past perhaps indicate that she is
not a determined or a wise individual? To challenge the attribution of a
quality to a person, idea, or object is always possible.

We might also ask if the quality, though present, is more clearly or
strongly represented somewhere else:

*Test 2:   Does someone or something else possess the
desired quality to a greater degree?*

In applying this test, we may be agreeing that the qualities of wisdom,
courage, and determination are present in Congresswoman Anderson,
and that they are desirable qualities. But we might respond to the example argument that Senator Billings is even more courageous, determined,
and wise than Congresswoman Anderson is.

Finally, we might oppose the concern for quality with a concern for
quantity, principle, or some other consideration. We can do this by asking:

*Test 3:   Does any other concern outweigh the quality in
this case?*

Even though Congresswoman Anderson possesses these rare qualities, is
Senator Philips backed by a larger number of people? In democracies this
quantity factor might be held to be more important. This last test points up

that, like principle and pragmatic arguments, arguments from quality and quantity are often opposed to one another in deliberative controversies.

WRAP UP

Arguments from quantity are category arguments that reveal a preference for size, longevity, weight, amount, or other similar factors. Arguments from quality often are in opposition to arguments from quantity. These latter arguments emphasize the unique or unusual qualities of some person, object, or idea, rather than considerations of quantity.

Chapter Review

Category arguments operate on the basis of relationships among groups or classes of things. One common category argument attempts to define a person, an object, an idea, or an action acccording to a specific category. These argumentative definitions might amount to euphemisms at times, if the effort is made to substitute an acceptable term for an unacceptable one.

Pragmatic and principle arguments are also category arguments, and these two often oppose one another. Pragmatic arguments urge that actions be taken or avoided strictly on the basis of their consequences. Arguments from principle, on the other hand, urge adherence to a value, a duty, or some other principle.

Two other arguments that often oppose one another are those from quantity and quality. Quantity arguments reveal a preference for things that exhibit longevity, size, number, or some other consideration of quantity. Arguments from quality show an opposing preference for the rare, the beautiful, the unusual, or some other expression of an unusual quality.

EXERCISES

A. Identify the following arguments by type. Employing the appropriate tests, suggest a possible weakness or response for each.

1. We should give Jones the new car because it would serve to motivate the other employees to work harder.

2. We should give Jones the new car because he has worked for the company longer than any of the other employees.

3. We should give Jones the new car because he is the best salesman on the team.

4. We should give Jones the new car because we have an obligation to help out our employees who are struggling financially.

5. We should give Jones the new car because the company bylaws state that new vehicles should go to the "most deserving" employee. This term "most deserving" should be taken to mean the employee who has done the most to advance the company's image, and that's Jones.

6. AIDS testing should be required of everyone applying for life insurance policies, because it would save insurance companies a great deal of money in the long run and thus bring down rates for everyone.

7. AIDS testing should not be required of those applying for life insurance policies, since it is a violation of a person's right to privacy.

8. AIDS testing should be required of all people applying for life insurance, since this plan has the backing of the vast majority of Americans.

9. Public schools should conduct their classes only in English, since education laws read, "Education should be provided in the common language of the people." "The common language" must be taken to mean the language common to the most people, and that's English.

10. Cultural relativism is an attractive philosophy to many people. However, few philosophers accept relativism as an adequate moral foundation.

11. "Death" is the utter and final cessation of consciousness. Thus, anencephalic babies—born with a brain stem but not a cerebral cortex—are dead, since they are not and never will be conscious.

12. Every year 2,000 to 3,000 children need organ transplants. Each year 2,000 to 3,000 anencephalic babies are born. With so many potential lives saved, shouldn't we allow organs from anencephalic babies to be used in transplants?

13. "Surrogacy" is just a polite term for baby selling, and selling people is clearly morally reprehensible.

14. The canyon ought to be preserved as a wilderness area, since wilderness areas are rare.

15. The canyon area ought to be developed, since more people then would have access to it.

16. Nuclear chemistry and biology have produced significant improvements in the human condition, especially in the areas of agriculture and medicine. Thus, even though there is still a threat of nuclear annihilation, it is more likely that you will be helped by nuclear medicine than that you will be killed by a nuclear explosion.

17. The scientific community bears the responsibility to educate as well as to expand our knowledge. Scientists must assist the rest of us in understanding the options presented by their discoveries. It is not enough that they make the discoveries.

18. Surrogacy is an acceptable practice. After all, in more than 500 cases of legal surrogacy, only three have resulted in lawsuits.

19. The suggestion that the new album by Slash and Trash should be banned from record stores amounts to censorship. Moreover, the critics misunderstand the musical intent of these sincere, sensitive young artists.

20. Why shouldn't college athletes be paid, and paid well? After all, they are primarily entertainers, and entertainers are paid well.

B. For the following examples, identify the term or phrase that is ambiguous. Explain and try to clarify the ambiguity.

1. Belmont HMO guarantees free delivery of your baby.

2. Student decapitated in accident before going to class.

3. I walked all the way across campus to hear the bacteria talk.

4. She judged from the man's dress that he was Finnish.

5. Safety commissioner recalls cars with reclining seats.

6. Perplexed by the disappearance of his sister, Vincent stood at the edge of the lake and thought, "Phyllis is at the bottom of this!"

7. A top executive of the firm made the tender offer, which was refused.

8. The shady dealings at the fertilizer factory finally got to Hal. "This whole business stinks," he said.

9. A professor reported to the university's president that the students were revolting.

10. Frank sat next to the Contessa, who had the most prominent seat at the banquet.

C. Identify and clarify the equivocation in the following arguments:

1. You say that faith in God can be logical. However, you can't show me a logical proof for belief in God, so faith must not be logical.

2. Bomb threats at the high school are no news, and no news is good news. So, as you can see, these bomb threats are actually good news.

3. My teacher said that Eskimos are disappearing. Mr. Smith is an Eskimo. Does that mean he is he going to disappear, Mommy?

4. You said the movie was good since the critics liked it. But it's obvious that it wasn't any good, since the studio lost money on it.

5. Susan said Fred passed the bar, but he's never willing to pass the bar when I go out with him.

D. Find an example of a category argument in an advertisement. Identify the type of argument being advanced and analyze it according to the tests discussed in this chapter.

E. Provide an instance of ambiguity or equivocation that you have encountered. Identify the ambiguous or equivocal term or phrase and, by rewriting the sentence or paragraph, suggest a solution to the problem.

ENDNOTES

1. For an interesting discussion of the "loci" of quality and quantity, see Chaim Perelman and L. Olbrechts-Tyteca, *The New Rhetoric*, translated by John Wilkinson and Purcell Weaver (Notre Dame, IN: University of Notre Dame Press, 1969), pp. 85–92.

9 DIVISION ARGUMENTS

Chapter Preview

DIVISION ARGUMENTS

Consideration of three arguments that divide options or alternatives and suggest a choice among the alternatives.

Key Terms

division arguments
disjunctive arguments
compatible disjuncts
incompatible disjuncts
contradictory statements
contrary statement
dilemma

trilemma
false dilemma
argument from inconsistency
enumeration arguments
arguments by partition
method of residues
tu quoque fallacy

The airliner's crash can only have been caused by pilot error or engine malfunctions or a terrorist's bomb. There is absolutely no indication that the pilots committed any errors, and examination of the engines reveals that they were working well at the time of the incident. Therefore, we are led to conclude that a bomb was planted on board just prior to takeoff.

The above example illustrates a **division argument**, *an argument that divides alternatives or possibilities and then urges a specific choice among those options.*[1] Division arguments are common when alternative solutions to a problem are being considered and also when one among a series of actions is being urged. They also are encountered in seeking explanations of events. Thus, these argument often are used in connection with hypothesis arguments. Several of the most common division arguments are:

1. Enumeration arguments and disjunctions.
2. Dilemmas and trilemmas.
3. Arguments from inconsistency.

❖ ENUMERATION ARGUMENTS AND DISJUNCTIONS

In **enumeration arguments**, *alternative accounts of an event or action are set out (enumerated), and a process of elimination is undertaken to arrive at the most likely account.* This type of argument is sometimes called **argument by partition** or the **method of residues**. When only two alternatives are presented, the term may be disjunctive argument, a special case of enumeration argument to be discussed later in this section. Because of the relationship among evidence, connective, and conclusion, enumeration arguments also are said to employ the process of elimination.

Enumeration arguments often are advanced in the effort to find the cause of some event. Thus, they frequently appear as one of the reasons lending plausibility to a hypothesis, as in the following example:

A: Only three employees were working that night: Bill, Sue, and Jack. B: Bill couldn't have opened the safe, since he never has been shown the combination. C: Sue left work before the money had been placed in the safe. This means that D: Jack is the only employee who both knew the combination and was

still in the building after the money had been deposited. E:
He must have stolen the money.

Some enumeration arguments attempt to eliminate all of the enumerated
possibilities:

The robbery would have been committed for only one of
three reasons: a desire to harm the company, revenge
against an individual within the company, or simply the
need for money. Jack always has shown himself to be a
loyal employee, and he wouldn't wish to harm the company. He doesn't have any reason to seek revenge against
anyone in the company, and he doesn't need cash badly
enough to risk stealing it from his own employer. I'm certain that Jack did not break into the safe.

Enumeration arguments may set out any number of possible causes, but
they always exhibit this effort to eliminate some or all from consideration—the *evidence* of enumeration arguments. The connective belief or
assumption for these arguments is the enumerative statement itself, from
which the argument gets its name. The following is a general statement
of that connective:

Connective: The only reasonable alternatives are [A, B, C,
etc].

The assumption that enumerates reasonable alternatives (and is thus the
connective) appears as the first statement in the first example and as the
first sentence of the second example. Thus, the first example could be
standardized:

Evidence: B: Bill couldn't have opened the safe, since
he never has been shown the combination.
C: Sue left work before the money had been
placed in the safe.
Connective: A: Only three employees were working that
night: Bill, Sue, and Jack.

	<u>This means that</u>
Intermediate Conclusion:	D: Jack is the only employee who both knew the combination and was still in the building after the money had been deposited.
Conclusion:	E: Jack must have stolen the money.

Several reasons may work together in an enumeration argument, though each by itself is a complete statement and makes sense without other statements to complete it. This interactive relationship can be represented by the use of brackets. A diagram of the above argument, then, takes the following form:

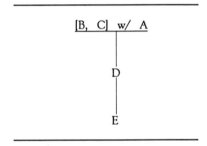

TESTS OF ENUMERATION ARGUMENTS

Because of their structure as arguments that articulate and eliminate possibilities, enumeration arguments absolutely must set out all of the plausible alternative accounts of the event in question. The first test of the enumeration argument asks:

Test 1:   Have all of the plausible alternatives been enumerated?

In the first example, a fourth employee could have been in the building. If this can be shown to have been the case, the argument is substantially weakened. In the second example, greed might constitute a fourth possible motive for the burglary, one not articulated in the argument. Because the argument is not reasonable if any plausible alternative has not been articulated, this test often provides an answer or a refutation for the enumeration argument.

Note that the connective asserts something about *reasonable* alternatives. The enumeration argument is not required to account for every *conceivable* alternative, only for those that are in some way probable. Therefore, in the first example the person advancing the argument would not be responsible for answering objections such as, "Perhaps agents of the KGB took the money, or aliens, or a ghost." Of course, what counts as a "plausible alternative" may itself be the subject of argument.

Second, in enumeration arguments the evidence that eliminates possibilities can be called in question. If some alternative that is treated as having been eliminated is, in fact, still a viable alternative, the argument loses some of its force as a reasonable argument. The second test of enumeration arguments asks:

> *Test 2:*   *Have all of the alternatives that were treated as eliminated actually been eliminated?*

If Jack could have been shown to indeed need some cash immediately, one of the possibilities in the second example would not be eliminated from consideration. Similarly, if Sue could have been shown to still be at work when the money was placed in the safe, she would not have been eliminated as a possible suspect in the crime.

DISJUNCTIVE ARGUMENTS

Disjunctive arguments are *enumeration arguments that set up two alternatives marked by an "either . . . or . . ." statement.* As an example:

A: Either the pilot forgot to extend the flaps or the mechanism was broken. B: The mechanism was not broken, <u>so</u>
C: the pilot did forget to extend the flaps.

In a disjunctive argument the connective is the either/or statement itself—statement A in our example. The disjunctive statement is made up of two disjuncts. In our example they are, "Either the pilot forgot to extend the flaps" and "or the mechanism was broken." When scanning or diagramming a disjunctive argument, the two disjuncts in a disjunctive statement should not be separated, because *together* they constitute one reason, the connective. Notice that in the example, the disjunctive statement is scanned as a single reason.

The evidence and the connective in a disjunctive argument are dependent. So our example is diagrammed as follows:

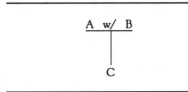

The tests of disjunctive arguments are the same two as are employed with other enumeration arguments, as discussed. But some special considerations come into play when testing disjunctive arguments as well. Disjuncts can have three relationships to one another. The example involves **compatible disjuncts**, or *disjuncts that can both be true of the same thing at the same time*. The pilot might have forgotten to extend the flaps, and at the same time the mechanism could have been broken. When disjuncts are compatible, it is not reasonable to affirm one of them in the evidence and then deny the other in the conclusion. This is because affirming that one of a pair of compatible disjuncts is true does not rule out the other one; they could both be true. Notice the problem when the example is changed slightly and one of the disjuncts is affirmed in the evidence:

A: Either the pilot forgot to extend the flaps or the mechanism was broken. B: The mechanism was broken, <u>so</u> C: the pilot did not forget to extend the flaps.

The first of the two disjuncts is *affirmed* in the evidence statement (the mechanism *was* broken), and the other disjunct is then denied in the conclusion. This is not a reasonable inference for a disjunctive argument with compatible disjuncts, because these are compatible causes of the plane's problems; they both can be true at the same time. Affirming that the mechanism was broken is not to say anything about the pilot's memory. It does not eliminate the pilot from consideration as a possible cause of the crash. Thus, affirming a disjunct does not allow us to deny the other disjunct in our conclusion if the disjuncts are compatible.

Some disjunctive statements, however, involve **incompatible disjuncts**, or *disjuncts that cannot be true of the same thing at the same time*. For example:

Either Elvis is dead or alive. From the available evidence, he clearly is dead. Thus, it is safe to conclude that he is not

still living, and therefore your cousin did not see him working at Burger Paradise.

In this example the disjuncts in the connective reason set up a particular
kind of incompatibility: The two disjuncts represent **contradictory
statements**, *statements that cannot both be true and cannot both be
false*. The statement, "Either Elvis is alive or dead," contains the two
contradictory statements:

Elvis is alive.
Elvis is dead.

One of these statements must be true, and one must be false. In the case
of contradictory disjuncts, then, it *is* reasonable to affirm one of the
disjuncts in the evidence and deny the other in the conclusion. They
can't both be true, and they can't both be false. As with compatible
disjuncts, it is still reasonable to deny one of the disjuncts in the evidence
statement and affirm the other in the conclusion.

But the disjunctive statement represents a second kind of incompatibility in the following argument:

The key was either in the desk or on the table. It was on
the desk, so it was not on the table.

The disjunctive statement in this argument represents **contrary statements**, *statements that cannot both be true but that can both be false*.
The contrary statements contained in this disjunctive statement are:

The key was on the desk.
The key was on the table.

These two statements could not both be true of the same key at the
same time, but they could both be false at the same time.

With contrary disjuncts, if one can be accurately affirmed as true
in the evidence, it is reasonable to deny or eliminate the other in the

conclusion. With these disjuncts, however, we must ensure that at least one of them is true.

WRAP UP

Enumeration arguments set out alternative accounts of an event or action and then eliminate alternatives until one or none is left. These arguments can be quite forceful provided that all of the plausible alternatives have been articulated and that the alternatives treated as having been eliminated actually have been eliminated.

Disjunctive arguments are enumeration arguments that seek to account for events or actions by advancing two alternatives in the form of an either/or statement. The two disjuncts in the statement may be compatible or incompatible, and there are two types of incompatible disjuncts: contraries and contradictories. When dealing with compatible disjuncts, it is reasonable to deny only one of the two in the evidence statement. When dealing with most incompatible disjuncts, it also is reasonable to affirm one in the evidence. As with other enumeration arguments, we must ensure that all of the alternatives actually have been accounted for in the two disjuncts, and that the one being affirmed or denied actually has been established as such.

❖ DILEMMAS AND TRILEMMAS

Disjunctive statements may show up in another kind of argument as well. *Arguments that advance incompatible disjuncts in the effort to force a choice between limited and often undesirable options* are referred to as **dilemmas**.[2] An example of a dilemma is:

A: Either we can intervene militarily in Central America or we can sit back and watch communism spread throughout this part of the world. <u>Because</u> B: the further spread of communism is unacceptable, C: we have only one course open to us—direct, immediate military intervention.

Because the two alternatives in a dilemma usually are undesirable, we may hear people speak of the "horns of a dilemma," suggesting that the choice is painful at best. When confronting a dilemma, we also often hear people speak of choosing the "lesser of two evils."

Sometimes a third option is added to the set of choices, in which case the argument might be referred to as a **trilemma**:

We can intervene militarily in Central America, or we can invest our energies in a pointless, hopeless peace process, or we can simply watch communism spread throughout this part of the world. The choice is clear. We must intervene.

The number of alternatives could be increased, resulting in quadrilemmas, quintilemmas, and so on. But at some point the effect of forcing a choice among a limited number of options is lost. For this reason these arguments usually present two or three options. Again, what is characteristic of these arguments is their division of options, which usually carry some liability, and their insistence on a choice among these. The insistence on choosing among limited and perhaps undesirable options is what differentiates dilemmas and trilemmas from the simple enumeration and disjunctive arguments discussed previously.

Like disjunctive arguments, the connective in dilemmas and trilemmas is an assumption about the nature and number of the options being faced. In most cases the options advanced in a dilemma are incompatible, so the argument suggests that pursuing both options at the same time is not possible; one of them must be selected. We cannot both intervene and *not* intervene in Central America.

Because the options are incompatible, the evidence attempts to show that one (or two, in the case of a trilemma) of these options has been eliminated, or the other recommended, or both. In a dilemma it is taken as reasonable that the evidence eliminates one option from consideration or affirms one as the least undesirable, or both. The conclusion of a dilemma is the resultant recommendation of one of the options for acceptance.

Because of its similarity of structure with disjunctive arguments, the connective reason for dilemmas and trilemmas is also similar. But the crucial element of pressing a choice also must be expressed in a dilemma's connective statement. Thus, in most dilemmas and trilemmas the connective can be formulated as a disjunctive statement something like this:

Connective:	The only alternatives available to us are [X and Y], and one must be selected.

In almost any dilemma or trilemma, this connective *will be stated* in some form or other, because this claim is what gives the argument its force by limiting the available options. In the first example this connective shows up in statement A, which advances the limited options of military intervention or the spread of communism. The evidence is statement B, which affirms that the further spread of communism is unacceptable. In standardized form our first example looks like this:

Connective:	A: Either we can intervene militarily in Central America or we can sit back and watch communism spread throughout this part of the world. <u>because</u>
Evidence:	B: The further spread of communism is unacceptable.
Conclusion:	C: We have only one option available to us—direct, military intervention.

This standardization results in a simple and familiar diagram:

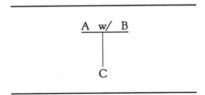

TESTS OF DILEMMAS AND TRILEMMAS

Like disjunctive arguments, dilemmas and trilemmas, to be reasonable, must advance *all* of the possible alternatives. Their connective must be accurate. If there is some unidentified alternative, the argument loses its force and is rendered unreasonable. Thus, the first test of the dilemma or trilemma is:

Test 1:   Are these the only alternatives?

Perhaps some other alternative has not yet been articulated. If so, we are faced with a **false dilemma**. In the first example, we might want to suggest that economic pressure and diplomatic efforts be used in Central America to help bring about democratic approaches to government in the region. A new option often develops by combining elements from two or more options already under consideration. Thus, it might be suggested that involvement in peace negotiations, combined with limited military assistance, is preferable to either approach employed alone.

Even if the dilemma or trilemma actually sets out all of the options, the argument may be flawed. The second test of dilemma arguments derives from the fact that one option often is advanced as the lesser of the evils:

*Test 2:   Is the choice recommended really the least
            undesirable of the options?*

We could answer the example argument by suggesting that what happens in Central America is not up to the United States to determine. If communism does take hold in these nations, so be it. That is preferable to our military involvement there, which amounts to meddling in the internal affairs of sovereign nations. This response of choosing the other horn of the dilemma is often a possibility when answering a dilemma argument.

WRAP UP

Dilemmas and trilemmas share language and structure with enumeration and disjunctive arguments, but the former have the characteristic of pressing a choice among limited, incompatible, and often undesirable options. For this reason, the dilemma is a popular argument in debate settings. For a dilemma or trilemma to be reasonable, the options advanced actually must exhaust the possibilities, and the option arrived at actually must be the more desirable one.

❖ ARGUMENTS FROM INCONSISTENCY

One type of division argument involves *an effort to catch an opponent in an inconsistency*. The **argument from inconsistency** places an opponent in the position of having to choose between self-contradiction and open inconsistency. For this reason, it may be thought of as a form of dilemma; the opponent must choose between limited and undesirable alternatives. The argument from inconsistency, however, probably deserves treatment as a distinct argumentative form within the general category of division arguments because it is common and has some unique qualities. Consider the following example:

A: The President has said that he desires peace in the Western Hemisphere. B: He also has advocated sales of arms to the Contras, a move calculated to bring not peace, but war. So C: the President must decide whether he is an advocate of peace or of war.

One intent of the argument from inconsistency is to point out and condemn an opponent's duplicity, and thus to discredit the opponent. This is a particularly common tactic in political argumentation and in other controversial settings in which personal character is an issue. To be inconsistent is generally held to be a sign of dishonesty or some other character flaw, such as weakness of will. Another typical goal of the argument from inconsistency is to try to force compliance with one of the two inconsistent actions or statements.

Inconsistency arguments involve as evidence the observation of inconsistent words or actions. In our example statements A and B are evidence. The connective in inconsistency arguments, a missing but clearly implied reason in the example, articulates a value for consistency by condemning inconsistency, and is therefore some form of the following:

Connective: Inconsistency is unacceptable.

Our example might be standardized as follows:

Evidence: A: The President has said that he desires
                  peace in the Western Hemisphere.
               B: He also has advocated sales of arms to
                  the Contras, a move calculated to bring
                  not peace, but war.
Connective: D*: Inconsistency is unacceptable.
               so
Conclusion: C: The President must decide whether he is
                  an advocate of peace or of war.

In a diagram of the argument, we should show the parallel relationship of the two claims that convey the inconsistent words or actions. Because inconsistency arguments advance these two claims as separate, we can divide them in a standardization and diagram but bracket them to reveal how they work together in the argument; how one could not appear without the other, though each by itself makes sense as a complete statement. A diagram for the argument then takes the following form:

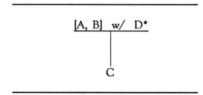

THE *TU QUOQUE* FALLACY

One special version of the argument from inconsistency is worthy of consideration. Most of us strongly reject what we take to be hypocritical advice, direction, or recommendation. We seem to believe that if someone is guilty of an offense, he or she has no right to instruct others not to do the same or some similar thing. For example:

How can you tell me to study harder and to apply myself at college? You weren't a stand-out student, and you spent more time golfing than studying.

This argument has been labeled the ***tu quoque* fallacy**, or the "you too" fallacy. It usually is treated as a fallacy because the connective assumption is so questionable: Advice of a hypocritical nature cannot be good advice. But the fact that someone is guilty of a particular offense does not automatically render his or her advice on the topic bad advice. The advice giver might be exactly right in what he or she has said. To reject hypocritical advice may be satisfying for other reasons, but it does not generally represent a good inference.[3]

TESTS OF THE ARGUMENT FROM INCONSISTENCY

The argument from inconsistency is often persuasive as long as the evidence of inconsistency is accepted as reasonable. Thus, we must ask if any inaccuracy has been contained in reporting the inconsistency. This means that we will want to ask the following question of an argument from inconsistency:

Test 1: *Are the apparently inconsistent statements or actions true to fact?*

We almost always can question the accuracy of evidence in an argument. If the President never advocated selling arms to the Contras, the evidence is faulty. Or, if he did advocate it, but not as a calculated effort to bring about war, then, again, the evidence is inaccurate. If either part of the inconsistency can be successfully called into question, the argument loses most, if not all, of its force as a reasonable argument.

If the evidence of inconsistency is clear to everyone, as when the statements or actions in question are a matter of public record, the evidence probably cannot successfully be challenged. But reasonably resolving the inconsistency still may be possible. Thus, a second test can be applied to the argument from inconsistency:

Test 2: *Can the inconsistency be resolved in any reasonable way?*

Two important possibilities can be explored here. First, we might ask if *circumstances have changed* from the time of the first action or statement to the second in such a way as to eliminate the inconsistency. Though, in the example, it is an unlikely possibility, the President might respond that he made his statements about world peace before a communist threat emerged in Central America, a development that required other than peaceful means of resolution.

Second, we can try to show that *consistency is present between the allegedly inconsistent actions or statements* and it simply is not immediately apparent. The President might respond that the best way to ensure bringing peace to the hemisphere is to topple certain governments, and that this can best be done by selling arms. In this way, selling arms and the commitment to peace can be explained as consistent.

WRAP UP

Because the argument from inconsistency involves charging an opponent with inconsistent statements or actions, it is closely related to the dilemma. The argument seeks to place an opponent in a position where no good choice can be made. This argument is common in political controversies. For the argument from inconsistency to be reasonable, however, the allegedly inconsistent statements or actions must be reported accurately, and there must be no reasonable way of resolving the inconsistency.

Chapter Review

The arguments discussed in this chapter have in common a tendency to divide alternatives or possibilities and then to urge a choice among the limited options presented. The enumeration argument seeks an explanation for an event by advancing all of the alternatives and eliminating all but one or, in some cases, all of them. This argument succeeds only when all of the reasonable alternatives have been advanced and when those treated as having been eliminated actually have been eliminated.

The disjunctive argument—like conditional arguments—is governed by rather strict rules of reasonable inference. In testing this argument, we have to ascertain the nature of the relationship between the disjuncts, whether they are compatible, contrary, or contradictory.

Dilemmas and trilemmas are like disjunctive arguments in their use of either/or statements, but these arguments attempt to force a choice between limited and often undesirable alternatives. In testing them, we have to ensure that all of the alternatives have been mentioned and that the least undesirable one is being urged for acceptance.

Finally, the argument from inconsistency attempts to catch an opponent in an inconsistency. As a result, it sometimes is thought of as a kind of dilemma argument. Of course, if a real inconsistency does not exist, the argument fails.

EXERCISES

A. Identify the following arguments by type. Employing tests discussed in the chapter, suggest a possible response or weakness for each argument.

1. a. Your money or your life!

   b. Your money, your life, or your season tickets!

2. One side or the other is going to win in this conflict, regardless of whether we are pleased with either. Admittedly, both sides have shown a willingness to disregard basic human rights, but we must back the one most likely to work for our interests in the region, and that means sending aid to the Contras.

3. The rapid drop in American production of goods witnessed in the past decade is not the result of "lazy blue collar workers." Blue collar production is actually up when output is compared to new hires. And government regulations are not the cause, since these regulations came into effect well after the sudden drop was already

in its advanced stages. This leaves only one possible cause: the addition of thousands of new white collar workers in many industries.

4. The U.S. government is clearly inconsistent in its activities in Nicaragua. We say we want peace in the region, but we send arms to the Contras!

5. *Context*: An outbreak of salmonella infection in eggs sold in New England was traced to its source, using the following process of reasoning.

   The salmonella infection was not the result of cracks in the eggs. All of the eggs had been washed, so the infection did not result from externally introduced bacteria. This leads us to the shocking conclusion that the bacteria are present in the eggs themselves, introduced during ovulation within the hen's body. Thus, salmonella bacteria are present in the chicken flocks and will take years to eradicate.

6. *Context*: The following argument has been advanced in the debate over using organs from anencephalic babies—children born with a brain stem but little or no cerebral cortex, and who often die soon after birth—to save the lives of other children who need organ transplants.

   We can let both children die, or we can save one by transplanting the organs of the other. Which is preferable, saving one life or losing two lives?

7. The Catholic Church is certainly in a bind on the condom issue. They're telling us that using condoms is OK if one partner in a marriage has AIDS but not OK if the idea is birth control.

8. Saving the economy will require cuts in either Social Security or defense. Defense is a vital part of the budget, but because we recently discovered that cuts in Social Security are not a possibility, defense will have to be drastically cut.

9. Senators are in a no-win situation here. If we vote against the new medical care package, we are voting against the senior citizens who stand to benefit from it. If we vote for the package, we are voting for an enormous tax increase for the average American. Nevertheless, a vote against taxes for everyone is preferable to a vote against benefits for a single group.

10. A nation's value system can be derived from either of two sources: a common religion or a general culture. America has not had a

common religion for a long time, and we can no longer claim to possess a culture common to most of our citizens. Thus, America is a nation without a source for common, unifying values.

B. In the evidence of each of the following disjunctive arguments, indicate what is occurring and whether each involves a reasonable inference:

1. Either Jones will have his contract renewed or he will look for a new job. He is looking for a new job, so his contract must not have been renewed.

2. Either Ms. Wilson is ignorant of the rules or she is deliberately trying to usurp the committee's authority. She is fully aware of what the rules require in such cases, so this is a deliberate attempt to circumvent the committee.

3. Either the school board is trying to deny our children a good education or the members are ignorant of educational principles. They obviously are ignorant of sound educational principles, so they clearly are not intentionally trying to deny our kids an education.

4. Either they had a boy or they had a girl. I heard the child was a boy, so they didn't have a girl.

5. Either the janitor left the water on all night or the pipe was broken. The janitor admits he left the water on, so the pipe is not broken.

C. Answer the questions for each of the following items.

1. *Question*: Is the following argument better explained as an instance of enumeration or of dilemma? Explain your answer.

    It's not that I think evolution is preferable because it is supported by a great deal of evidence. In fact, I know it's not. However, the whole idea of creation is simply impossible to believe.

2. *Question*: Is the following argument claiming that macroevolution has never occurred? If it is not making this claim, what is the argument's conclusion? An argumentative definition is implied in the argument. What term is a definition suggested for?

    Evolution from one species to another has never been directly observed to occur in nature, nor has anyone been able to bring it about in the laboratory, nor has a convincing model ever been presented. Thus, I am led to conclude that there is no way to scientifically verify macroevolution.

3. *Question*: The following example includes an argument from this chapter. It also includes an argumentative definition of the term "religion." Which division argument is advanced? Referring back to chapter 8, determine which source of definitions is appealed to in defining "religion" in the second sentence.

The Freedom from Religion Foundation charges that teaching creation science violates the doctrine of separation of church and state. But its worldview of scientific humanism was ruled a religion in a recent Supreme Court decision. This religion is taught in all of our schools, and I don't hear the Foundation objecting.

4. *Question*: What argumentative definition is advanced in this example? What kind of division argument does it support?

Affirmative action is justified injustice. It is a tragic choice but one that has to be made because the alternative of racial discrimination is unacceptable in a civilized society.

5. *Context*: In the following example President Bush is reportedly attacked with one of the arguments discussed in this chapter. What argument is the President being confronted with, and what test of that kind of argument does he employ in his own defense?

The firearms lobby accused President Bush of having modified his opposition to restrictions on the importation of weapons. He previously opposed all restrictions on the import and sale of firearms. He now favors restrictions on the import of some semi-automatic weapons. Challenged on the point, he replied, "Times have changed."

D. Dilemmas and trilemmas are common in public debate. Provide an instance from arguments you have read or heard of one of these arguments. Analyze your example according to the tests suggested in the chapter.

ENDNOTES

1. For an interesting discussion of several arguments covered in this chapter, see Chaim Perelman and L. Olbrechts-Tyteca, *The New Rhetoric*, translated by John Wilkinson and Purcell Weaver (Notre Dame, IN: University of Notre Dame Press, 1969), pp. 234–241. Aristotle also discusses several similar arguments in *Rhetoric*, translated by W. Rhys Roberts (New York: Modern Library, 1954), book 2, chapter 23, topics 9, 12, 14, 15, 19.

2. Richard A. Lanham discusses two types of dilemmas in his book *A Handlist of Rhetorical Terms* (Berkeley: University of California Press, 1969), p. 36.

3. For a discussion of the *tu quoque* fallacy, see T. Edward Damer, *Attacking Faulty Reasoning*, 2d ed. (Belmont, CA: Wadsworth, 1987), pp. 109–110.

10 ARGUMENTS FROM ESSENTIAL NATURE

Chapter Preview

ARGUMENTS FROM ESSENTIAL NATURE

A discussion of an interesting set of four arguments that seek to discover and reason from the essential nature of objects, events, ideas, and people.

Key Terms

genetic argument

genetic fallacy

argument from intent

argument from function

irrelevant functions

sources of function

prescription

common understanding

form

current need

person/act argument

This organization should not be advocating a position on abortion. Its founders made it clear in the charter that the organization exists strictly to provide counsel to those who intend to become parents. To make the organization a lobbying force is to violate its very reason for existence.

In the argument above the essential nature of the organization is being invoked as a reason for objecting to a certain set of activities. Its nature is held to be revealed in the intentions of those who initiated it, and that nature is treated as governing how the organization should be understood and what it should do.

There are several important *arguments that exhibit a concern for the fundamental character of the thing in question.*[1] These arguments from essential nature may refer in their connectives to the origin, intent, function, or acts of an object, document, institution, or person. The nature of the thing apparently is taken to be expressed in where or how it originated, what its creators intended it to do or be, the particular function that is appropriate to it, or how it behaves. In these arguments this essential nature is seen as governing interpretations, judgments, and uses of the thing in question. The arguments to be considered in this chapter are:

1. The genetic argument.
2. The argument from intent.
3. The argument from function.
4. The person/act argument.

❖ THE GENETIC ARGUMENT

This argument takes its name from an ancient word for beginnings or origins, the word that names the first book of the Bible—"genesis." The **genetic argument** can be described as *an argument that claims that the origin of a thing reveals its essential nature,* regardless of how much time has elapsed from the time of its origin. An example of the genetic argument is:

A: The yin and yang symbol originated with ancient Eastern religious groups that have little in common with Christianity. <u>Thus,</u> B: it is an inappropriate symbol for a Christian church youth group.

In this example the origin of a symbol is said to reveal its nature, even though that origin is temporally and culturally distant. The evidence in this and other arguments is some claim regarding origins. In this case the symbol's origin is advanced as evidence in statement A. The conclusion is that the symbol is inappropriate for the youth group, statement B. The connective is an unstated assumption about the connection between origins and a thing's essential nature. We can try to formulate that connective as follows:

Connective: The essential nature of a thing—its meaning,
               interpretation, or use—is revealed in its
               origins.

If we supply this connective in the example argument, we get the following standardization:

Evidence: A: The yin and yang symbol originated with
                  ancient Eastern religious groups that have
                  little in common with Christianity.
Connective: C*: The essential nature of a thing—its
                   meaning, interpretation, or use—is revealed
                   in its origins.
Conclusion: B: The symbol is inappropriate as a symbol
                  for a Christian church youth group.

This brief argument yields the following diagram, which reveals the dependent relationship of the evidence and the connective:

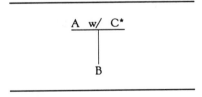

TESTS OF THE GENETIC ARGUMENT

The genetic argument relies on the connective from which it derives its name. The assumption expressed in this connective is, of course, open to question. As a first test of the genetic argument, then, we would want to ask:

Test 1:   Does the origin of the thing in question reveal its essential nature?

Leaders of the church in question might answer the question yes. They might take the position that in the case of this particular symbol, its nature as an aspect of Eastern religious thought can never be erased or altered. Thus, as a symbol for a Christian youth organization, it is and always will be inappropriate. Members of the youth group might argue in response that the origin of the yin and yang symbol is completely irrelevant to the symbol's present meaning or uses, that it has no essential nature or no such nature is revealed in its origins. They might argue that time and changing context affect the meanings of many symbols, including this one.

Some people hold that the origin of a thing is always irrelevant to its present value or uses, and thus that all genetic arguments always fail this first test. These people label the argument the **genetic fallacy**.[2] Nevertheless, apparently reasonable people advance these arguments often enough to lead us to want to treat each case of the argument separately, to weigh the merits of each application of the principle involved in the connective reason. Associations with the origin of a practice or object may be so strong that they never become irrelevant to some people, and this may be, in some instances, reasonable.

Whenever a historical claim is made, as is inevitably the case with the genetic argument, the possibility is inherent that the claim is historically inaccurate. The accuracy of that historical claim should be ensured, as far as this is possible. The second test for assessing the reasonableness of genetic arguments is:

Test 2:   Has the origin of the thing in question been related accurately?

Perhaps the yin and yang symbol did not originate with the ancient Eastern religious groups in question but was simply an available symbol those groups used to symbolize a religious view. If this is the case it could be argued that, in like fashion, the youth group can employ a symbol whose origins are either unknown or innocuous.

It also is possible to acknowledge that somehow origins and nature are linked but to suggest that this does not preclude some evolution in the thing's essential nature or meaning. Thus, a third test of the genetic argument balances current meanings or uses against origins:

Test 3:   *Is the present meaning, interpretation, or use of the thing in question more important to consider than its origin?*

In the example, the leader of the youth group might concede that the yin and yang symbol did originate with ancient religious groups. It might be pointed out, however, that the symbol now enjoys much broader meaning than spiritual dualism and seems to convey to contemporary people notions such as harmony, peace, and balance. Because these notions are not at odds with Christian ideas, it might be affirmed that the symbol should not be found offensive. This approach denies that essential nature is revealed in origins, and it tends to find essential nature revealed in present uses or meanings. Of course, the church leaders might still respond that the symbol's current meaning is irrelevant and that its origin is clearly pertinent to its use as a church symbol.

WRAP UP

The genetic argument finds the essential nature of a thing in its origin. Thus, this argument reveals a value for beginnings, and perhaps also a mistrust of changes that occur over time. Since discussions of origin usually are historical in nature, a thing's origin has to be accurately recounted in the genetic argument. Before accepting a genetic argument, we also would want to be sure that we accept that the thing's origin is more important than its current uses or associations.

❖ ARGUMENTS FROM INTENT

Occasionally we encounter *arguments that assume that the essential nature of a thing is revealed in the intent of its authors or designers*. These arguments may be advanced regarding objects, institutions, documents, or even people and nature itself. In the intent of the creator or designer of an object is found its essential nature, and thus its ultimate meaning, its uses, and its value. An example of an **argument from intent** is:

A: It is ridiculous to prevent access to these records by historians on the basis of Freedom of Information Act.
B: The people who drafted the Act intended it to control access to recent documents that have a direct bearing on na-

tional security matters. <u>But</u> C: these documents are now
thirty to forty years old, <u>and for that reason</u> D: could not
possibly affect national security.

The evidence in this argument is the assertion concerning the original
intent of the authors of the Act and the observation about the age of the
documents in question. The conclusion concerns the ridiculous nature
of restricting historians from the documents on the basis of the Act,
which is to say that historians should not be restricted from access. The
unstated connective reason in this example is some variation on the assumption from which the argument derives its name. We can try to formulate that assumption in the following way:

Connective: The essential nature of a thing—its meaning,
               interpretation, or use—is revealed in the
               original intent of its designers.

Standardized, then, the argument looks like this:

Evidence: C: These documents are now thirty to forty
                       years old.
                       <u>and for that reason</u>
Intermediate   D: [These documents] could not possibly
Conclusion: affect national security.
                       [and]
Evidence   B: The people who drafted the Act intended
                       it to control access to recent documents
                       that have a direct bearing on national
                       security.
                       [and]
Connective: E*: The essential nature of a thing—its
                       meaning, interpretation, and use—is
                       revealed in the original intent of its
                       designers.
                       [thus]
Conclusion: A: It is ridiculous to prevent access to
                       these records by historians on the basis
                       of the Freedom of Information Act.

Diagrammed, the argument reveals the following form:

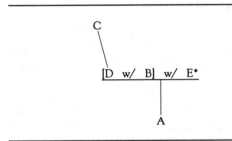

The argument from intent is especially common in argumentation about legal matters or interpretations of the law, as this example illustrates. In fact, arguments from intent may show up in any argumentation about the proper interpretation of documents or artifacts. It is often affirmed that the intent of a document's author is important to an accurate interpretation of that document. The focus of this argument is on the author or designer of the thing in question, not on the object itself.

A common instance of the argument from intent occurs in debates over interpretations of the Constitution. Here the focus of the debate is on the framers of the Constitution, and the nature or meaning of that document is held to be revealed in the original intent of the persons who wrote it. Most of us have encountered some version of the following argument:

A: The Constitution guarantees the right of every citizen to "keep and bear arms." <u>Thus,</u> B: the intent of the framers was to ensure that the citizenry always have free access to arms with which to defend themselves and their country, <u>and therefore</u> C: the right to own a gun must not be violated.

Standardized, the argument appears as follows, with the connective added as reason D*:

A: The Constitution guarantees the right of every citizen to "keep and bear arms."
   <u>thus</u>
B: The intent of the framers was to ensure that the citizenry

have free access to arms with which to defend
themselves and their country.
[and]

D*: The nature of a thing—its meaning, interpretation, or
use—is revealed in the original intent of its designers.
therefore

C: [The right to keep and bear arms] must not be violated.

A diagram of the argument takes the following form:

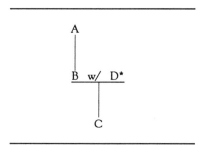

In response to this argument, some variation on the following argument
often is advanced:

A: The Constitution states that a well-ordered militia being
essential to the defense of a country, the right of the citizen to keep and bear arms must not be infringed. Thus, B:
the intent of the framers was to ensure the existence of a
militia, such as the National Guard. Therefore C: there is no
Constitutional injunction against gun control.

Standardized, this argument takes the following form:

A: The Constitution states that a well-ordered militia being
essential to the defense of a country, the right of the
citizen to keep and bear arms must not be infringed.
thus

B: The intent of the framers was to ensure the existence of
a militia, such as the National Guard.

D*: The essential nature of a thing—its meaning,

interpretation, or use—is revealed in the original intent of its designers.

<u>therefore</u>

C: There is no Constitutional injunction against gun control.

A diagram of this argument takes the following form:

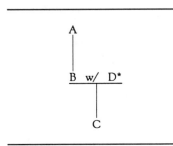

Each of these examples involves the argument from intent. Evidence is linked to conclusion on the basis of some version of the assumption that the essential nature of a thing—its meaning, interpretation, or use—is revealed in the original intent of its designers. This argument, as we have noted, is particularly important in controversy surrounding the interpretation of documents. It also shows up often in arguments about the design of nature when God is posited as the designer of nature.

TESTS OF THE ARGUMENT FROM INTENT

The connective reason for the argument from intent suggests one possible test of the argument. The connective assumption is not always reasonable and can be called into question by asking:

Test 1:   Does the original intent of the authors or designers of the thing in question reveal its essential nature, meaning, and uses?

Responding to nearly any argument from intent is certainly possible by questioning the correctness of the connective reason. To the example concerning the Freedom of Information Act, a respondent might reply that the original intent of those who wrote the Act is now irrelevant, that all laws are adapted and interpreted in accordance with current need, and that the current need is for the Act to regulate access to documents that are older than those to which the Act originally controlled access.

A similar response could even be made to either of the arguments about the right of citizens to keep and bear arms and its protection in the Bill of Rights. A respondent to those arguments might argue that the intent of the framers is irrelevant to current uses of the Constitution, that the circumstances in America have changed so drastically in the past two centuries that what Jefferson or Madison thought about the citizen's right to bear arms is absolutely irrelevant to current interpretations of the Constitution. This response could be made by someone who believes strongly in Constitutional government but at the same time rejects the idea that interpretations of the Constitution ought to be governed by reference to the framers' intentions.

Of course, the original intent of a designer or author could have been understood wrongly. Knowing someone else's intent is often difficult at best. The two examples concerning the right to keep and bear arms suggest this second test:

Test 2:   Has the intention of the individual(s) in question been represented accurately?

Notice that the argument about whether the Bill of Rights ensures a right to own a gun is not about whether the authors' intent ought to govern interpretation of the Constitution. On that point these two disputants are in general agreement. What they disagree about is *what* the framers intended, each claiming that the other misrepresents that intent. Each of these persons is employing the second test of arguments from intent. Resolving a dispute such as this would involve ascertaining, with as much accuracy as the situation allowed, the actual intent of the authors in question. This may require a good deal of historical research, because terms such as "militia," and even "keep and bear arms," may change in meaning over time.

Finally, even when one is inclined to find some interpretive value in the author's intent, it can be argued that other considerations outweigh intent as the governing principle of interpretation. Accordingly, the third test of the argument from intent asks:

Test 3:   Does some other consideration outweigh original intent in this instance?

Concerning interpretation of the Bill of Rights on the question of gun ownership, it might be urged that, whereas the framers' intent is important, more critical to our present societal situation is the need to control the number and distribution of firearms. Thus, societal need would be advanced as a consideration outweighing original intent in interpreting the Constitution.

WRAP UP

The argument from intent is found in disputes surrounding the meaning, value, interpretation, or use of documents or other objects. The nature of the thing in question is seen as revealed in the intent of the individual or individuals who wrote, constructed, or designed it. This argument, then, exhibits a value for consistency over time in the nature of objects; as the object originally was, so it is now. The argument also demonstrates a value for creative ownership; what the creator of a thing meant it to be, so it is. Recognizing the place of these values in the argument from intent is important to fully understanding the argument.

❖ THE ARGUMENT FROM FUNCTION

Some arguments *develop around the assumption that function reveals the nature, and thus the appropriate roles or expectations, of objects, institutions, and people.* Consider the following example of an argument about the function of police forces:

A: The mayor is wrong to suggest that the police are not doing enough about the crime situation in our city. B: The police simply don't have the role of controlling the real causes of crime: poverty, unemployment, access to guns, lack of proper role models for kids, abuse and neglect, and tolerance for drug use.

The evidence in this argument consists of the problems that police cannot correct. The argument concludes that the mayor is wrong for criticizing the police for failing to do enough about crime in the city:

Evidence: B: The police simply don't have the role of controlling the real causes of crime: poverty, unemployment, access to guns, lack of proper role models for kids, abuse and neglect, and tolerance for drug use.

Conclusion: A: The mayor is wrong to suggest that the police are not doing enough about the crime situation in our city.

The connective assumption linking the evidence to the conclusion in this case seems to be some version of the following:

Connective: The nature of a thing, and any judgment or expectation of it, is determined by its proper function.

Adding this connective as statement C*, the standardized argument might look like this:

Evidence: B: The police simply don't have the role of controlling the real causes of crime: poverty, unemployment, access to guns, lack of proper role models for kids, abuse and neglect, and tolerance for drug use.

Connective: C*: The nature of a thing, and any judgment or expectation of it, is determined by its proper function.
                <u>therefore</u>

Conclusion: A: The mayor is wrong to suggest that the police are not doing enough about the crime situation in our city.

TESTS OF THE ARGUMENT FROM FUNCTION

As with most arguments, we can question the connective of the **argument from function**. Maybe the nature of the thing in question—judgments and expectations of it—is not revealed in its function. Thus, the first test of such arguments asks:

Test 1:   Is the nature of a thing, and any judgment or expectation of it, determined by its function?

Using this test, the function typically assigned to a person, an object, or an institution might be called into question as a factor limiting the expectations we have of that thing. The nature of the thing in question might be affirmed as involving more than its principal, prescribed, or agreed-to function.

Though the "role" of police may not be to deal with the social problems outlined, they still might be expected to help address some of the problems mentioned. Even though their job description might not include "providing a role model for children in the community," can they not legitimately be expected to help out in this regard? Is there possibly something in the "nature" of police work that extends beyond the widely recognized functions of police? This would not be an adequate answer to the argument in the example, but it perhaps illustrates the point that the connective reason in arguments from function can be questioned in some cases. Nature, and thus judgments and expectations, are not in all cases reasonably limited to typical function.

Another test of the argument from function develops from a concern for the accuracy with which the function of the thing in question has been described:

Test 2:   *Has the proper function of the thing in question been described accurately?*

It is always possible to challenge the function attributed to a group, a person, an institution, or an object. In our example, the contention that the activities mentioned are not part of the proper function of the police could be challenged. For instance, one might reply: "It seems that the police *do* have some responsibility to help control access to guns and the availability of drugs on the street. And why should we not expect the police to provide a role model for children in the community? To say that these things are outside the proper function of the police is to unreasonably limit their proper function."

Under this test, another possibility should be considered. Sometimes arguments are advanced based on some wrong conception of the function of an object or an institution. Someone might argue that a book on successful business people was no good because it did not help them to become successful. This is an example of **assigning an irrelevant function,** and constitutes one potential problem arising from a failure to accurately describe the function of the thing in question.[3]

SOURCES OF FUNCTIONS

This raises the question of the **sources of claims about function.** Attributions of function may develop from a number of sources, four of which are particularly common:

1. *Prescription.* Function is sometimes prescribed, that is, written down somewhere. The function of a police officer, for instance, may be written down in a job description. This **prescription** of function may be referred to in making arguments from function.

2. *Common understanding.* Claims about function often are based on what the function of a person, an object, or an institution is commonly taken to be. Thus, schools commonly are understood as functioning to provide education, police to enforce the law, hospitals to take care of sick people. **Common understanding** often is linked closely to tradition; a thing's function is known by what it has done in the past.

3. *Form.* Sometimes function is attributed on the basis of the form a thing takes. Thus, police officers' "**form**"—wearing a military-style uniform, carrying a weapon, driving a specially equipped car—all seem to indicate a function having something to do with enforcement, literally with the use of force, to bring something about. A school's form—seats arranged in rows, blackboards, teachers addressing students—seems to indicate a function of delivering something (education) to an audience. Of course, the form of a thing may have originated in an earlier "common understanding" of the thing's function. Form originally may have followed function. Once form is established, however, function can just as easily follow form.

4. *Current need.* Claims about function may be based on what currently is understood to be a need. Though police traditionally may be understood as enforcers of the law, **current need** may require them to function as mediators or role models. Although the schools traditionally may be seen to function as providers of education, the current social situation may suggest that their function should be expanded to include providing personal counseling. As needs change, functions also may change.

Knowing the source of a claim about a thing's function can assist in analyzing or responding to an argument from function. If we know that the claim is based on common understanding, for instance, we can point out that common understanding may be too limited or suggest other ways of assigning function, such as current need.

WRAP UP

In the argument from function, the essential nature of a person, an object, or an institution is revealed in its appropriate function and it proceeds to render judgments or assign expectations. Sources of functions include prescription, common understanding, form, and current need.

❖ THE PERSON/ACT ARGUMENT

Genetic, intent, and function arguments usually are advanced about objects and institutions, although occasionally they are made about people. One argument from essential nature is concerned strictly with establishing and evaluating the nature of a person. The person/act argument looks to a person's acts or behaviors to find the nature of that individual, what the person is like, and how he or she ought to be evaluated.[4] The following is an example:

A: Mr. Brown is a civic-minded and kind-hearted individual.
B: After all, he recently donated $1,000,000 to St. Anne's Children's Hospital, and $5,000,000 to State University's basketball program.

The evidence in this argument consists of the acts of Mr. Brown, specifically his donating money to a hospital and to an athletic program. The conclusion is that he is a "civic-minded and kind-hearted individual," which is a claim about his essential nature as a person. The evidence and conclusion are connected here by the assumption that somehow persons' natures are revealed in their activities or behaviors. We can try to formulate this connective as follows:

Connective: The nature of a person is revealed in his or her acts.

The example argument can be standardized as:

Evidence: B: [Mr. Brown] recently donated $1,000,000 to St. Anne's Children's Hospital, and $5,000,000 to State University's basketball program.

Connective: C*: The nature of a person is revealed in his or her acts.

Conclusion: A: Mr. Brown is a civic-minded and kind-hearted individual.

TESTS OF THE PERSON/ACT ARGUMENT

As with other arguments from essential nature, the connective reason in the **person/act argument** can be questioned. In this case we would be asking the following question:

*Test 1:   Is the nature of a person revealed in his or
            her acts?*

It may seem obvious that if we want to know the kind of person we are dealing with, we can simply look at what that person has done. We all probably accept this connective reason to some extent. But we also are aware that acts can be intentionally or unintentionally deceptive, that people can mask their true nature by behaviors not in keeping with it. Each case of the person/act inference, then, has to be judged on its own merits.

In the case of Mr. Brown, someone might respond: "How do you think he got all of that money in the first place? Mr. Brown's ties to organized crime are well known, and his apparently charitable activities are only an effort to distract attention away from the charges that recently have been brought against him." In this statement Mr. Brown's true nature is affirmed as *not* revealed in the acts of generosity that have been reported. This response suggests that Mr. Brown's true nature may be revealed in an entirely different set of acts, which would bring us back to the connective as a reasonable one.

The charge against Mr. Brown suggests a second test of the person/act argument. Because people engage in many activities, we should ask:

*Test 2:   Are the acts in question consistent with other
            acts this person performs?*

To establish that an act reveals a person's nature, generally it must be clear, or we must be able to show, that the act in question is somehow consistent with other acts attributed to that individual. The response to the argument about Mr. Brown's benevolence suggests that the act of giving money to a charitable cause is inconsistent with other acts he has performed, though these other acts are not specified. If, in fact, his charitable acts are inconsistent with other things he has done, especially if these other things are well known, the argument is severely weakened.

An act always carries some question of interpretation. Was someone's refusal to answer a question an indication of anger or of shyness? Accordingly, the person/act argument can be tested for accuracy of interpretation of an act. We can phrase that test as follows:

Test 3:   Has the act in question been interpreted accurately?

Nearly any act is subject to more than a single interpretation. Still, we feel confident in most of our judgments about what acts or behaviors reveal about people, especially people we know well. Consistency of the act with other acts is one good clue assisting accurate interpretation. Consistency with what a person has said is another.

In the case of Mr. Brown, the act of giving money to the hospital and the university have been interpreted by one person as kind-hearted acts, by another as perhaps something else. Certainly acts such as these can be efforts to create a false image or to distract attention from other events or activities. When an interpretation of an act is advanced, it may require additional support, especially if the interpretation is called in question.

WRAP UP

The person/act argument finds the essential nature of a person to be revealed in his or her acts. This is a common means of ascertaining the value of a person, but, as the tests of this argument suggest, it is not always reliable.

Chapter Review

Some arguments seek the essential nature of a person, an object, an institution, or an idea to justify judgments or interpretations. Four of the more common means of establishing a thing's essential nature are: the genetic argument, the arguments from intent and function, and the person/act argument.

The genetic argument finds a thing's essential nature in its origins. This argument sees origin as stamping things indelibly. Whether this is true can be questioned. The argument from intent shows respect for the intent of designers, authors, legislators, and other creators of documents and objects. The nature of a thing is held to be revealed in the author's intent. Again, whether their creators leave an indelible mark on the nature of documents and other objects can be questioned.

The argument from function looks to the thing itself for its nature. This argument affirms that function—assigned in various ways—reveals essential nature. Finally, the nature of people often is held to be revealed in what they do—their acts. The person/act argument operates on the basis of this assumption. As powerful as this assumption is in argument, however, it still can be challenged.

EXERCISES

A. Identify the following arguments from essential nature by type. Employing the appropriate tests, suggest a possible weakness or response for each.

1. The church cannot be expected to deal with social problems. That is simply not its role in society. The church ought to provide a haven from those problems.

2. You cannot justify the interpretation you just gave to that poem. It is not a poem about the tragedy inherent to all human life. To understand the poem, we must understand that the author intended it as a pro-Marxist statement, a statement about the ongoing struggle among the classes and the eventual triumph of the working class.

3. I don't give my kids Easter eggs, because they originally were a sign of fertility in various religious cults associated with the goddess Ishtar.

4. The only reason we have public schools is to ensure that people can participate in democratic government. This implies that citizens must speak the same language. Though I am all for preserving ethnic heritages, it is not the function of the public schools to preserve and perpetuate these heritages. The schools must, however, teach all students a common language.

5. The press was very hard on Nancy Reagan, calling her shallow and aloof. But she is not. Her loyalty to Ronald Reagan and her friends and her unwillingness to stage events reveal a person who is caring and has her priorities straight.

6. It's a waste of taxpayers' money to have the fire department hand out food to needy people. That department is supposed to put out fires!

7. You're asking if homosexuality is wrong? Let me ask you: How many sexes did God create?

8. Catholics shouldn't throw rice at weddings. Didn't you know that this is an ancient pagan fertility custom?

9. The job of the Supreme Court is not to decide who is right but, rather, to decide what is constitutional.

10. Lee Iaccoca's character should be clear to all. Only a man of the highest moral character could do what he has done at Chrysler.

B. Provide answers for the following questions.

1. *Question*: Is the following argument better identified as an argument from function or as an argument from intent? Explain your answer.

   Surrogate parenting deliberately severs a natural link between intercourse and procreation, a connection that ought not to be broken, simply because doing so opposes God's design of nature.

2. *Question*: What functions are assigned to science in this argument, and what function is denied it? What function is assigned to individuals?

   Science provides options by educating us and by expanding our knowledge. But individuals must make choices; that is not science's responsibility.

3. *Question*: What test or tests of the person/act argument might the following argument be susceptible to?

   A lot of people have criticized Frank Sinatra for his alleged ties to the Mafia. I think he's OK. After all, look at all the nice things he's done for people.

4. *Question*: What function is allowed parents in this argument, and what function is denied them? What function is assigned to the schools, and what is denied as a function of the schools?

   Parents have a moral role to play in the rational development of their children, but I don't think this gives them the right to ban books from public school libraries. The schools are not supposed to stamp perfect little moral duplicates. The purpose of schools in a free society is to prepare students to think critically about a wide range of topics, and this cannot be accomplished if parents are allowed to determine the content of books students read.

5. *Question*: What source of function is appealed to in the following argument from function?

   Don't open the paint can with those scissors! Can't you see that they have sharp blades, and so are meant to cut things, not to pry things open?

6. *Question*: To which of the tests of the genetic argument do you find the following example to be particularly susceptible?

I never read the fortunes in fortune cookies. Did you know that originally people believed these fortunes actually controlled their destinies?

7. *Question*: Is the following argument better identified as an argument from function, as an argument from intent, or as a genetic argument? Explain your answer.

The present welfare system can't work. It began as a temporary pension for widows. Today it is asked to accomplish an entirely different task.

8. *Question*: What source of function is appealed to in the following argument from function?

It is obvious that assault rifles are not hunting weapons. Just look at the way they are designed. Clearly these weapons are intended to do only one thing: kill large numbers of people. Therefore, they should not be available to the general public.

9. Provide a rationale for your identification of the following argument from essential nature:

Medical malpractice suits have gotten out of hand and threaten to drive thousands of doctors out of the profession. We must return the system to its original role: providing reasonable compensation when there has been genuine malpractice, proven beyond a shadow of a doubt.

10. *Question*: To what test of the argument from intent do you find the following argument to be most susceptible?

I don't like the way basketball is played today. All this showboating gets the game away from what the guys who originally put it together meant it to be: a sport that emphasized teamwork.

C. Standardize the following arguments, and provide the missing connective for each.

1. To criticize the college for failing to solve your daughter's personal problems is simply not fair. The college seeks to provide education.

2. It's downright criminal that city officials are using the new immigration laws to scare legal immigrants out of the city. The bill's authors wanted to ensure that legal immigrants could hold jobs in the city, and the author's intentions are being grossly violated.

3. The beat of rock music originally was the beat of music used in demon-worship rituals. Thus, rock music cannot escape condemnation as demonic.

4. The role of a public health system is to keep people well. The system should not exist for the purpose of making a profit. Thus, our current system should be radically overhauled to better reflect its reason for existing.

5. I never read the fortunes in fortune cookies. Did you know that people originally believed these fortunes actually controlled their destinies?

6. Despite the accusations against him, I believe that Jones is a respectable attorney. He has always worked strenuously to protect the rights of the poor in this city, and his efforts on behalf of professional athletes are legendary.

D. Provide one example of an argument from essential nature that you have heard or read. Analyze your example according to the tests discussed in this chapter.

ENDNOTES

1. Chaim Perelman and L. Olbrechts-Tyteca discuss the "locus" of essence, a closely related concept, in *The New Rhetoric*, translated by John Wilkinson and Purcell Weaver (Notre Dame, IN: University of Notre Dame Press, 1969), pp. 94–95.

2. For example, see T. Edward Damer's treatment of the argument in *Attacking Faulty Reasoning*, 2d ed. (Belmont, CA: Wadsworth, 1987), pp. 101–102.

3. See also Damer, pp. 102–103.

4. For a detailed discussion of the relationship between persons and their acts, see Perelman and Olbrechts-Tyteca, pp. 293–305.

11 NONPROPOSITIONAL ARGUMENTS

Chapter Preview

NONPROPOSITIONAL ARGUMENTS

Discussion of four nonpropositional arguments and consideration of some of the linguistic means used to conceal arguments.

Key Terms

emotional appeals
translating obscure
 statements
ridicule
reductio ad absurdum

suggestion
paralepsis
linguistic conventions
accent
innuendo

selection
arrangement
rhetorical question
appeals to authority
power

---

*The charges against my client are simply ridiculous. He is
the victim of a witch-hunt being carried out by unscrupulous
opponents whose own crimes will soon come to light. But
we refuse to bring up those crimes at this time.*

So far in this text we have been thinking about arguments that have
easily fit the definition of argument as a reason or reasons advanced
in support of some conclusion. This chapter considers nonpropositional arguments, *arguments in which reasons and conclusions are
obscured by form or manner of presentation.* The arguments to be
discussed are sometimes not seen as arguments at all, and this perhaps
is because they do not appear in propositional form, that is, as a series
of statements that are clearly related as reasons to conclusions.

Four types of nonpropositional arguments are especially common:

1. Emotional appeals.

2. Ridicule.

3. Suggestion.

4. Appeals to authority.

❖ EMOTIONAL APPEALS

We are all familiar with *the effort to gain adherence to an idea or to
induce action by arousing an audience's emotions,* or **emotional appeals.** For example:

A: Drunk drivers murder 25,000 innocent people each year.
B: How many more children like Janet are to be left without a mother before we act?

Fear, anger, and pity are appealed to frequently in argumentative discourse, and it may be helpful to look at some of the approaches employed
when appealing to these emotions.

SOURCES OF EMOTIONAL APPEALS

The most common emotional appeals are to fear, anger, and pity.[1] The
example contains elements of all three. Fear appeals often derive from
three fears common to most of us:

1. Fear of death or physical harm, either to ourselves or to loved ones.

2. Fear of loss of health, wealth, or security, as in the loss of occupation.

3. Fear of deprivation of rights or freedoms.

Anger appeals frequently have their source in one or both of the following notions:

1. The suggestion that someone is doing or will do to us what we fear.

2. That injustices are being done to us or to someone we care about.

Pity appeals usually involve suggesting or stating:

1. That someone or something helpless is being harmed, and these appeals are intensified if

2. The harm is being done carelessly or intentionally by another.

In accordance, children and defenseless animals often are the sources of pity appeals.

Emotional appeals frequently are dismissed as unreasonable, as having no place in reasonable argumentation. I will not take this approach, recognizing that at times each of us employs or is influenced by emotional appeals, finding them not only persuasive but also reasonable. These appeals often are the actual basis for decisions to take action on a matter. It is necessary, however, to seek some guidelines for determining when to accept an emotional appeal—understood as a type of argument—as reasonable.

In our search for guidelines, we must understand that emotional appeals have an underlying argumentative structure. Because these appeals usually are not presented as propositional arguments—they do not appear as a series of reasons supporting some conclusion—we have to clarify their argumentative nature and structure.

The initial example clearly contains some evidence, expressed in statement A, although the evidence itself has some emotional content, communicated in the choice of the word "murder" and in the large number of deaths reported. In addition, the argument in statement B, the example of a child who has been orphaned, also advances a kind of evidence with emotional power. The image of an orphaned child, especially one orphaned as a result of the careless actions of another, evokes powerful emotions.

In all of this is the clearly suggested conclusion that action must be taken against drunk driving, which is a conclusion that should be supplied in a standardization of the argument. Some **translation**—restatement in a clearer form—of the three statements is necessary to arrive at a standardization:

A: Drunk drivers murder 25,000 innocent people each year.
B: Many children like Janet are left without a mother [by drunk drivers].
[therefore]
C*: [Action must be taken to stop drunk driving.]

A diagram of this argument is relatively simple to provide:

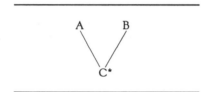

Consider another example:

A: Mr. Welch savagely beat this innocent three-year-old, while the child and her mother pleaded for him to stop.
B: Even after the child was unconscious, Welch continued the brutal beating. C: Is it not clear, therefore, that he deserves the most severe penalty the law allows?

The evidence in this argument appears in the observations expressed in statements A and B, and the conclusion is contained in statement C. But this argument entails more than simply, "Mr. Welch is guilty of a serious case of child abuse and therefore should be severely punished." An effort is made to arouse our emotions by pointing out the child's age, her innocence, her mother's presence, the defendant's callous nature, his brutality.

This example also shows some effort to forge a link between the emotional response that is affirmed as appropriate to such a terrible crime and the appropriate punishment. This argument, like others involving emotional appeals, involves a strongly implied connective reason, which works to link evidence to conclusion in a particular way. To ascertain the exact content of this implied connective is not easy. I suggest that the connective is some form of the belief or value that, in some circumstances, to feel and even to be guided by emotions is only reasonable. In fact, these arguments may suggest that *not* to be guided by emotions in such cases would be unreasonable. Thus, the connective for emotional appeals may be some version of the following:

Connective: To experience and respond to [anger] in such
a case is only reasonable.

"Anger" is placed in brackets, because the connective has to reflect the particular emotion targeted in a given argument.

In such a case we might even object to an argument that did not make appeal to our emotions, or we may deem morally insensitive a person who could hear about such a case without feeling some anger. The following standardization of this argument is suggested:

A: Mr. Welch savagely beat this innocent three-year-old
while the child and her mother pleaded for him to stop.
B: Even after the child was unconscious, Welch continued
the brutal beating.
D*: To experience and respond to anger in such a case is
only reasonable.
    therefore
C: Welch clearly deserves the most severe penalty the law
allows.

This argument leads to the following diagram:

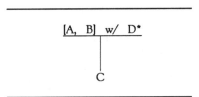

Statements A and B are advanced to establish the cruel and brutal nature of the beatings, although they are not in a dependent relationship. These reasons are dependent upon the connective, D*, for drawing the conclusion expressed in statement C.

Here is another example of an argument involving an emotional appeal:

The first thing you notice is a little shortness of breath, and some pain in your chest. Then you cough and can't stop. The pain gets worse and you go to your doctor. He examines you and gives you the news: cancer. You've got a year to live, a year filled with painful, frightening treatments. Your hands tremble, and you reach for a cigarette. If you hadn't ever reached for a cigarette, you wouldn't be where you are today.

This whole passage, if viewed argumentatively, is *evidence*. It is intended to arouse fear—but fear that leads to action. The connective reason is some form of the statement suggested above:

Connective: To experience and respond to [fear] in such a case is only reasonable.

The strongly implied conclusion of the argument is:

Conclusion: Don't smoke cigarettes.

Like the previous examples of arguments involving emotional appeals, this one seems to imply that to fear the results of smoking is reasonable and, in fact, not to fear the results of smoking would be unreasonable.

Admittedly, the examples we have looked at do not have a clear argumentative structure; we have had to impose a structure on them. Looking at emotional appeals argumentatively, however, may be helpful in deciding whether a given appeal is reasonable or not. We at least become more aware of the hidden assumptions we are accepting in accepting the appeal.

TESTS OF EMOTIONAL APPEALS

When people object to emotional appeals as unreasonable, they usually have in mind the power of these appeals to attract attention away from good reasons and good inferences. There is also a concern that emotional appeals may be employed in the absence of other arguments or as a substitute for arguments. In most cases it is reasonable to require some balancing of arguments based on emotional appeals with other types of argumentative forms and other types of evidence.

These reservations regarding emotional appeals can be formulated into tests. The first test of emotional appeals is:

*Test 1:   Does the emotional appeal appear in the absence
of other arguments and evidence?*

As we already have suggested, to make a decision strictly on the basis of an emotional appeal is probably not reasonable. Such appeals, however, often are embedded in and accompanied by other arguments and evidence. In the example concerning drunk driving, evidence is advanced concerning the number of fatalities attributed to drunk drivers each year. The second example advances evidence concerning Mr. Welch's acts. In each case, however, we might wish for more evidence, or other arguments, before we are willing to accept the argument's conclusion.

Just as the emotional appeal probably ought not to appear as the sole support for a conclusion, so it ought not to be presented in such a way that the audience is prevented from exercising reason at all. Some speakers and writers are so skilled at arousing our emotions that they run the risk of preventing critical thinking in the process of making a decision. Again, a balance between the critical faculty of reason and the ability of emotion to prompt us to action is desirable. The second test of emotional appeals is:

*Test 2:   Is the appeal so powerful that the audience will
have difficulty reaching a reasonable decision?*

In most cases we would rightly object to an emotional appeal so powerful that it subverts reason. The example concerning a case of child abuse, because it involves injury to a child, might run the risk of altogether circumventing reason. Because the implied context is that of a criminal trial, we would want to be sure that any decision we would make as members of a jury would be based on the best available evidence and arguments, as well as on our strong feelings about the nature of the crime. When issues are emotionally charged, we have to be careful about what we respond to and also how we ourselves argue. We have to be responsible in using emotional appeals in such cases. This is one way of respecting other people as reasonable beings, as discussed in chapter 2.

Perhaps the best defense of emotional appeals as part of an argumentative case is their ability to place an audience in the appropriate frame of mind for making a decision and acting on it. Therefore, we should ask whether a particular appeal is likely to accomplish this goal. The third test of emotional appeals, then, is:

Test 3:   *Does the appeal place the audience in the proper frame of mind for making a reasonable decision on the issue?*

Unless we reject all emotional appeals out of hand, we may believe that these appeals are employed properly at times, and even that they have an important role to play in making reasonable decisions. Perhaps we should feel some anger and fear when making decisions about drunk driving laws, some fear when deciding whether to smoke, some pity and anger when deciding how to deal with child abusers. This test asks the critic or the individual presenting an argument to consider whether a particular emotion is in fact appropriate to deciding an issue.

WRAP UP

Emotional appeals seem to have an argumentative structure; they advance evidence and arrive at or strongly imply conclusions. They probably should not be rejected *a priori* as unreasonable attempts at persuasion, though they do have to be accepted with some caution. These appeals should not appear in the absence of arguments and evidence and should not be so powerful as to prevent the exercise of reason altogether. In some cases they can put an audience in the right frame of mind for making a reasonable decision and acting upon it.

❖ RIDICULE

Ridicule is one of the most intriguing arguments we encounter; it is *the effort to discredit an idea by suggesting that it is laughable.*[2] Is ridicule even an argument? Well, like emotional appeals, ridicule has an underlying argumentative structure that we can get at with a little effort. Let's consider an example of an argument advanced by Senator Smith in a debate with Senator Jones over how to solve the AIDS crisis:

A: Senator Jones has proposed that the only way to deal
with the AIDS epidemic is to create a vast holding area in
the Southwest for all people confirmed as having the AIDS
virus. Essentially, an area the size of New Mexico would be
set aside, and all AIDS victims would be sent there to live
out their lives in isolation from society. Thus, B: this ridiculous proposal should be rejected without further discussion.

This is an argument, although at first glance it may not appear to be one.
The evidence is presented in statement A, which describes the proposal
under consideration. Statement B asserts that the proposal is ridiculous
and thus should be rejected. On what basis, though, is Senator Jones's
idea held to be ridiculous?

Ideas that are affirmed as ridiculous usually are taken to be violations
of common knowledge or common experience—that which all people
know or experience. The unreasonableness of these ideas is taken to be
immediately apparent to everyone, and they therefore are held to be
ridiculous—laughable or not worthy of serious consideration. Other terms
often employed to express that an idea is ridiculous include: absurd,
ludicrous, preposterous, crazy.

Senator Smith, then, apparently finds Senator Jones's idea to be a
gross violation of common knowledge or accepted opinion, perhaps a
violation of the belief that people who have not committed a crime cannot be denied basic rights and freedoms for the sake of the safety or
convenience of other people. This is a guess, and Senator Smith might
not even be able to supply the actual connective which leads from the
evidence advanced to the conclusion stated.

The argument then asserts that Senator Jones's proposal, because
of its ridiculous nature, deserves to be rejected. The implied connective
that seems to be at work in ridicule is some version of the following:

Connective: Ideas that clearly violate common knowledge
or common experience are ridiculous and
should be rejected.

If this connective is at work in the example, it would look like this in
standardized form:

Evidence:	A:	Senator Jones has proposed that the only way to deal with the AIDS epidemic is to create a vast holding area in the Southwest for all people confirmed as having the AIDS virus. Essentially, an area the size of New Mexico would be set aside, and all AIDS victims would be sent there to live out their lives in isolation from society.
Connective:	C*:	Ideas that clearly violate common knowledge or common experience are ridiculous and should be rejected. thus
Conclusion:	B:	[Jones's] ridiculous proposal should be rejected without further discussion.

A diagram of this argument appears as follows:

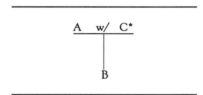

Ridicule suggests that an argument or idea is extraordinarily unreasonable, and that this is clear to any thinking person. In fact, the idea has achieved such a low degree of reasonableness as to excite laughter. This argumentative approach apparently operates on some notion of a spectrum of reasonableness; it suggests that some things are so unreasonable as to be worthy of laughter rather than serious consideration. Perhaps the other end of the spectrum of reasonableness suggested by ridicule is the self-evidently reasonable or the demonstrable idea. In between these poles we might locate ideas that are highly probable, probable, possible, improbable, and highly improbable.

Ridicule assumes that most or all reasonable people readily, perhaps immediately, recognize a given idea or argument as unreasonable. Ridicule is risky if the audience is at all inclined to treat the assertion of ridiculousness critically. To ridicule an idea that the audience is inclined to find even possible is to put yourself at odds with the audience, and perhaps to make yourself appear to be ridiculous.

THE *REDUCTIO AD ABSURDUM*

One method of answering or refuting arguments, the **reductio ad absurdum**, is similar to ridicule. This method attempts to show that an idea is absurd or ridiculous by one of two means. The first involves assuming that the idea is true, and seeing where this assumption leads. For example, in Plato's dialogue *Gorgias*, Socrates refutes an argument advanced by the sophist Callicles that the best, strongest, and most intelligent people should have the biggest and most of everything:

> The man who is best and most intelligent about shoes should have the advantage. The shoemaker should, no doubt, have the biggest shoes and walk about shod in the largest possible number.[3]

The second approach involves setting up an argument parallel to the one advanced, in which the parallel is clearly unreasonable. For example:

> You have argued that because Communists backed the guerrillas, and church leaders backed the same guerrillas, this proves that the leaders of the church are Communists. This is like saying that because all dogs are mammals, and all cats are mammals, all dogs are cats.

Propositions can be considered to have been reduced to absurdity if they result in a contradiction, a clear violation of common sense, or some offense to common experience such as an impossibility.

TESTS OF RIDICULE

When should we accept ridicule? The discussion to this point suggests that two assumptions are at work in ridicule, and that these assumptions should be tested before accepting someone's ridiculing an idea.

The connective involved in ridicule affirms that the idea in question is a violation of common knowledge or common experience. The claim that the idea being considered is clearly unreasonable should be tested in one or both of these ways. The first test of ridicule asks:

Test 1:   Is the idea being ridiculed a clear violation of common knowledge or common experience?

Only in cases in which we think the idea ridiculed is plainly ridiculous should we accept the argument uncritically. In most cases we will want to take a careful look at the object of ridicule before accepting or rejecting it. The argument from ridicule says that *the idea is so unreasonable that one does not even have to examine it*. Unless we are willing to take someone else's word for this, we had better check out the idea for ourselves.

Although an idea may appear to be patently unreasonable to others, we still may want to consider it further or even accept it. Each of us holds to some ideas that others would find ridiculous. The second test of ridicule asks:

> *Test 2:   Even if the idea is ridiculous to others, do I*
> *want to reject it?*

Historically a lot of ridiculous ideas have turned out to be quite reasonable. That the world is round, that there are living things which cannot be seen by the unaided eye, that people would one day walk on the moon—these and thousands of other notions started off as "ridiculous" ideas. Therefore, we probably should be careful about rejecting ideas just because someone has affirmed them to be ridiculous, or even has been able to get an audience to laugh at them.

WRAP UP

Ridicule is a common approach in controversial settings, and it seems to have an argumentative structure. Ridicule assumes that ideas clearly in violation of common sense or experience are ridiculous, and that such ridiculous ideas should be rejected. The argument implied in ridicule should be accepted only when a clearly unreasonable idea is under consideration, and when we have determined for ourselves that the idea is not worthy of our acceptance.

❖ SUGGESTION

Another important type of nonpropositional argument is **suggestion**, or *implying an argument without directly stating it*. Nearly every word we read or hear is presented from a point of view, though sometimes that point of view is not clear. Arguments always represent a point of view on some topic, and again, the point of view may be concealed. When reading an argument that is only suggested, we may accept reasons or conclusions uncritically because we have not recognized their actual content. Thus, we have to be able to translate suggested arguments into statements that accurately represent the concealed or suggested argument is important.

At this point it will be helpful to look at an example of suggestion:

A: Of course, Senator Smith does have his wife on his payroll, <u>but</u> B: I'm not accusing him of any wrongdoing in this regard.

Clearly, in this example, the claim "I'm not accusing him of any wrongdoing in this regard" is disingenuous. This is an argument masquerading as a simple observation.

Standardizing this argument means translating the second statement so as to reveal its actual nature as a claim about Senator Smith. An important reason is also missing and has to be supplied in a standardization. The following standardization works to reveal the argument being suggested here:

A: Of course, Senator Smith does have his wife on his payroll.
C*: [It is wrong for senators to have their spouses or other immediate family members on their payrolls.]
[therefore]
B: [I *am* accusing him of wrongdoing in this regard.]

This standardization results in the following diagram:

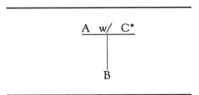

The suggestion in this example, achieved by a device with the Latin name *paralepsis*, involves *making a claim about something by stating that you will not bring up the topic, or that it is insignificant.*[4] The concealed argument is not difficult for us to ascertain, because suggestion usually is achieved by means of **linguistic conventions**—*recognized ways of indirectly expressing a meaning*—with which we are familiar. These conventions enable one to say something implicitly without stating it explicitly, so all suggestion depends to some extent on linguistic conventions.

A second way of achieving suggestion is the use of **accent**, or *emphasizing certain parts of a statement to make a point*. For example:

A: Joe's position in the company is secure, *even though*
B: his name was *the very last one on the list* for promotion.

Standardizing this example also involves some translation:

[since]
B: [Joe's] name was *the very last one on the list* for promotion.
[thus]
A: Joe's position in the company is [not] secure.

A third means of achieving suggestion is by **innuendo**, or *making a claim indirectly by insinuation*:

A: I don't doubt that the Senator is faithful to his wife, even if B: he has been seen with other women at his private Washington apartment late at night, and C: these women haven't been seen to leave the apartment building until early the next morning.

Standardized, this example would look like this:

[because]
B: The Senator has been seen with other women at his private Washington apartment late at night.
and
C: [The women with whom the Senator has been seen] have not left the apartment building until early the next morning.
[therefore]
A: [I don't believe that the Senator has been faithful to his wife.]

Suggestion also can be achieved by **selection**, which means *presenting only some of the available evidence so as to achieve a particular impression*. Suppose that Senator Wilson knows that his opponent in the election, State Representative Clark, donated more than $30,000 of her personal income to medical charities, and thus paid less in taxes than her income of $85,000 would suggest. In a campaign speech, however, Senator Wilson argues:

Anyone who wonders whether Representative Clark can identify with the middle-income taxpayer should compare her income to her taxes. Last year she made more than $85,000, but she paid only $5,000 in taxes!

By selection—in this case, failing to provide the audience with a piece of relevant information of which he was fully aware—Senator Wilson has suggested that Representative Clark has not paid enough of her income in taxes. Although he is not exactly lying, he is creating the impression that the Representative has done something unscrupulous or even illegal. How did he accomplish this? By allowing the audience to assume that her deductions for charitable donations are similar to those of others with relatively large incomes, when this is not the case. Thus, a standardization of his argument would have to show an important, and false, missing reason:

B: Last year [Representative Clark] made more than $85,000, but she paid only $5,000 in taxes!
C*: [Her deductions for charitable donations are about the same as those of others with similar incomes.]
[therefore]
A: Representative Clark can [not] identify with the middle-income taxpayer.

Suggestion can be achieved easily by means of **arrangement**, or *creating an impression by the ordering or placement of items in an argument*. We tend to assume that points placed next to one another in a statement have equal status, or that the ordering of items in a list reflects their relative merit. These are two of several assumptions that allow suggestion to be achieved by means of arrangement.

The following example exhibits the use of arrangement to suggest a conclusion about the significance of the work done by a city's Committee on Human Relations:

A: The Committee on Human Relations has, they tell us, important work to do. I doubt it. <u>Listen to the three items on the agenda for the last meeting</u>: B: The problem of race relations at Jackson High School, C: the problem of racist language in the city's hiring policy, <u>and</u> D: the problem of finding a new name for the mascot of the city's junior-high school!

Because the three items on the agenda are phrased similarly, they might be assumed to have equal significance. Because the third item does not seem to be especially significant, it has been used to make the other two sound less significant than they may be. In fact, the third item might be quite significant—people may be offended by the current mascot's name—though its description in the argument doesn't sound that way. Moreover, placing the least significant item last is more effective in making it sound typical than would be placing it first or second. The last item heard or read tends to reflect on earlier items in a list. Standardizing this argument, we would want to point out the assumption that allows the conclusion to be drawn from the "evidence":

    <u>Listen to the three items on the agenda for the last meeting</u>:

B: [One item was] the problem of race relations at Jackson High School.

C: [Another item was] the problem of racist language in the city's hiring policy.
    <u>and</u>

D: [A final item was] the problem of finding a new name for the mascot of city's junior-high school!

E*: [This last item is typical of the other items on the agenda.]
    [therefore]

A: The Committee on Human Relations [does not have] important work to do.

Finally, suggestion often is accomplished by the use of **rhetorical questions,** or *statements presented as questions with strongly implied answers.* This type of suggestion is not as difficult to interpret as some of the other types may be, because rhetorical questions represent a widely accepted and understood linguistic convention. For instance, when we hear someone say, "Are we going to stand for four more years of the same anemic leadership from Washington, D.C.?" the intent of the question is usually clear enough. Nevertheless, it is useful to recognize that evidence, connectives, and conclusions in arguments may appear as questions rather than as direct statements, their actual content being suggested by the implied answer to the question.

In standardizing the arguments in such cases, we have to translate the rhetorical question into a statement to see its actual content and its place in the argument. For example:

A: The prosecution's approach suggests that my client should be denied due process in these proceedings simply because he is male. B: Does the Constitution allow equal protection to vary with gender?

In this argument the evidence advanced is the prosecution's alleged suggestion that someone on trial be denied due process on the basis of his gender. The connective is the principle that the Constitution guarantees equal protection under the law to all people. The conclusion, only implied, is that the defendant should be guaranteed due process. Standardized, the argument looks like this:

A: The prosecution's approach suggests that my client should be denied due process in these proceedings simply because he is male.
B: [The Constitution does not allow equal protection under the law to vary by gender.]
C*: [Equal protection under the law must not be denied my client in this case.]

TESTING SUGGESTION

In each of the examples of suggestion, the implied argument revealed in the standardization is probably closer to the actual intent of the person arguing than is a literal interpretation of their arguments. We should be aware of suggestion and its common manifestations such as *paralepsis*, accent, innuendo, selection, arrangement, and rhetorical question. Testing suggested arguments requires first translating them into propositional form so that we know their actual nature and content as arguments. Thus, the first test of suggestion is:

> *Test 1:   Do I have an accurate translation of the argument?*

For each of the preceding examples, a suggested translation is given that brings out the probable nature and content of the argument. Because the actual argument is only suggested and not directly stated, whether a specific translation is accurate is only a guess. In these cases we have to use our judgment and understanding of factors such as the speaker's orientation and the effects of context on the argument's presentation. What position is the speaker likely to take on the topic under discussion, and does the setting or medium of presentation have any effect on what can or cannot be stated directly? We must be sure not to "read into" someone's statement sentiments that are not actually present there. If an argument is presented less than directly, however, we have a right to interpret and clarify that argument.

The second test of suggestion follows directly from our translation of the argument:

> *Test 2:   Do I accept the actual argument, including any unstated assumptions?*

For each of the examples, we have had to supply assumptions that the arguments' authors hoped their readers or listeners would supply. Often it is these assumptions with which we might take issue. Before accepting a suggested argument, we should be certain that we really want to be aware of all that we are being asked to accept.

WRAP UP

Arguments often are presented indirectly. Their actual content is only suggested, by carefully chosen phrasing or arrangement of terms. Six types of suggestion are: paralepsis, accent, innuendo, selection, arrangement, and rhetorical question. In dealing with suggestion, we must try to arrive at an accurate translation of the argument, including any unstated assumptions. Only when we know the argument's actual nature and content—and agree with these—should we be willing to accept it as reasonable.

❖ APPEALS TO AUTHORITY

We are all familiar with **appeals to authority**—*arguments that urge compliance with the directives of an authority*. Appeals to authority always involve the notion of power, or some implied or stated threat or reward associated with either accepting or rejecting the authority's directives. As an example of an appeal to authority:

A: The professor said this paper must be turned in by Monday, <u>so</u> B: we had better get it in on time.

This simple argument has one reason and one conclusion. Notice that it is not an appeal to the professor's expertise in some area. In this argument the professor is seen as wielding power based on position, and that is all.

Appeals to authority likely employ as connective some variation on the following assumption:

Connective: To respect authority in this case is reasonable.

With its connective reason in place, the example looks like this when standardized:

Evidence:	A: The professor said this paper must be turned in by Monday.
Connective:	C*: To respect authority in this case is reasonable.
	<u>so</u>
Conclusion:	B: We had better get it in on time.

Regardless of whether we agree with the notion that respecting authority is reasonable in certain cases, some version of this assumption seems to be operating as a connective reason in appeals to authority. Lurking in the background in most appeals to authority is a threat of some kind of sanction if the authority is not heeded.

TESTS OF APPEALS TO AUTHORITY

When either using or evaluating an appeal to authority we have to determine whether the argument is appropriate in the case at hand. At some times and under some circumstances, many people find that heeding authority is fully reasonable, and at other times and under other circumstances, most of us would find it unreasonable. When deciding whether to accept an argument from authority, the first consideration involves asking whether this is an instance in which heeding authority is reasonable. We can formulate the test as follows:

Test 1:   *Should authority be heeded in this particular case?*

We must be certain that we either ought to or want to heed authority in a particular case, that we find this basis for decision making reasonable in the situation at hand. Sometimes, deviating from the recommendations of authorities is actually the more reasonable course.

In the case of the professor's authority to require that an assignment be turned in, I might choose to not turn in the assignment for any number of practical reasons, such as the need to study for an exam that to fail would mean failing an entire course. On the other hand, I may find myself to be morally opposed to what the assignment requires of me. Civil disobedience is often action taken on the basis of moral objection to the requirements of authority.

Reducing these objections to a couple of broad principles, the following questions might be asked as elaborations on this first test of appeals to authority:

1. In this case is there a compelling *practical* reason for rejecting authority?
2. In this case is there a compelling *moral* reason for rejecting authority?

Some instances may have compelling practical *and* moral reasons for rejecting authority.

A compelling practical or moral reason for rejecting authority is one that outweighs the authority's claim to legitimate power and leaves us willing to endure the consequences. Refusing to pay a speeding fine because it is not practically beneficial for you at the time must be balanced against judicial power to have you arrested for failing to pay the fine. Telling the IRS that it wasn't convenient to pay taxes last year won't get you very far in an audit. But feeding yourself or your family with money that was required by either authority might be a compelling practical reason for not complying with the requirements of either authority. For some, refusal to pay a tax because the money will be used to buy armaments is a compelling moral reason for rejecting the authority of the IRS.

Next, in testing appeals to authority, we should concern ourselves with the actual authoritative status of the individual or group in question. In keeping with that concern, the second test of appeals to authority is:

Test 2:   Is this individual or group in fact an authority for me in this case?

This test asks about my relationship to the authority in question. In the first example we would want to be certain that professors actually have the authority to require students in their classes to turn in papers by a particular time. In most cases they seem to have this authority. The **power** of an authority—the ability to gain compliance with a directive—is based on either voluntary or coerced acceptance of the authority. The power of authorities, then, is based on willing acceptance of the authority, the threat of some punishment or other sanction as a consequence of rejecting the authority, or the promise of some reward for following the authority.

In asking whether a person or a group is an authority, we might try to clarify the nature of the claim to power, and to ensure that we accept the source of power as legitimate. It almost goes without saying, but probably should be noted, that being an authority in one jurisdiction does not qualify one as an authority in other arenas. Therefore, in accepting authority, we want to be sure that the authority in question is wielding authority in an appropriate area. A church leader may have authority regarding uses of the church building but may not have authority to tell parishioners how to spend their money. A Marine colonel's authority in the military does not make him or her an authority in civilian contexts.

In some cases an authority's advice or direction may conflict with that of other authorities. To test this appeal to authority, the third question is:

Test 3:   Is this authority consistent with other relevant authorities?

Authorities may be in conflict. When a religious leader instructs people to do something the political authorities forbid, whose authority is most reasonable to heed? This kind of question can be answered only within a framework of personal values, and within a specific context. At least, we should ask in such instances: "Which authority do I accept as the higher authority in this case?" The student directed to turn in a paper on a subject that his or her religious leaders forbid inquiry into is faced with a choice of this nature.

> ## WRAP UP
>
> Appeals to authority make reference to some individual or group that wields power based on office, rank, or title. If we accept the authority appealed to in an argument from authority, we should be sure before complying that we find no compelling practical or moral reasons for not following the authority's direction.

Chapter Review

Some arguments do not appear *as* arguments. Nevertheless, we should understand the structure and sometimes hidden assumptions of these nonpropositional arguments. Four of the most common are: emotional appeals, ridicule, suggestion, and appeals to authority.

To be guided by our emotions is appropriate and reasonable at times, but *emotional appeals* have to be tested before accepting these highly persuasive nonpropositional arguments. *Ridicule* is the effort to discredit a person or an idea by suggesting that it is laughable. This argument also has some hidden assumptions that have to be tested before deciding to accept it. Sometimes arguments are only suggested, and this can be accomplished by a number of means. When dealing with *suggestion*, we must ensure that we have an accurate translation of the argument before deciding whether to accept or to reject it. *Appeals to authority* recommend that the directives of some people should be accepted on the basis of the position they occupy. These appeals also have an underlying argumentative structure that has to be assessed before they are accepted as reasonable.

Nonpropositional arguments are common in public controversies. Because they do not appear as arguments, we have to be especially attentive to their presence and their impact.

EXERCISES

A. Find an example in the media of each type of nonpropositional argument discussed in this chapter. Test your examples according to the guidelines presented, and be prepared to discuss your examples in class.

B. Identify the type of nonpropositional argument taking place in each of the following examples; standardize the examples and apply the appropriate tests:

1. I'm sick and tired of the way your paper tears apart the President. The city's other paper is much fairer in this regard. I get both papers but am thinking of going to just one. Want to guess which one?

2. *Context*: A candidate in a mayoral race in a small midwestern town was criticized in letters to the editor of the local paper for his youth—he was twenty-two—and interests. A respondent to these criticisms advanced the following argument.

    The claim that Phil Pinkus is unqualified to be mayor because he listens to rock music is absurd. The kind of rock Phil listens to is intelligent music written and performed for thoughtful and sensitive young adults.

3. Why do *you* think that he stays up there so late every night and pays his aides so much money, and that their only apparent responsibility is to keep quiet about their boss?

4. All one need do in deciding which side to back in the surrogacy controversy is to think of the children involved. What does it do to a child to be shuttled back and forth from one family to another, called by different names in each, and never assured that either family is really her family?

5. The Pope has condemned the use of contraceptives. As Catholics, we clearly cannot approve their use.

6. No way would I condone his use of campaign funds to pay for vacations for himself and his family, but I also refuse to make that an issue in this campaign.

7. The St. Francis of Assisi Baptist Church burned to the ground this morning, and the causes of the fire are under investigation. Without speculating about the fire's origin, it should be noted that the church was recently insured for $2,000,000, and the congregation is known to have debts of about $1,500,000.

8. Ohm's law expresses the relationship between current, voltage, and resistance in electrical circuits. As scientist Paul Davies has suggested, the idea that this law has existed in some timeless, ethereal realm forever, just waiting for someone to build an electrical

circuit, is preposterous. This example proves that physical laws do not exist independent of physical events.

9. I'm not saying that Mr. Smith is a member of the Mafia. But how do you explain the fact that his name regularly shows up in the indexes of books on the mob?

10. It may be wrong, but the Captain said to do it.

C. Provide answers for the questions regarding the following examples of ridicule.

1. *Question*: On what basis does the individual writing this argument find President Bush's statements on the environment to be "laughable"?

   George Bush's recent statements on the environment are simply laughable to anyone who has been paying attention to the President's environmental record: fewer and more relaxed regulations for industry, failure to clean up toxic waste sites, no action on acid rain. Does he think the voters of this state are brain dead?

2. *Question*: What kind of argument underlies the claim to the ridiculous in the following? What are you told about the actual content of the laws being ridiculed?

   In New Hampshire it is against the law to take a cow up in a hot air balloon on Sunday. The laws governing banking in this state make about as much sense. If the American banking industry is to compete with foreign banking concerns, it must be released from the tyranny of these ridiculous regulations.

3. *Question*: In the following argument, what practice is Mr. Thurmond arguing in support of? What idea or practice does he hold to be "patently absurd"? What kind of argument does he use to support this claim?

   "In this body we begin our workday with the comfort and stimulus of voluntary group prayer. Recently, such a practice has been constitutionally blessed by the Supreme Court. It is patently absurd, in my judgment, that the opportunity for the same beneficial experience is denied to the boys and girls who attend public schools." (Senator Strom Thurmond, *Congressional Digest*, 1983, 63 [5], p. 140)

4. *Question*: What idea is Mr. Gorbachev trying to discredit by his claim that it is "not serious"? On what basis is he suggesting that the idea is not serious?

"I have to laugh when I hear the suggestion that the Sandanista regime in Nicaragua threatens the security of the United States. This is not serious, it's not serious." (Mikhail Gorbachev, November 30, 1987)

5. *Question*: How has the head of the Fish Advisory Board interpreted the FDA's claim in the following example? What possible problem with ambiguity is presented in this example?

The FDA reported that eating fish may be hazardous because fish is the only flesh food that is not subject to inspection. The head of the Fish Advisory Board replied: "The idea that beef and pork are better for you because they are inspected is simply ludicrous."

D. Refer back to any items in exercise B that you identified as suggestion. Looking at your standardization, try to identify the type of argument (e.g., argument from principle) that the suggestion concealed.

E. Provide an example of a nonpropositional argument that you have read or heard. Analyze your example employing tests discussed in this chapter.

ENDNOTES

1. This discussion of the sources of emotional appeals is suggested by Aristotle's analysis of these topics in *Rhetoric*, translated by W. Rhys Roberts (New York: Modern Library, 1954), book 2, especially chapters 2, 5, and 8. Aristotle's idea that *pathos* (appeals to the emotions) serves to put hearers "in the right frame of mind" is behind the later discussion of experiencing an emotion appropriate to the decision at hand.

2. Of the few discussions of ridicule as an argumentative form, the best is found in Chaim Perelman and L. Olbrechts–Tyteca's *The New Rhetoric*, translated by John Wilkinson and Purcell Weaver (Notre Dame University Press, 1969), pp. 205–209.

3. Plato, *Gorgias* translated by W. C. Helmbold (Indianapolis: Bobbs-Merrill, 1952), p. 60.

4. This and other common rhetorical devices and linguistic conventions are discussed in Richard Lanham's helpful book, *A Handlist of Rhetorical Terms* (Berkeley: University of California Press, 1969).

12 ADAPTING ARGUMENTS TO AN AUDIENCE

Chapter Preview

CONSTRUCTING A PICTURE OF THE AUDIENCE

A consideration of ways in which we can get some idea of the beliefs and values of an audience to which you might be presenting an argument.

CLARIFYING LANGUAGE AND INFERENCES

A look at how to write and speak in language that is understandable to the audience.

PAYING ATTENTION TO LANGUAGE

A consideration of some common language pitfalls that lead to confusion in the presentation of arguments.

Key Terms

invention	political perspective	unintentional humor
adapting an argument	demographic analysis	choosing the wrong word
psychological commitments	eliminating irrelevant reasons	misusing a common expression
attitudes	shared commitments	tangled sentences
beliefs	redundancy	
values	mixed metaphor	

T he process of **invention**, *coming up with the arguments we will present in support of some claim*, considers the audience for which our arguments are intended. In most cases, arguments are advanced in an effort to persuade an audience—even if the audience consists only of a single individual—and this usually means that our arguments are *adapted* to that audience. Moreover, the goals of clarity and propriety dictate that we modify or adapt our arguments, and the language in which they are cast, before they are presented to an audience.

To **adapt arguments** to an audience, then, we must know something about arguments and the clear and effective use of language, topics that already have been discussed in this text. But effectively adapting arguments to audiences also means that we must know something about the audience we are addressing. This chapter begins with a discussion of how to think about audiences and how to adapt arguments to specific audiences. It then draws on ideas presented earlier in the book to show how arguments and language can be used to adapt our ideas to an audience. Finally, it considers some common pitfalls of language to be avoided in presenting our arguments.

❖ CONSTRUCTING A PICTURE OF THE AUDIENCE

Even though our reasoning may be largely private, our arguments are very often public, and constructed with some person or group in mind. This is the case whether we are presenting an argument to a friend or roommate, the local board of education, or a national television audience. We all adapt our arguments to audiences, but we are not always certain how to effectively go about this process.

In thinking about adapting arguments to an audience, the best place to start is to try to construct a mental picture of that audience—to have an audience in mind as you go through the inventional process. In beginning to think about your audience, you may wish to ask questions such as: Who am I writing for or speaking to? What is their interest in my topic? What do they think of my position on this topic? What do they think of me?

These general questions can be answered more specifically by asking other questions about the psychological and demographic make-up of your audience, about their knowledge of and interest in your topic, and about their attitudes toward your topic and toward you. As far as the audience's **psychological commitments** are concerned, you may wish to ask:

1. What are their *attitudes* toward my topic?
2. What are their *beliefs* that have bearing on my arguments?
3. What *values* do they hold that bear on my position?
4. What is their *political perspective?*

Clues to answering these questions are sometimes found by doing a **demographic analysis** of your audience. The demographic nature of your audience can be revealed by asking some or all of the following questions:

1. What *groups* do the audience members belong to?
2. What is the general *age* of the audience?
3. What mix of *gender* is found in the audience?
4. What *races* or *ethnic groups* are represented in the audience?
5. What *occupations* are represented?
6. What *religious views* are present in the audience?

Once you have done an initial psychological and demographic analysis of your audience, you can ask some specific questions regarding their interest in and likely feelings about your topic. The following questions can be useful:

1. Is this audience likely to be *interested* in this topic, or does the topic even concern them?
2. Does the audience have to *make a choice* on the topic?
3. Is the audience likely to *need or want information* on the topic?
4. If my topic does concern the audience, are the feelings likely to be *hostile or friendly* toward my position?

Finally, audiences do not have feelings about topics only. They also have feelings about speakers and writers. For that reason, you might want to think about your audience's attitude toward you. Your thinking can be guided by the following questions:

1. Does the audience *know* me?
2. Does the audience *accept* me? Am I viewed as "one of their own," a friend, a guest, an outsider, or an enemy?
3. Does the audience consider me to be a *credible source* on the topic I am addressing in my arguments?

4. How is the audience likely to *react* when I speak? Will the audience listen politely, shout me down, believe every word I say?

With these considerations in mind, you should be able to make an intelligent guess about the nature of your audience. In many cases, you can get a clear picture of your audience by considering their psychological make-up, demographic profile, feelings about the topic, and attitudes about you.

Can asking this sort of question about an audience actually be helpful in adapting an argument to an audience? In many cases, the answer is yes. For example, a university student named Brad was going to make an argumentative speech on the question of art censorship before two audiences. Brad, an art major, had been bothered by suggestions from certain conservative members of Congress that the National Endowment for the Arts should be restricted from providing funding for artists whose work is offensive to some members of the public. Here is a brief profile of Brad's two audiences:

Audience 1

The audience is made up of members of one of Brad's classes at his university. The class, "Art in Society," has thirty-four members. About half consists of art majors, and the other half represents a cross-section of the campus. The campus itself is a large, public institution located in a major eastern city with a liberal political tradition. About twenty-five of the students are between ages eighteen and twenty-three; the others are older, ranging in age from twenty-four to fifty. The class is evenly divided by gender, and about half is composed of racial and ethnic minorities. Brad is an active member of the class and is well-liked by the other students.

Audience 2

This audience is a local service club in Brad's hometown. The club is known to be politically conservative. It often invites members of the community to speak on a variety of topics. A typical meeting attracts about fifty people, and most of these—forty or more—are male. All but a few of the members are white, and all but a few are over age thirty, with many of the members being over sixty. Most members of the club also are active in local religious organizations,

and most own or work for businesses in the town. The
town, with a population of 50,000, is located in a central
midwestern state. Brad is not a member of the club and, as
a student just back from his junior year at a major urban
university, he may be viewed with a little suspicion.

Brad was going to address both groups and present arguments in opposition to restricting NEA funding on the basis of the content of artists'
works. He probably would not make exactly the same arguments before
each group, and his linguistic tone likely would be different for each.
For which group would the following portion of his argumentative case
be more appropriate?

Most of the people behind the drive to censor artists by limiting the federal funds available to them are narrow-minded
fundamentalists. Their political conservatism and cultural bigotry should not be allowed to prevail in these matters.
They are offended by works such as one portraying a cruci-
fix in a jar of human urine, or Robert Mapplethorpe's homo-
erotic art. Because these works offend them, they seek to
prevent artists from exercising their right to artistic expression. This is not right, and the right wing should be put in
its place. I propose that the review board for all NEA funding be made up of a majority of artists. This is the only
way of assuring that bigotry will not prevail, and that art
and the Constitution will.

Well, believe it or not, Brad presented this argument to the second audience. They were not receptive. Having written the speech originally
with his university class in mind as an audience, he made absolutely no
changes in the presentation when speaking to the service club. You can
look at this event in two ways. You might say, "Good—they needed to
hear that!" But then you are, of course, admitting that little or no persuasion took place and that the argument was rejected. Or you might
conclude that, with some efforts at audience adaptation, the speech could
have been much more persuasive without sacrificing its point or its integrity as an argument. What could Brad have done differently while
remaining true to his belief that the NEA should not restrict funds on
the basis of artistic content?

Keeping in mind the balance between conviction and content, Brad might have carefully adapted his argument to his second audience. He could have taken into consideration this audience's psychological and demographic profile: They are politically conservative, middle-aged, religiously oriented, white males living in a large town in the Midwest. They are also members of a group known for its political conservatism. Their values are likely to be influenced by these factors, and they may believe, for instance, that artists ought not to get federal support for art that offends some members of the general public.

Brad also could have considered that these people might be more interested in the issue of federal spending—which they are likely to understand as taxation—than they are in artistic freedom. Moreover, Brad should have known that he was coming as something of an outsider, and one advocating an unpopular position. Nevertheless, the fact that he was born and grew up in the town perhaps could have worked to his advantage if approached correctly.

Knowing these things about his audience, what could Brad have done differently while still remaining true to his convictions? Almost certainly, Brad should not have used the label "narrow-minded fundamentalists" to describe those favoring restrictions on the NEA, or the label "bigotry" to describe their attitudes. Members of his second audience might feel that they are themselves being attacked by the use of such labels.

In addition, Brad could have sought to identify with his audience in a couple of different ways. First, his value for artistic freedom might have been linked more clearly to values the audience accepted—such as freedom of speech, or a value for a "loyal opposition" in a democratic society. Had Brad given more thought to his audience's values and anchored his arguments in those values, his case probably would have been better received. Moreover, Brad might have identified himself as a member of the community, and a person who understands some of the reservations the members have about provocative works of art.

Brad also might have chosen his examples more carefully, especially because the examples he did choose are not any more representative of the art causing concern than are other examples that might have been less offensive to his audience. Or he might have introduced some other examples along with these, to balance the effect. Brad also might have introduced testimony from sources that the club would likely find credible, sources affirming either the value of freedom of artistic expression or the need not to tie federal funding to local preferences.

Finally, Brad might have developed an analogy to some case on which the people in his audience are likely to have strong views already.

For instance, he might have developed an analogy to the federal government telling business people what kinds of products they can sell, and to what groups, how they can advertise, and other limitations on what they might see as their ability to compete.

These are just some ideas as to what Brad might have done to adapt his argument to a new and different audience. You probably can think of other ideas that would have helped to make his arguments more effective before this audience. Though Brad's failure to consider his audience led to a rather obvious error, incidents such as this are not at all uncommon. By taking some time to think about our audience as we write our arguments, we can avoid many of the more obvious mistakes.

WRAP UP

Arguments should be adapted to the audiences for which they are intended. The process of adaptation requires that we have in mind some picture of our audience. Psychological and demographic audience analysis can help in constructing this picture. We usually want to know whom we are speaking or writing to and what our audience is likely to think about us and our topic.

❖ CLARIFYING LANGUAGE AND INFERENCES

Part of the problem in the previous example was a failure to adapt the argument to a particular audience. Moreover, problems of clarity arise when preparing arguments for presentation to an audience.

Suppose that a friend of yours has the assignment of presenting before a class at her university a brief argument in support of an idea. Although she thinks she knows what she wants to argue, she has come to you for advice about writing the speech. She isn't satisfied that she is saying exactly what she wants to, and she is concerned that she will be misunderstood or won't get her point across. What will you tell her? You could offer some advice about constructing and testing her arguments. You might also mention the techniques for getting a picture of the audience, as described earlier. But even when we know something about the types and tests of arguments, we may not present our own arguments in a way that is clear and easily understood by our audience. Several additional considerations, presented as a series of questions, can be helpful in preparing clear and effective arguments for presentation to an audience.

You might begin by noting that when we set out to construct our own arguments, we have to be absolutely clear about the point we are trying to establish. This may seem obvious, but perhaps the most common mistake of speakers and writers is to fail to make clear their conclusions. Suppose that your friend showed you the argument she intended to present to her class at the university. This is her argument:

Many scientists accept creationism as a valid theory of origins. And evolution is just that—a theory. You can't say that one is a better theory than the other, so students should know they are both possible alternatives for intelligent people. The people who oppose teaching creationism in our schools are the same people who oppose school prayer, and I am highly suspicious of their motives. Opposition to religious instruction in schools is causing untold damage to our nation. Religious instruction always has been an important aspect of education.

An argument clearly is intended here, but what is not at all clear is the conclusion. Is the conclusion that creationism should be taught in the public schools or that religious education is important? Or perhaps that some conspiracy is afoot to neutralize religious influences in education? Without knowing the conclusion, the argument is difficult to understand, let alone to analyze. To the extent that your friend intends this "argument" to persuade anyone, the effort expended inventing and advancing it probably will have been wasted because its conclusion is not clear.

You suggest that your friend ask herself the following question:

What is my main point or conclusion? This is a question we have to ask ourselves as we invent and adapt our own arguments. It is entirely possible that the friend would not be able to give a clear answer to the question because she is expressing a loosely connected set of ideas that don't seem to involve a single main point.

After some discussion, and the elimination of several possibilities, you and your friend agree that the conclusion she is trying to establish is:

Conclusion: We must not allow the erosion of religious
ideas in education.

This is a simple, declarative statement of a normative conclusion. The members of her class would be able to assess whether she had or had not advanced a good argument in support of this conclusion. Her audience would be able to understand the claim being made and defended and decide whether they would accept the accompanying arguments.

When constructing arguments, we need to ask ourselves, "What is my point?" But the language in which the conclusion is presented must be clear if the audience is to easily understand it. We also must be sure that we are stating our conclusion precisely as we wish it to be understood. Thus, you also might recommend that your friend ask:

Have I accurately and clearly stated my conclusion? At this point you might ask your friend whether preventing the erosion of religious ideas in our schools is really the point of her argument. After all, because religious ideas currently are not much represented in public schools, not much erosion is left to take place. Moreover, preventing erosion does not suggest a positive plan of action but, rather, a defensive effort in response to a process already taking place. After considering these objections to the conclusion as stated above, your friend agrees to the following formulation of her point:

Conclusion: Religious ideas should be afforded a place of
importance in the educational process.

This statement may accurately express the point of her argument, but recall that our emphasis is on the audience to which the argument is directed. Will this audience easily understand the language in which the conclusion is presented? The statement, "Religious ideas should be afforded a place of importance in the educational process," perhaps would not be as clear and direct for that audience as would:

Conclusion: Religious ideas ought to be given an
important place in the educational process.

You and your friend agree, let us suppose, that this is an accurate, clear, and direct statement of the conclusion of her argument.

Your friend's argument is intended to lead to the conclusion: "Religious ideas ought to be given an important place in the educational process." Looking at the argument again, and scanning it, we find that it contains the following statements:

A: Many scientists accept creationism as a valid theory of origins, and B: evolution is just that—a theory. C: You can't say that one is a better theory than the other, so D: students should know that both are possible alternatives for intelligent people. E: The people who oppose teaching creationism in our schools are the same people who oppose school prayer, and I am highly suspicious of their motives. F: Opposition to religious instruction in schools is causing untold damage to our nation. G: Religious instruction always has been an important aspect of education.

We can now add the missing conclusion:

Conclusion: Religious ideas ought to be given an
               important place in the educational process.

Though the conclusion may be clear, the reasons leading to it are not. Looking at the argument again, your friend should probably ask about the *relevance* of the first seven statements to her conclusion. She might ask the following question:

Is it clear how my reasons support my argument's conclusion? It is not clear that statement E has much to do with the conclusion of the argument. The argument's point might be clearer if this statement were eliminated. **Eliminating irrelevant reasons** is an important aspect of writing arguments. Statement E only tends to draw attention away from the conclusion and to confuse the argument. Eliminating it leaves the argument with six rather than seven statements.

The other statements in the argument seem to have some bearing on the conclusion. The first four statements have to do with the rational legitimacy of religious ideas for the educational setting, and the last two statements have to do with the place and function of religious ideas in education.

Whether we agree or disagree with the argument, we perhaps can see some connection between the remaining reasons and the conclusion.

Let's look just at the first four statements in your friend's argument:

A: Many scientists accept creationism as a valid theory of origins, <u>and</u> B: evolution is just that—a theory. C: You can't say that one is a better theory than the other, *so* D: students should know that both are possible alternatives for intelligent people.

Statements A, B, and C apparently are intended as reasons for D. It also seems that statements A, an observation serving as evidence, and B, an assumption or belief serving as a connective, are reasons for C, although this is less obvious as no indicator word is present to tell us this.

We can test our thoughts about the structure of this part of the argument by inserting an indicator word between statements B and C:

Evidence: A: Many scientists accept creationism as a
                    valid theory of origins.
                    <u>and</u>
Connective: B: Evolution is just that—a theory.
                    <u>thus</u>
Intermediate
Conclusion: C: You can't say that one is better than the
                    other.
                    <u>so</u>
Conclusion: D: Students should know that both are
                    possible alternatives for intelligent people.

At this point, statement C seems to require a connective reason in order to yield statement D. Your friend apparently assumes something like:

(*): Ideas that are reasonable alternatives for intelligent
     people should have a place in the educational system.

We can insert this connective in the argument in an effort to clarify the connection between statements C and D:

Evidence: A: Many scientists accept creationism as a
                        valid theory of origins.
                        and
Connective: B: Evolution is just that—a theory.
                        thus
Intermediate
Conclusion: C: You can't say that one is better than the
                        other.
Connective: (*): Ideas that are reasonable alternatives for
                        intelligent people should have a place in
                        the educational process.
                        so
Conclusion: D: Students should know that both are
                        possible.

This set of reasons and conclusions now tends to support the final conclusion:

Conclusion: Religious ideas ought to be given an
                   important place in the educational process.

Designating this as statement G, we now have the following argument:

Evidence: A: Many scientists accept creationism as a
                        valid theory of origins.
                        and
Connective: B: Evolution is just that—a theory.
                        thus
Intermediate
Conclusion: C: You can't say that one is better than the
                        other.
Connective: (*): Ideas that are reasonable alternatives for
                        intelligent people should have a place in
                        the educational process.

<u>SO</u>

Intermediate
Conclusion: D: Students should know that both are
                     possible.
Conclusion: G: Religious ideas ought to be given an
                     important place in the educational
                     process.

The diagram for this argument is:

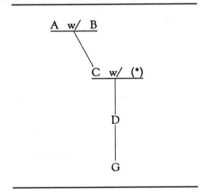

Let's look again at what are now statements E and F:

E: Elimination of religious instruction from our schools is
    causing untold damage to our nation.
F: Religious instruction always has been an important
    aspect of education.

These statements do not seem closely related to one another—one
deals with consequences, the other with tradition—but each could be
construed as support for the conclusion of the argument. Statement E
suggests a practical concern, and statement F seems to be based on a
value for maintaining tradition, or continuing to do those things that have
been done for a long time. Suppose your friend agrees that this is what
she intended by including these reasons. You might suggest that inserting
the linguistic cues "moreover" and "and" would clarify the separate nature of these reasons. Then we could standardize this part of the argument as:

Moreover
because
E: Elimination of religious education from our schools is causing untold damage to our nation.
and because
F: Religious instruction always has been an important aspect of education.
therefore
G: Religious ideas should be given an important place in the educational process.

Adding these new reasons to the standardized argument, we get:

Evidence:	A:	Many scientists accept creationism as a valid theory of origins. and
Connective:	B:	Evolution is just that—a theory. thus
Intermediate Conclusion:	C:	You can't say that one is better than the other.
Connective:	H*:	Ideas that are reasonable alternatives for intelligent people should have a place in the educational process. so
Intermediate Conclusion:	D:	Students should know that both are possible. moreover because
Evidence:	E:	Elimination of religious education from our schools is causing untold damage to our nation. and because
Evidence:	F:	Religious instruction has always been an important aspect of education. therefore
Conclusion:	G:	Religious ideas should be given an important place in the educational process.

A diagram of the complete argument now looks like this:

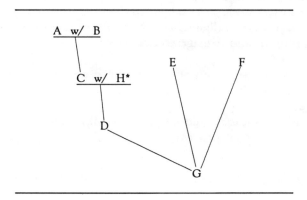

Our example argument would now appear as follows, with a few modifications to make it a little more appealing to read:

Many scientists accept creationism as a valid theory of origins. And evolution is just that—a theory. Thus, you can't say one is better than the other. Ideas that are reasonable alternatives for intelligent people should have a place in the educational process. So students should know that both creationism and evolution theory are possible alternatives for reasonable people. Moreover, eliminating religious instruction from our schools has caused untold damage to our nation, and religious instruction always has been an important aspect of the educational process. For all of these reasons, I conclude that religious instruction ought to be given an important place in the educational process.

Notice that we have arranged the reasons so that they precede the conclusion they support. They also appear in order, so that audience members do not have to struggle to track the argument. Finally, it is helpful to ask:

Have I emphasized common values and important ideas? Perhaps you and your friend now notice that her argument emphasizes the values of justice (equal treatment of the two theories and, by implication, of people holding the different views), religious belief, and tradition. If presented to an audience already adhering to these values, she might emphasize the values by stating them outright. For example, because the value for adhering to traditions is still hidden in the argument as it is currently formulated, before an audience for whom adherence to tradition is also an important value, she might choose to draw it out by articulating it:

Moreover, eliminating religious instruction from our schools has caused untold damage to our nation. In addition, religious instruction always has been an important aspect of the educational process. It is an American tradition, and we abandon our traditions at our peril.

When adapting an argument to an audience, one question we might ask is: Have I emphasized commonly held values? In some cases, as noted earlier in the text, we might choose to emphasize a shared commitment of audience and speaker, *by intentionally leaving it unstated*. Recall that Aristotle called an argument with an unstated value premise an "enthymeme." Enthymemes involve the audience in the argument by supplying the unstated but shared value, and at the same time affirm the unity of speaker and audience regarding a strongly held value—one so strongly held that it is understood without being stated directly. Whether to state or to not state a shared value, then, is a choice a writer or speaker must make, given the situation and the audience being addressed.

Emphasizing the important ideas in an argument is also crucial; to set them off from the less important ones. One way in which speakers can emphasize important ideas is by *using rhetorical questions*. A rhetorical question can accomplish nearly the same goals as an enthymeme. For example, your friend might emphasize the idea that evolution and creationism deserve equal consideration by using the following rhetorical question:

Many scientists accept creationism as a valid theory of origins. And evolution theory is just that—a theory. Can anyone say one idea is better than the other?

By asking this rhetorical question, the speaker emphasizes a commitment to a principle of justice on the part of speaker and audience. Recall that rhetorical questions are actually contentions, and they should be treated as such. The use of rhetorical questions and enthymemes could, of course, be combined to further emphasize mutual commitment to some value or idea.

Suppose one were addressing a hostile or perhaps neutral audience. In such a circumstance, arguments still can be adapted to the audience on the basis of **shared commitments**, or beliefs held in common with the audience. This can and should be done without sacrificing our own commitments or misleading the audience regarding them. In these circumstances, shared commitments and important ideas may have to be presented in a somewhat different way; unstated reasons and rhetorical questions may not be appropriate. Directly stating points of agreement, and candidly admitting the disagreements between you and your audience, may be more effective. Thus, if your friend's university class were likely to be unfriendly to her ideas, she might take the following tack:

I know that we disagree about the place of religious instruction in the educational process and, in particular, the place of creationism in instruction about the origins of the universe. But many scientists do accept creationism, whereas evolution theory cannot claim to be any more than that—a theory. I think you would agree that ideas that are reasonable alternatives for intelligent people should have a place in the educational process, and so it seems only fair that students should know that both creationism and evolution theory are possible alternatives for reasonable people.

Here, the shared value for fair treatment of different ideas is emphasized as a commitment common to people who disagree about application of the principle. Candor is employed to encourage audience members to lower their defenses for a moment so the argument can be made. The argument itself has not been altered much, but its manner of presentation reflects the speaker's awareness that the audience is not initially inclined to agree with her position on the issue at hand.

WRAP UP

Not only does the content of our arguments have to be adapted to our audience, but so does the language in which we present those arguments. The goals here are clarity, precision, and persuasiveness. We have to ask whether we have made a clear statement of our conclusion, clarified the relationships among reasons and conclusions, emphasized important ideas, and made some effort to include the audience in the reasoning process by stressing common values.

❖ PAYING ATTENTION TO LANGUAGE

One important aspect of adapting argumentation to an audience is simply paying attention to what we are saying. Occasionally we hear or read a sentence that strikes us as odd, although we may not be sure why. For instance, a speaker says that "Child abuse is a widespread, uncontrollable crime that is difficult to enforce." This person probably meant to say that "Child abuse is a widespread, uncontrollable crime, and the laws regarding it are difficult to enforce," but it didn't come out that way. The problem in this sentence might have been identified and solved had the writer asked: Does the sentence say what I want it to say?

In some instances we run into the problem of **redundancy**, or repeating an idea unintentionally. For example, a speaker states: "We are in danger of developing wrong misconceptions about this." The idea of wrongness is stated twice here, both in the word "wrong" and in the word "misconceptions." What this speaker meant to say was: "We are in danger of developing wrong conceptions (or ideas) about this" or perhaps, "We are in danger of developing misconceptions about this." In developing your arguments, be careful not to be unintentionally redundant.

Another common problem in writing arguments is known as the **mixed metaphor**. For example, a reporter states that, "The governor didn't focus on one direction but offered a smorgasbord that adds up to a lot of money." Here the metaphors of "focus," "direction," and "smorgasbord" are all used as if they present a similar picture, but they don't. Each word introduces a different picture, and by introducing three different pictures in the same sentence, an unpleasant clash develops which can be distracting to readers or listeners. Here's another example from a Congressional candidate speaking to the press: "When you add up all the pieces, the pie makes a bigger loaf than you planned, and you can't get a handle on it." Here we have pieces of a pie that's really a loaf with a handle on it!

A third frequently encountered problem with language is **unintentional humor**. For example, one student claimed in a speech on animal rights and medical experimentation: "I don't think we should be using animals for guinea pigs." Of course, the student did not intend this statement to be funny. But guinea pigs are animals, so the statement doubles back on itself in an amusing way. This is a real problem when the point being made is serious. And it may present a problem even in less serious situations, such as when we are simply making an observation about the inevitability of defeat or failure: "Even Napoleon met his Waterloo." Of course he did!

Sometimes the problem is **choosing the wrong word**, as in the following example: "I know it sounds like an old touché, but the cream always rises to the top." That the cream always rises to the top is not a touché; it is a cliché. *Touché* means "touch" in French and is clearly not the word this person wanted to use. Speakers must be careful to use the word they want and not something that sounds like it. Sometimes we just have the wrong form of the right word, as in this example: "Criminals who break the same law repeatable should be punished so they can never commit the crime again." Here the word "repeatedly" was intended, not "repeatable."

Another problem that occurs with some frequency is **misusing a common expression**. For instance, we might hear someone say in praise of a famous person, "Clearly, she stood head and tails above the others." The expression is "to stand head and shoulders above," not "head and tails above," though the latter suggests an interesting mental picture. Heads and tails go together when flipping coins, and this, no doubt, is what led to the confusion.

Finally, there are **tangled sentences**, complex statements that get mixed up as we say them. The problem seems to arise from losing track of the sentence, or switching parts of it as we speak. Tangled sentences end up sounding odd, and even funny. For instance, a Vietnam veteran reported to a group of listeners: "We were ordered to burn houses, blow up bunkers, and kill livestock. Burning houses was common, and blowing up livestock was not unheard of." This person probably meant to say that "killing livestock was not unheard of," but this is not what he actually said. The unintentional humor of his tangled sentence—a result of the image of blowing up a cow or a pig—is unfortunate given the serious nature of his topic.

WRAP UP

Using language well means paying close attention to what we are saying. In writing arguments, we should be careful not to commit some common errors that can render our arguments less effective: redundancy, mixed metaphors, unintentional humor, using the wrong word, misusing a common expression, and tangled sentences.

Chapter Review

The process of adapting arguments to particular audiences involves getting a clear picture of the audience through psychological and demographic analysis. Adapting arguments to an audience involves making contact with the audience through various means—for instance, emphasizing the things you and they have in common—as well as avoiding unintentionally offending them.

The language in which we present our conclusions should be clear and precise, and our reasons and conclusions should be clearly related. Important ideas should be emphasized, and some effort can be made to directly involve the audience in the argumentative process by stressing common values. Finally, language errors that can hinder the success of argumentative efforts should be avoided.

EXERCISES

A. Write an argument of about a page in length defending any one of the controversial statements in exercise C. Write the argument with your class in mind, and employ the suggestions in this chapter in adapting the argument to your audience. In the margins of the paper, note the places where particular suggestions have been followed.

B. Write a paragraph in opposition to, and another in support of, any of the controversial statements in exercise C. Follow the guidelines set out for exercise A.

C. For each of the following controversial statements, suggest three beliefs, values, or assumptions that a person accepting the statement might hold.

1. The minimum wage should be increased.

2. First-time conviction for drunk driving should carry a mandatory jail sentence.

3. Adoption records should be made readily available to adoptees.

4. Genetic engineering research should be stopped immediately.

5. Development of nuclear power should be pursued aggressively.

6. Animal experimentation should be halted.

7. Violence in sports should be prosecuted under local criminal statutes.

8. Retirement at age sixty-five should be mandatory for all jobs.

9. Insurance companies should be allowed to ask insurance applicants if they have AIDS.

10. Registration should be required for all guns.

D. With each of the following statements, suggest the problem and provide a reformulation of the sentence that avoids the problem.

   1. A news reporter sums up a report by saying, "And so, the winds of Washington are blowing again over another political hot potato today."

   2. I know it sounds like crying over sour milk, but that's the whole kettle of fish in a nutshell.

   3. The very thought of it sent curdles up my spine.

   4. When they arrived, I felt condescended upon.

   5. He's getting a lot of hot water over his decision.

   6. These laws hurt more than they harm.

   7. Poverty in America today is academic.

   8. Government statistics prove that alcohol is responsible for half of all automobile fertilities.

   9. To coin an old saying, You Rip What You Sew.

   10. I've investigated the topic from one end of the political pole to the other.

   11. Oh, it's right on the tip of my head!

   12. Let's burn that bridge when we get to it.

   13. And never the two twains shall meet.

   14. He was pulling in money hand over foot.

   15. On the third side of the coin. . . .

   16. She prefers diet-free drinks.

   17. This new faith has gone to the four corners of the globe.

   18. I worked my bones off on that paper.

   19. Although the lack of communication pointed in the direction of truth, it still has major complications.

   20. In Ft. Lauderdale, Florida, during spring break drinking while being intoxicated is not allowed.

E. Guided by the questions suggested at the beginning of this chapter, write a thorough description of an audience you have spoken to, or of which you were a member. Discuss the relationship between speaker and audience in this situation, and how arguments either were or were not adapted to this audience.

13 ANALYZING LONGER ARGUMENTS

Chapter Preview

ANALYZING LONGER ARGUMENTS

An analysis of a longer argument, using the types and tests of arguments discussed throughout the text.

Most of the arguments we have analyzed and evaluated have been relatively short—one or two paragraphs—but the analytic skills and tools developed in the text can be employed to evaluate longer arguments as well. In this chapter a longer argument originally presented in class by a student will be analyzed, employing some of the critical tools developed in earlier chapters. The student's entire argument is presented first, followed by a discussion of it. The exercise section has another argument for you to analyze using a similar approach.

❖ ARGUMENT

Buried Alive!
Wes Anderson

1   Americans are being slowly buried alive. Our life as a society is being suffocated little by little, and we aren't even aware that it's happening. Who is this insidious enemy that is burying us alive? The enemy is us: We are burying ourselves—in garbage! While we are directing our attention at Colombian drug lords, an equally serious enemy is waiting in our own backyards—millions of tons of solid waste. We already have declared war on drugs, and now it's time—past time—to declare war on garbage!

2   The simple fact is that we produce too much waste and we have no place to put it. Wisely, we made ocean dumping illegal. But available landfills are closing at an alarming rate. If we do not reduce the level of waste output soon, available landfill will reach capacity, municipalities will have nowhere to dump garbage, and garbage trucks will be dumping their contents anywhere—in national parks, in the streets, even in your backyard! Thus, it is imperative that we do something about this threat now. We can't rely on the government to solve the problem for us, and industry has been dragging its feet. That means it is up to each and every American to become part of the solution. In addition, you have a duty to become part of the solution in order to save our nation and our future. We must take a stand against our common enemy, and avert the impending waste disposal crisis by voluntarily recycling.

3   Let me begin by presenting the problem. America has too much waste and no place to put it. *Newsweek* reports that "Americans collectively toss out 160 million tons [of garbage]

each year—enough to spread 30 stories high over 1,000 football fields, enough to fill a bumper-to-bumper convoy of garbage trucks halfway to the moon."[1] The January 2, 1988, issue of *Time* magazine finds Americans throwing away 16 million disposable diapers, 1.6 billion pens, 2 billion razors and blades, and 220 million tires each year. "[We] discard enough aluminum" writes one reporter, "to rebuild the entire U.S. commercial airline fleet every three months."[2]

4   Not surprisingly, we are running out of room for our garbage. The current number of landfills in the U.S. is estimated at 6,000, but 3,000 others closed in the past five years. Moreover, out of the current 6,000 landfills, 2,000 more are expected to close by 1993.[3] With no place to go, the waste is being loaded onto barges, which remain at sea until the ship's captain can finally find a dumping place for the waste. Unfortunately, these sites are usually poor Third World countries, which have almost no way of dealing with the waste. John Langone of *Time* writes that "international dumping is the equivalent of declaring war on the people of a country."[4] This is a terrible injustice perpetrated against people who sometimes have no choice but to accept American garbage, an injustice we must actively oppose.

5   Can there be any doubt that we are being buried alive! Solid waste has become for the 1980s and 1990s what air pollution was to the 1960s and 1970s—an environmental tragedy that threatens our entire nation. And what is the cause of this problem? We are, with our consumerist and materialist lifestyle, which considers only our convenience and gives not a thought to the impact of our habits on other people and on the earth itself. When each one of us throws out 50 gallons of trash a week, we together create a national and international crisis.

6   America clearly has an environmental crisis of the greatest magnitude on her hands, and the time has come to recognize that it is a problem and that it must be dealt with. We must have a national plan of action to deal with solid waste. If we fail to develop such a plan, we will witness a decline in the American standard of living unparalleled in our history. It may be time for a tax levied according to the amount of waste we each produce. This already has been implemented in Seattle, Washington, and the results are very encouraging—a 25 percent reduction in waste since the tax was instituted two years ago.[5]

7   But we as individuals can begin to reverse the trend to-ward burying ourselves by a relatively simple life-saving ma-neuver—recycling waste. There are measures that any one of us can take. What can you do to get involved with recy-cling? There are four simple steps that almost anyone can take to begin recycling. For starters, in many states there is a 5-cent to 10-cent refund on beverage containers. It is vital to turn these in. Not only do you earn money, but the aluminum and glass are then recycled. Second, don't throw away items such as old televisions or couches just because you don't need them anymore. Plenty of families would welcome an old black-and-white television—even if it needs some repair. Organizations such as the Salvation Army will accept, repair, and distribute such items. Third, separate your garbage into the following groups: clear, brown, and green glass; plastic; aluminum; news-paper. Return these separated items to recycling centers. Fourth, if your city doesn't provide for recycled items to be picked up by local garbage collection companies, lobby to make this a requirement. In addition to recycling, Americans of voting age must support legislation that favors recycling.

8   The benefits of recycling extend beyond saving ourselves from being buried in garbage. Because America is slow to re-cycle, we have yet to see the benefits of recycling—benefits clearly evident in the world's leader in recycling waste: the country of Japan. The Japanese recycle roughly 50 percent of all waste, whereas America recycles only a meager 10 percent of its waste. Some Japanese towns separate their trash into thirty-two different categories. By recycling, their cost of alu-minum is reduced by 10 times the current cost, glass is made much cheaper, and plastics are given multiple lives.[6] Not only do they benefit from cheaper prices, but the strain on their landfills is also eased. Clearly, the Japanese have shown us that recycling can work—and work very well indeed—with numer-ous benefits to individuals and to society.

9   In sum, America is faced with an environmental crisis: We have too much waste and no place to put it. It is time for Americans to recognize this problem, take action, such as re-cycling, so we may reuse resources and benefit from reduced costs of recycled materials. I urge you to do your part by fol-lowing the four suggestions mentioned. Americans throw out about 160 million tons of garbage a year—3.5 pounds apiece each day.[7] Where are we going to put it all?

Notes

1. Melinda Beck, "Buried Alive," *Newsweek*, November 27, 1989, p. 67.

2. John Langone, "A Stinking Mess," *Time* (reprint), January 2, 1989, p. 22.

3. Langone, p. 22.

4. Langone, p. 23.

5. Beck, p. 75.

6. Beck, p. 71.

7. Langone, p. 67.

❖ ANALYSIS

In the first paragraph, Anderson introduces the problem of solid waste with several analogies. He begins with a figurative analogy, suffocation, which probably is intended to create some sense of fear in his readers. He also personifies the problem with a second figurative analogy; the problem is referred to as an enemy, an analogy he develops further in the paragraph. These first two analogies are principally attention-getting devices and may not be particularly consequential to the argument as a whole. Nevertheless, we can see relationships developed among the sets of terms in these figurative analogies, as discussed in chapter 5:

Evidence Relationship		Conclusion Relationship
suffocation/individual		garbage/the nation
	and	
an enemy/the nation		solid waste/the nation

Just as suffocation stands in the relationship of threatening the life of the individual by cutting off a source of life, so garbage threatens our lives in a similar fashion. As an enemy threatens us as a nation, so garbage threatens us in a similar way.

The more consequential analogy in this paragraph, however, occurs in the next sentence, which builds on the figurative analogy of solid waste as an enemy. At this point Anderson compares the war on drugs, his evidence case—something most Americans are familiar with—to our country's approach to solid waste, his conclusion case. This argument is perhaps best understood as a judicial analogy, because it calls for similar treatment of the two cases. Because we have "already declared war on drugs," he concludes that it is past time to declare war on garbage. Following the type of analysis suggested in chapter 5, we might see the analogy as looking like this:

Evidence Case
Drug problem
1. Serious threat
2. Declared war
* Similar cases should be
   treated similarly.

Conclusion Case
Problem of solid waste
Serious threat

[Therefore]
We should declare war
on garbage.

Another point worth noting about this paragraph is that Anderson places us in the role of being our own enemy, and in this way associates us with Colombian drug lords as a threat to our own security. This is an interesting and effective approach. But his analogy works only if the audience is willing to accept that the two problems—drugs and garbage—are of equal magnitude. If we are not willing to accept this, the analogies of the first paragraph begin to break down.

In the second paragraph Anderson begins to more specifically outline the problem. In this way he is adhering to the structure of an argument arriving at a normative conclusion, or defending a proposition of policy. This paragraph advances an argument from direction—discussed in chapter 7. The argument affirms a progression beginning with a failure to reduce the level of solid waste output, which in turn causes a severe shortage of places to put garbage, which results ultimately in a crisis in which garbage may be dumped anywhere. The conclusion of this argument is that "it is imperative that we do something about this threat now." If this argument is to be a reasonable one, each step in the progression must be accepted as causing the next—test 1 of the argument from direction. We might object that the progression itself is not likely to occur as predicted. This particular argument also might be attacked as exaggerating the consequences of the progression, a possibility suggested by test 2 of the argument from direction.

This paragraph also advances an enumeration argument, discussed in chapter 9. Anderson asks by implication: Who can solve this terrible problem? He then sets out three possibilities: government, industry, and individuals. Test 1 of the argument from enumeration asks whether all of the alternative sources of solutions to the problem have been advanced. For example, perhaps a combination of government, industry, and individuals would provide a better solution than any one factor taken alone.

The first of his enumerated alternatives is eliminated by simply asserting, "we can't rely on government to solve the problem for us." Test 2 of the enumeration argument asks if all of the alternatives treated as eliminated have been actually eliminated. This one doesn't appear to have been eliminated unless we are willing to agree with him without seeing any evidence. The same might be said of the alternative of industry, though he does at least suggest here that it is "dragging its feet."

His conclusion from this enumeration argument is that "it is up to each and every American to become part of the solution," a conclusion which may be unobjectionable, but which may not find much support from his enumeration argument.

Anderson now turns to an argument from principle, discussed in chapter 8: "You have a duty to become part of the solution. . . ." The principle appealed to in this argument is the duty to work to save one's nation and its future. To accept this argument, we must be willing to accept that this principle is appropriate to this question (test 1), and that pragmatic factors do not outweigh it (test 3). We also would have to be willing to accept that the problem is as serious as Anderson has indicated—something for which he has as yet given us little evidence.

At the end of paragraph 2, we get a statement of Anderson's more specific conclusion. He is urging us to participate in voluntary recycling. This is a normative conclusion, and its presentation seems to raise the question of whether such a serious problem can be solved by individual action. This is a question to keep in mind as we read the rest of the essay.

Paragraph 3 begins to advance some evidence of the problem. Anderson draws on a well-known news magazine as a source, *Newsweek*. As noted in chapter 3, these magazines are considered generally reliable sources of evidence, although the authors of the articles are not themselves experts on the topics they report on. They rely on other sources of evidence. Anderson advances a striking interpretation of the evidence of a solid waste problem, one presented by Melinda Beck of *Newsweek*. *Time* is also introduced as a source of evidence (in paragraph 4), and statistical evidence is offered to show the magnitude of the problem. This paragraph does an effective job of suggesting the seriousness of the problem, a requirement of arguments arriving at normative conclusions, as discussed in chapter 4. Although the evidence is not from original sources, there is probably no good reason to doubt its accuracy, and we could check other sources to see if they report a problem of similar magnitude. The evidence is probably accessible, and it is recent.

Paragraph 4 further develops the problem. The number of landfills is shrinking and will continue to shrink. The seriousness of the problem is now compounded. An unacceptable temporary solution—dumping garbage in Third World countries—is condemned by the use of another analogy. John Langone of *Time* is quoted as comparing international dumping "to declaring war on the people of a country." Is this a literal or a figurative analogy? The answer to this question probably depends on what Langone (and perhaps Anderson) intended. The fact that the reporter calls it "the equivalent" probably brings this analogy into the realm of the literal. Thus, we might ask about any relevant dissimilarity between the two acts. Langone might discuss obvious ones—such as the fact that dumping does not involve guns and bombs—as irrelevant because the eventual impact of the two acts is essentially the same: The weaker countries are seriously harmed by the invasive tactics of a stronger country. Still, the analogy is not unassailable.

Anderson closes paragraph 4 by developing a second argument from principle. The act of dumping garbage on weaker nations is "a terrible injustice," and one "we must actively oppose." The principle of opposing serious injustice is invoked, and the argument is reasonable if we accept the principle, and accept that it applies in this case.

In paragraph 5 Anderson sums up the problem of solid waste and makes yet another analogy, this time to the air pollution problem of the 1960s and 1970s. Provided that we accept the severity of the problem, the literal analogy to air pollution—his evidence case—is a reasonable one. Anderson probably is hoping that the usually accepted judgment that air pollution was serious enough to address as a national problem will be carried over to solid waste, his conclusion case.

At this point the author makes a rather abrupt shift to the causes of the solid waste problem: "And what is the cause of this problem?" This question seems to introduce a hypothesis argument, as discussed in chapter 7. All of the claims about solid waste stand as observations, which in turn raise the question he now poses. The hypothesis is stated immediately: "We are [the problem], with our consumerist and materialist lifestyle." A cause is identified, and plausibility reasons are advanced—consumerism, materialism, selfishness. Corroborating evidence comes in the form of the claim that "each one of us throws out fifty gallons of trash a week." Is this a plausible hypothesis? Perhaps, but its focus is on individuals, and not, for example, on government or industry. This may be a strategic choice on Anderson's part, because he is recommending an individual solution to the problem. Nevertheless, an alternative hypothesis may better explain the situation. The problem has many causes, self-ish consumerism being only one.

Paragraph 6 calls for a national plan of action, one that matches the seriousness of the problem. Now Anderson has moved beyond the earlier call for recycling alone. It might have been more persuasive to have announced this part of the plan earlier so that it does not at this point appear as almost an inconsistency on his part. This paragraph moves quickly into a pragmatic argument from the negative consequences of failing to develop a comprehensive plan for dealing with the problem. Pragmatic arguments are discussed in chapter 8, and we would accept this one if we accept that the consequences are in fact as serious as Anderson suggests—test 1—and no principle is violated by taking action against them—test 3.

This paragraph calls for a tax on individuals according to the amount of garbage we produce. The example of Seattle is advanced, along with the success of that experiment. Here we encounter an argument from example—discussed in chapter 6—and the unstated connective that the example, as should be clear, represents the population. That is, this argument is reasonable only if we are willing to accept that what is true of Seattle also can be true of other cities, that Seattle is somehow representative of other cities. This is test 2 of arguments from example. If, on the other hand, Seattle is in some way uncharacteristic, the argument is weakened. Note how the pragmatic argument and the argument from example are employed together in this paragraph to strengthen one another.

In paragraph 7 Anderson moves from a national approach to an individual one. The plan is recycling, and the means of getting involved are explained. It appears as a practical plan that does not involve anything unethical. The question the plan raises is: Will this—along with a tax—solve the problem? Nevertheless, the recommendations are clearly presented, and they do represent actions that most people can take which probably would have some impact on the overall problem.

In paragraph 8, Anderson returns to the analogy to burial or suffocation with which he began. This does lend a certain consistency and symmetry to the essay as a whole. Anderson is now stating some of the benefits of his plan, in keeping with the structure of arguments arriving at normative conclusions (chapter 4). A statement of benefits usually is going to amount to a pragmatic argument and will be subject to the same tests (chapter 8). Japan is now introduced as part of another example argument. Japan's success with recycling is advanced as support for the notion that individual recycling efforts can make a difference in the solid waste problem. A significant question to ask at this point is: Does the fact that the Japanese have been successful with recycling mean that we will as well? If you accept that it does mean this, his example argument is a good one. At this point Anderson has linked each of his major proposals—a tax and recycling—to an example argument. In this way he has sought to establish the workability of his proposals.

Two specific benefits of recycling in Japan are mentioned here, and the example argument becomes intertwined with the pragmatic argument that recycling should be pursued because of the benefits it offers. This brings Anderson to the end of his argument, and the last paragraph is devoted to again calling his readers to do their part. He reviews only the recycling part of his plan, not the tax aspect, and in this way may miss an opportunity to urge all of his suggestions as a single, integrated plan.

Overall, the argument presents a problem and some evidence to support the contention that a serious problem exists. Wes Anderson has tried to show that the problem is inherent to the way we do things as a society, and he urges changes that might make a difference. Moreover, he has presented a plan, along with some of the benefits he believes would accompany its implementation. In these ways he has adhered to the expected structure for arguments arriving at normative conclusions. He also has advanced a variety of types of arguments in support of his major contention, and we have suggested some ways these might be tested. Though the argument is not unassailable and at points may contain some significant weaknesses, it has some merit as well.

Chapter Review

In this brief chapter some of the concepts from the text have been applied to the analysis of a longer argument. The procedure followed here can be used in reading arguments, or in doing more detailed written analyses of arguments. You might also want to attempt an analysis like this with some of your own arguments. Critical reading and listening—two major aspects of critical thinking—can help us make more reasonable decisions about which arguments we will accept. The same analytic skills can help us construct stronger arguments of our own.

EXERCISES

A. Find an argument in a magazine or newspaper, and do the kind of analysis done in this chapter with the essay "Buried Alive!"

B. Analyze the following argument, in the same way as was done with Wes Anderson's argument:

Canada's Acid Rain Dilemma
Daniel Sneep

1   When one thinks of Canada, images of lofty, rugged mountains, crystal blue lakes and rivers, and broad expanses of evergreen forest come to mind. Yet this fragile ecological setting is threatened by a deadly shower of pollution known as acid rain, most of which originates from U.S. industry. The U.S. government must take decisive and drastic action on pollution from its industries in order to control the potentially disastrous effects of acid rain on the Canadian environment. I'll go over what acid rain is and what it does, what should be done about it, and the potential benefits of this solution.

2   So what exactly is acid rain, and what are its effects? Acid rain results when the gases of industrial pollution react with moisture in the atmosphere and fall back to earth as rain. The deadly rain's impacts include killing aquatic animal and plant life, withering vegetation, scarring trees, deadening soil, retarding crop growth, eating away stone and concrete, corroding metal, forming smog, contaminating water, and contributing to human respiratory disease. These are all serious and dangerous effects.

3   Acid rain potentially affects every component of the environment, and all living things dependent upon that environment. In an article in *Scientific American*, V. A. Mohnen wrote, "Acid rain, or more correctly the pollutants that cause it, represents a large-scale interference in the bio-geochemical cycles through which all living things interact with their environment."[1] Acidic components from this pollution are carried by clouds and wind, inevitably crossing the border into Canada. According to Robert Norton, in a *U.S. News and World Report* article, as much as 75 percent of acid rain falling on Eastern Canada originates in the U.S.[2]

4   This deadly rain has numerous effects on Canada's environment and livelihood. Canada's forests, farmland, and lakes are all affected by acid rain. Trees are killed, farmland polluted, and lakes rendered unable to sustain life. This has posed serious threats to the farming, forestry, maple sugar, fishery, and tourism industries in Canada. Moreover, the fact that America allows these effects to continue to grow amounts to a violation of Canadian sovereignty. How would Americans feel if Mexico

were to start dropping its industrial waste products on American soil? This is essentially what the U.S. is doing to Canada.
5   What should be done about the acid rain problem? Two approaches are possible: urging voluntary compliance on the part of industry, or forcing their compliance. Urging voluntary compliance has not worked. American and Canadian industry have both shown an unwillingness to take the expensive though necessary steps to control the acid rain problem. Thus, the only way to control acid rain is to force industries to take action on pollution. Industries can use certain methods to control acidic emissions. Cost, lack of availability, and lack of initiative have prevented their widespread use. These obstacles can and must be overcome to significantly reduce pollution causing acid rain.
6   The U.S. and Canadian governments must initiate and support programs to reduce industrial emissions. Canadian provincial and federal leaders have reached agreements on the problem. They promise to increase current reductions in air pollution to 50 percent by 1994. The task now lies in getting American government and industry to take similar action.
7   Though initially expensive, many benefits would result from such action. Government action on pollution in both the U.S. and Canada would have two major benefits. First, Canada's beautiful, fragile environment and vital industries would be preserved. Second, Canada's friendly relationship with the U.S. would be boosted. An official of Environment Canada put it appropriately when he said, "Acid rain is the litmus test of bilateral issues."[3]
8   To sum up, acid rain results from pollution in the air falling to the earth as rain, and its deadly effects are felt throughout the environment. The U.S. and Canadian governments must cooperate in forcing industries to reduce pollution that causes acid rain. This kind of action would preserve Canada's environment and economy and strengthen American-Canadian relations. I hope I've enlightened you on this very serious issue and urge you to recognize what can and should be done to deal with the threat of acid rain.

Notes

1. Volker A. Mohnen, "The Challenge of Acid Rain," *Scientific American*, August 1988: 30–38, n.

2. Robert E. Norton, "Yes, They Mind If We Smoke," *U.S. News and World Report* July 25, 1988: 43–45.

3. Mark Mardon, "Canada's View on Acid Rain," *Sierra*, July/August 1987: 20–22.

C. Do an analysis of some argument you have yourself advanced. Suggest changes that you might make in the argument.

BIBLIOGRAPHY

Aristotle. *Rhetoric*. Translated by W. Rhys Roberts. New York: Modern Library, 1954.

Beardsley, Monroe C. *Thinking Straight*. 4th ed. Englewood Cliffs, NJ: Prentice Hall, 1975.

Billig, Michael. *Arguing and Thinking*. Cambridge: Cambridge University Press, 1987.

Bitzer, Lloyd F. "Aristotle's Enthymeme Revisited." *Quarterly Journal of Speech* 45 (1959): 399–408.

Black, Edwin. *Rhetorical Criticism*. Madison: University of Wisconsin Press, 1979. Original work published 1965.

Browne, M. Neil, and Stuart M. Kelley. *Asking the Right Questions*. 3d ed. Englewood Cliffs, NJ: Prentice Hall, 1990.

Damer, T. Edward. *Attacking Faulty Reasoning*. 2d ed. Belmont, CA: Wadsworth, 1987.

Foss, Sonja K., Karen A. Foss, and Robert Trapp. *Contemporary Perspectives on Rhetoric*. Prospect Heights, IL: Waveland Press, 1985.

Golden, James L., Goodwin F. Berquist, and William E. Coleman. *The Rhetoric of Western Thought*. 3d ed. Dubuque, IA: Kendall Hunt Publishing Company, 1984.

Govier, Trudy. *A Practical Study of Argument*. Belmont, CA: Wadsworth, 1985.

Johannesen, Richard L. *Ethics in Human Communication*. 2d ed. Prospect Heights, IL: Waveland Press, 1983.

Lanham, Richard A. *A Handlist of Rhetorical Terms*. Berkeley: University of California Press, 1969.

Loftus, Elizabeth F. "Eyewitnesses: Essential but Unreliable." *Psychology Today* (February 1984): 22–26.

O'Keefe, D. J. "Two Concepts of Argument." *Journal of the American Forensic Association* 13 (1977): 121–128.

Perelman, Chaim, and L. Olbrects-Tyteca. *The New Rhetoric.* Translated by John Wilkinson and Purcell Weaver. (Notre Dame, IN: University of Notre Dame Press, 1969).

Plato. *Gorgias.* Translated by W. C. Helmbold. Indianapolis, IN: Bobbs-Merrill, 1952.

Richards, I. A. *The Philosophy of Rhetoric.* Oxford: Oxford University Press, 1979. Original work published 1936.

Smith, Mary John. *Contemporary Communication Research Methods.* Belmont, CA: Wadsworth Publishing Company, 1988.

Thomas, Stephen N. *Practical Reasoning in Natural Language.* 2d ed. Englewood Cliffs, NJ: Prentice Hall, 1981.

Tompkins, Phillip K. *Communication as Action.* Belmont, CA: Wadsworth, 1982.

Toulmin, Stephen. *The Uses of Argument.* Cambridge: Cambridge University Press, 1958.

Warnick, Barbara, and Edward S. Inch. *Critical Thinking and Communication.* New York: Macmillan, 1989.

Whately, Richard. *Elements of Rhetoric.* Edited by Douglas Ehninger. Carbondale: Southern Illinois Press, 1963. Original work published 1828.

Williams, Frederick. *Reasoning with Statistics.* 3d ed. New York: Holt, Rinehart and Winston, 1986.

Ziegelmueller, George W., Jack Kay, and Charles A. Dause. *Argumentation: Inquiry and Advocacy.* 2d ed. Englewood Cliffs, NJ: Prentice Hall, 1990.

INDEX